Memories of the Revolution

TRIANGULATIONS
Lesbian/Gay/Queer ▲ Theater/Drama/Performance

Series Editors
Jill Dolan, Princeton University
David Román, University of Southern California

Memories of the Revolution

The First Ten Years of the WOW Café Theater

Holly Hughes, Carmelita Tropicana, and Jill Dolan, Editors

University of Michigan Press ANN ARBOR

Published in the United States of America by the
University of Michigan Press
Manufactured in the United States of America
⊚ Printed on acid-free paper

2018   2017   2016   2015   4   3   2   1

A CIP catalog record for this book is available from the
British Library.

ISBN 978-0-472-09863-7 (hardcover : alk. paper)
ISBN 978-0-472-06863-0 (pbk. : alk. paper)
ISBN 978-0-472- 12149-6 (ebook)

Contents

Jill Dolan

Preface
Watching WOW

Putting together this collection has been something of an elegiac process for Holly and Carmelita and me, in part because as the years recede the halcyon days of the WOW Café seem harder and harder to recapture. Thirty-five years on, the landscape of the East Village performance scene and the outré, politically incorrect pocket of feminist and lesbian resistance that WOW represented both seem hard to fathom. The new terrain of downtown New York has gentrified so dramatically that many of the places to which the artists featured here refer are long since gone, covered over by New York University dorms, fancy foodie restaurants, and hipster bars. The cheap rents and numerous off-the-radar communities of artists and writers and audiences hungry to work made possible the creative and political ferment that the first ten years at WOW represent. Now, Under the Radar is a performance festival sponsored by the staunchly institutionalized New York Shakespeare Festival/Public Theatre. As parts of the margins become centralized (though emphatically only parts), it becomes more and more important to remember the radical creative ferment of historical performance that's sometimes homogenized by more mainstream attention.

Rereading these collected scripts and statements and interviews, I find myself nostalgic for a moment that passed much too quickly, even as we all lived it. Who knew that artists would be pushed farther and farther out of Manhattan, until Brooklyn and Queens became, in the 2010s, the "new downtowns" with their own bruising gentrifications? Who knew that the keen sense of possibility and community these pages represent was so tenuous, so dependent on the capricious movements of lesbians and feminists and artists and all of the above into a neighborhood where they could find one another? As performer/writer Sharon Jane Smith says to Carmelita

Tropicana during their interview, "Where would I ever have met you if there hadn't been WOW?" That serendipity created a cauldron of imaginative possibility and political potential that fired the desire and delight of generations of artists and audiences alike.

I first came to WOW in its 330 E. 11th Street incarnation, in what became its home after Peggy Shaw and Lois Weaver hosted the Women's One World International Theatre Festivals, in 1980 and '81, which became the Café's origin. 330 E. 11th was a tiny, narrow space with a jerry-rigged stage and an odd collection of places for the ragtag audience to sit. On November 30, 1984, I was one of the many journalists writing for *TDR: The Drama Review* who fanned out across the East Village to describe the many concurrent out-of-the-way performances being staged all over what we then called "ABCland" (in honor of Avenues A, B, and C in Manhattan's far East Village). I'd been assigned to write about Club Chandalier; Kate Davy—who was my partner at the time—was assigned to write about WOW. We went to Chandalier first, where I was put completely off-kilter by my impression that this was a community to which, as a lesbian, I should belong but one to which, as a journalist and stranger, I was clearly an outsider. My desire to be part of what I saw that night, at Chandalier and later at WOW, actually gave me a stomachache. But it also compelled me to return, again and again, to see the women at WOW work. I followed them to their new space on E. 4th Street, climbing the stairs with anticipation because I never knew what I'd find up those three flights, as I passed shuttered warehouse spaces and hoped my path wouldn't be crossed by rodents. I just knew that WOW's vernacular was one I wanted to speak, and that the communion on display among the performers and much of the audience was something I, too, wanted to experience.

Before WOW, I'd seen *Split Britches,* the first production by what became the eponymous troupe, at another Off-Off-Off-Broadway downtown theatre around 1981 or '82. I recall that performance—and all the ones I saw later at WOW—with a keen acuity that attests both to how vivid those productions were and how necessary and revolutionary they felt. Who were these three odd old characters, who seemed perhaps sisters or perhaps lovers? What did their eccentric stories mean? As Della, Peggy Shaw's description of the fire in her pocket resonated for me and so many others as a powerful metaphor for lesbian desire, which in the early '80s was still reviled. To see a commanding performer like Peggy speak those lines onstage, as Della shed her clothes, protesting the confinements of patriarchal culture, felt like looking into a mirror in public for the first time. I'd been writing about feminist and lesbian theatre since 1978, but I'd never seen anything at all like *Split Britches.* That experience of jaw-dropping recognition and that sense of necessary community continued over my years as a spectator at WOW. Many people whose work is collected in this book describe similar foundational experiences. Writer/performer Lisa Kron, one of the cofounders of the Five Lesbian Brothers, said, "I saw Split Britches do their show *Split Britches* at one of the non-WOW spaces they performed it in. Well, what can I say? It changed my life." And writer/performer Moe Angelos, one of Lisa's Lesbian Brothers, concurs: "Seeing the show *Split Britches* for the first time, I realized that theatre could be what I wanted it to be; and if I had the pluck, I could even make it myself. I didn't need some dead guy to have written a play that if I was lucky, some other guy would cast me in."

Other early WOW participants share similar testimony about the early performances. Writer/performer Alice Forrester said that the work at WOW was so determining that people's lives veered in completely unexpected directions after their time there. Eileen Myles and Claire Moed understood themselves as "fish out of water," as "boy-girls," as people whose desires and yearnings made them different. Until they found WOW, they felt like they were living their lives in the wrong key. At WOW they recognized themselves in others.

That surprise and delight are visible in the photos we've collected. The 1984 retreat, for which WOW collective members left the city for upstate New York to hash out their ideas and plans, is documented with photographs that show the WOW women gathered for the camera with their shirts off, proudly displaying their breasts, arms around one another, laughing. The image emanates pleasure, playfulness, and mutual recognition. The photo captures indelibly the rare wonderfulness of that moment. The women's faces shine with glee and pride and pleasure, outlined by the erotics of being friends and lovers in all the blurry messiness of lesbian relationships. The intimacy of that picture evokes the attitude of the moment. The WOW women worked for themselves and for one another in those days, liberated by the knowledge that no one but themselves was paying attention.

Soon enough, though, WOW's invisibility in the dominant culture became irksome. As their archive of work mounted, the women in these pages attest to their frustration that local newspapers with authority and power wrote about the male artists in their neighborhood but not about the women at WOW. When Holly Hughes programmed BOW/WOW (Boys at WOW/ Women at WOW), the men got the attention, just as Charles Ludlam's Ridiculous Theatre—housed over in the West Village on Sheridan Square and crafted from a parodic, irreverent, do-it-yourself aesthetic similar to WOW's—regularly saw its work reviewed in the *Village Voice* and the *New York Times*. The invisibility that had felt empowering began to feel constraining, as the radical performance work of WOW's women was ignored in favor of that of men. Sadly, that part of WOW's story remains too familiar. The most powerful, authoritative media outlets and producing venues in New York and beyond still marginalize theatre and performance work by women, lesbians, transmen, queers, and feminists.

But one of WOW's contributions to the history of American theatre and performance is the way so many of its artists redefined what it means to succeed. The artists at WOW wanted their work recognized on their own terms, without compromise. They wanted visibility in mainstream media outlets for the work's pioneering originality, a value consistently assigned to men but not to them. Sure, the Five Lesbian Brothers moved to a larger, more visible venue where they were reviewed by the *Times*; Moe Angelos, now working with the Builders Association, continues to perform at New York Theatre Workshop, most recently in *Sontag: Reborn* (2013), which she adapted from Susan Sontag's journals and created with director Marianne Weems. That show also got good reviews, although it's yet to be picked up by a larger theatre. Sure, Lisa Kron's solo performance *2.5 Minute Ride* (1996), an autobiographical story that crosscuts between Kron's visit to Auschwitz with her father, who survived the camps, and her visit to Cedar Point, an amusement emporium in Ohio, with her non-Jewish then girlfriend and her girlfriend's family, was presented at various regional theatres before landing at the Public Theatre on Lafayette Street. Kron also wrote a musical adaptation of Alison Bechdel's graphic novel *Fun Home*, composed by Jeanine Tesori, which was successfully produced at the Public before it moved to Broadway in Spring 2015. Angelos, Kron, the other Brothers, and many other WOW artists deserved their own HBO specials and subscription TV series, none of which were forthcoming because out lesbians doing the politically and aesthetically edgy work made famous at WOW scared off mainstream entertainment moguls. And for the most part still does.

Success, though, can be measured in other, perhaps more important ways. Many of the WOW artists represented here from the first ten years went on to enjoy lives in the arts that maintained their off-beat social and artistic commitments. Peggy Shaw, Lois Weaver, Deb Margolin, Carmelita Tropicana, and Holly Hughes, as well as Angelos and Kron and many others, have continued to create vital new work and ply their trade as teachers, passing on radical, antihierarchical strategies for creating feminist and queer art. Some of these artists make more money than others; some struggle to pay their rent; some don't have health insurance. Some found teaching positions in academic institutions that pay them a comfortable wage and give them benefits. Some went on to work with other theatre collectives and organizations—Carmelita with INTAR (one of the longest running Latino theatres producing work in English) and PS122, Moe with the Builders Association, Shaw with the United Kingdom's Clod Ensemble, and Madeleine Olnek as a filmmaker, among others—moving the radical strategies of WOW's work into other forums, sharing their techniques with other artists and audiences alike. The work at WOW, which might have begun by "preaching to the converted," became instead a feminist, lesbian, queer *method*, one that in certain circles remains more foundational and influential than Lee Strasberg's or Stanislavski's. That measure of "success" seems most relevant.

One of the stories this book tells, in fact, is how a scrappy theatre collective that began as a social club where who you were dating was as important (if not more) than the size of your role grew into a laboratory for experimentation that had a lasting impact on future generations of theatre makers and critics. The mainstream press may not have been looking, but a nascent crop of feminist and lesbian academic critics began to take note. Some of the funniest stories in this book, in fact, describe clueless academics like Kate Davy and me coming to see performances, for which the choice of props or staging had been made from sheer necessity, that we read—perhaps ponderously and certainly pretentiously—as politically, ideologically, and aesthetically meaningful. Alice Forrester may have performed in *Heart of the Scorpion* against a video talking head of another character, with the monitor propped up on a chair, because the actor slated to play the part suffered a sudden onset of Bell's palsy and couldn't go on. But on the other hand, the critically significant way Kate read that moment in her *TDR* write-up was in fact fair enough. All the work at WOW, for many of us watching, made profound and far-reaching statements about how lesbians could steal the means of theatre production and utterly reenvision how gender and sexuality played onstage and beyond. Heady times. I'm not surprised by how many people in this book describe their days at WOW as a replacement for going to church. Its work was motivated by faith and belief in the possibility of social, as well as theatrical and often spiritual, transformation.

We've stitched together many pieces to create a necessarily partial archive of the first ten years, and whenever we can we've let artists speak in their own voices to evoke the chorus of artists who then comprised the WOW Café. The group interview with some of the earliest principals, with which the collection begins, took place in 1984, less than five years after the first Women's One World Festival. The group interview that bookends the collection took place in 2004, twenty years after the first interview and already over ten years before this book's publication. Theorists like to call this "queer time," which—if I can paraphrase a complicated concept—suggests that lesbians and gay men often radically reorder conventional linear time. We reject all the markers of "normal" (that is, heterosexual, middle-class) life cycles. Or some of us do. In the 1980s, when WOW was founded, and over the ten years chronicled here, lesbians didn't expect to get married. Some of us even embraced the difference of our romantic or domestic relationships, proud that they didn't necessarily have to be long term, monogamous, or reproductive (that is, they didn't necessarily have to last or produce children to be considered important). Queer time, in fact, throws doubt on conventional futures (as J. Jack Halberstam, Elizabeth Freeman, and Lee Edelman suggest, in different ways, in their scholarship). WOW claimed that sense of tenuous, important if ephemeral productivity long before theorists coined "queer time" as a radical concept. Time was ordered by the present production and the one right after; the work wasn't geared to posterity but to the pleasures and potentials of the "now." "Sweat equity" was the only currency—you work on my show, I'll work on yours or neither of us will last long enough to create another production at WOW. Relationships formed around the work, around the necessity of serving the common project, around the insistence that anyone who came around should embrace the collective's pride in their homespun work with its can-do spirit, which didn't need outside critical evaluation to underwrite its importance.

But as our own sweat equity on this long-in-the-making collection attests, the story of artistic production and community building that the first ten years of WOW exemplifies needs to be told, remembered, and perhaps even emulated in some revised, hopeful way. Holly and Carmelita and I—along with all the artists who have contributed their scripts, their ideas, their words, their photographs, and their time to creating this book—fervently believe that the early history of WOW should be remembered instead of actively erased or allowed to fade from neglect. We've opted to do this in several ways. We've included edited interviews with women who worked at WOW and snippets of conversations and statements shared over the years we've been curating this material. We've excerpted numerous scripts to give readers the flavor of the work during those first ten years. Some excerpts are longer than others, mostly because they needed more space to give readers a sense of their tone, genre parodies, or style. We've also excerpted bits from three previously published performances—Split Britches' landmark *Split Britches*, Holly Hughes's *The Lady Dick*, and Carmelita Tropicana and Uzi Parnes's *Memories of the Revolution/Memorias de la Revolución*—because no anthology describing the WOW Café would be complete without them. We've included one full script: Ana Maria Simo's *Pickaxe*, which has never been published before. We're honored to include it here. For anyone eager to perform or produce one of these pieces in its entirety, we're happy to connect you with the playwright to facilitate your work.

As Carmelita says in her introduction to the book, before the more recent milestones of popular culture put (some) queers on the map, there was WOW—there was a group of far-sighted, creative, talented, fearless, energetic women committed to playing with one another in ways that demonstrated how happily we could overturn the expectations of heterosexuality and middle-class "success," in the theatre and in our lives. That story should be told, not just to honor the labor but to remind new generations of other models, to assure them that applying to expensive masters of fine arts programs or auditioning for regional theatres or workshopping a play until it doesn't resemble your original impulse aren't the only ways to be an artist. In her introduction to this book, Holly describes attending a meeting at WOW more recently; the collective continues to meet every Tuesday, and anyone interested in working there is welcome. At this meeting, only one of the fifteen people present knew who Holly was. That Holly was unrecognized in a place where her presence was once so crucial breaks my heart. But she reads the moment differently, suggesting that it's important for women to re-create themselves over and over again and not feel beholden to someone who looks like she's there to collect the rent.

Maybe, maybe not. What we do with our history is a recurring conflict in the feminist and queer movements. Even the language we use to describe history implies replacement, "queer time" aside, and the "waves" of feminism suggest that new ones obliterate the old. The replacement of LGBT with *queer* elided something particular about that earlier acronym. I know that to reinvent ourselves we have to keep renaming. But we erase our history at our peril. That said, Carmelita, in her introduction, admits to her anxiety about curating the archive of a place that steadfastly refused to choose one thing over another. The most complicated moments of WOW's history reflect those refusals, which played out as struggles over resources, power, and authority; acting as a collective didn't mean that those fault lines disappeared. In her introduction, Holly remembers that WOW was always an uneasy site of "family," that those who had been kicked out of their birth families because of their sexuality or their gender performances and couldn't quite make a place for themselves in the world didn't find all those struggles magically assuaged at WOW. These pages detail many of the conflicts the collective negotiated. The stories and interviews also describe WOW's growing pains. The collective decided early on not to apply for grants that would require them to bend their commitments to those of outside funders. But once some artists began to receive more public recognition—when, for instance, the Five Lesbian Brothers began presenting their work at the New York Theatre Workshop, down the block from WOW on E. 4th Street—they fought to sustain their collective work as they navigated a theatre industry that prizes individual artists over intimately connected collaborators.

This collection, then, is haunted by the real ongoing struggle during the first ten years of WOW to craft new ways of working together as women, as lesbians, as artists (amateur or eventually professional) with a desire for art and erotics, for politics and play, for pleasure and the sustaining labor of hard, resource-poor, idea-rich theatre work. That struggle is reflected with surprising sweetness in the scripts we've collected. Rereading the WOW plays thirty years after seeing them, I'm struck by their earnestness. They twist genre conventions and comment with a light touch but poignant insight on the political and emotional betrayals caused by conventional gender roles. The scripts read to me now as almost romantic when, at the time, I found them so radical. That they spoke to, by, and about women and reveled in loving and lusting after women, was so wholly new in theatre at the time that it felt revolutionary. I remember this work as fierce, but it was also really fun. And funny. Because it proved that lesbian comedy could be fierce and funny and radical all at the same time. That's what we hope this volume will remind readers.

When she interviewed Sharon Jane Smith in 2001, Carmelita asked her why she continued working at WOW long after many of the original collective members had moved on. Smith responded that she needed a place like WOW, where women are the default, where the ethos is collective, where you have to give back if you want to get something out. At other theatres, Smith said, people put up their work and leave; they don't stay to watch other people's performances or to talk or to labor or to engage with the larger canvas on which the work makes its interventions or just, even, makes sense. That's what WOW did during its first ten years and what it continues to do now. We hope this book offers an appetite-whetting taste of how to create and see theatre and performance differently.

Holly Hughes

Introduction

Secret WOW

I'm working on the WOW book, the long-awaited, long-overdue anthology. Should have been done, um, ten years ago. I thought it would be easy to spin boxes of typewritten scripts, old photos, and Xeroxed flyers into ninety thousand words safely locked between two covers. I thought I had made my peace with what it meant to edit, a kind of violence I would have to inflict in the name of history. Deciding what would go in and out, absolving myself of responsibility for taste, for memory lapses, because even a partial record of the past is better than none.

But I just couldn't get over the fact that WOW saved my life. Nothing as dramatic as that line suggests; I wasn't teetering on the edge of a bridge when a group of thespians showed up to talk me down. But at WOW I began to imagine a life that I might want to live.

Last winter I was interviewed by an Australian playwright who was researching American lesbian theater. She kept asking me how my life would be different if I were a man. Would I be more successful? What would my life look like if I were a man? I kept dodging the question, maybe because it's not really a question, just as climate change, Obama's citizenship, and evolution aren't really questions you can debate but bottomless sinkholes that will swallow you whole if you get anywhere close. And I don't want to dwell on the facts of sexism because I will find myself stripped down to my aging skin in the cold room of regret, nothing to hold on to but the slight hope of becoming a historical footnote. Why stop there, why not skin yourself alive, thinking you could have done it differently, worked harder, faster, better? Had you not wasted so many nights drinking Rolling Rock and laughing, perhaps you could have made yourself into the exceptional woman.

Listen, there's no doubt in my mind that if the women in those first ten years had been what we were in terms of class and race and educational opportunity—that is, mostly white, mostly middle-class with some college—with only a change of gender, a Google search for WOW would force you to wade through pages of links to World of Warcraft and all the other WOWs that are better known than the one founded thirty-some years ago by a handful of lesbians who slyly called it "a home for wayward girls."

Bitterness, I speak its many dialects. WOW is the story of women who lived with the knowledge of exclusion, erasure, and indifference, who carried the visible scars of prejudices that continue unabated, a few exceptions notwithstanding, and decided to make art anyway. This is not a decision you can make on your own. A monarch butterfly doesn't decide that Mexico seems like a good place to winter; you're part of a flock, and the flock decides to go. If you are a butterfly on your own, you're not a butterfly for long. You're dinner. I was lucky enough to find this flock, to allow myself to get so lost that I could stumble into WOW, and I was lucky that Peggy Shaw ordered me to make a show. You have to understand that I didn't know it was Peggy Shaw who was telling me; I thought it was a woman who looked like James Dean, who was, maybe, really James Dean, and so I should do what I was told.

Who am I now to edit the flock? To merely say "Peggy Shaw" or "Carmelita Tropicana" or "Lynn Hayes" without telling you everything, without bringing you, the reader, into the room, the night, and getting you drunk and young enough so it all makes sense?

This isn't a historical narrative, not in the sense that it recounts what happened and rewards you with a sense of closure, of progress you can count on. In my current position as a professor (yes, a full professor) at a major research university, I see what looks a lot like the past. Our students are overwhelmingly female. At all levels. They are also, at my school, becoming more affluent, whiter. This imbalance is much remarked on. Efforts are sometimes made that look suspiciously like affirmative action for white men, even as efforts toward racial and economic inclusion are denounced. Some of my younger female colleagues whose careers would have been unimaginable without feminism grouse about teaching so many female students; they don't come out and say women are "bitchy," but it's implied. Some of the men are exceptional, and many of the women are drifting through the BFA program with little intent of becoming artists. But the law of averages suggests that there will be more exceptional women than men.

But something happens after graduation. The few teaching jobs almost always go to men. The men get shows. They get better shows. They make work that is sexier and more fashionable, work that involves technology and gadgetry. The women start making decisions about their lives that will make the life of an artist even harder, and no one begs them not to. Contemporary feminism, such as it is, is all about "choices." And you gotta support a sister's "choices."

Okay, maybe this is just the situation at my school, but this is my book, and I'm telling you it's not, okay, you can listen or not. You can choose to think Obama was born in Africa or that the world is six thousand years old or you can face the facts. Even though years of these facts sink to your bones, make you ache, make it difficult to get out of bed in the morning or find a reason why.

These are decisions you can't make on your own.

WOW is a secret. It's easy to miss. You have to know what you're looking for. No sign announces you're standing outside one of the longest continuously running lesbian art organizations. Let's just say it's the oldest, shall we? It's November 2010; I'm in the East Village, looking for WOW, and even I walk by the building at least once before I find it. How I mourned that we were unmarked and therefore unrecognized; how happy I was that no one came in the door who didn't really want to be there. No one to tell us what we were doing was bad, trivial, offensive, a waste. We carried those voices inside our own skins, but here they got drowned out by the sounds of women trying to learn the lines written moments before, by double entendres volleying back and forth over the sound of power tools, by fights over who was and was not a member, a man, and who would take out the trash.

Now, I ring the buzzer. A relatively new feature. For much of my time at WOW, you stood in the street and called up, hoping to be heard over car alarms. East 4th Street was always crowded and loud. There were many villages in the East Village, and you had to make yourself heard above them all, in a way that your tribe might recognize. We had our own rebel yell, our mating call. Then you would wait, till someone struggled to open the reluctant window, to drop a key wrapped in a sock to the street four flights below.

There's no foyer, no space to receive you. This shabby but sturdy building doesn't have time for that kind of nicety. You're inside or you're outside, there's no liminal space. The building seems solid, substantial, able to support whatever else goes on inside the other rooms. The Lower East Side print shop. Light manufacturing converted to artists' studios, small businesses. I never made it my business to know what else went on there, beyond strategizing with other WOWettes about the crazy lady upstairs who always complained about us. We weren't loud; she was crazy. And she wasn't supposed to live there anyway, that's how we saw it.

New York City is full of secrets, full of rabbit holes opening to parallel universes. The tragedies of sweatshops, of too many undocumented workers crammed into too little space. There are the people who have half-decomposed bodies stashed beneath their antediluvian ottomans, or who share a studio with a couple of tigers, or with piles and piles of ancient newspapers carved into canyons. But there's the sweetness of secrets there, too. Clubs, speakeasies, abandoned piers enlivened by another species of abandonment. New York is the place you go to be seen and the place you go to disappear, to be anonymous, as E. B. White acknowledged at the beginning of *Here Is New York*: "On any person who desires such queer prizes, New York will bestow the gift of loneliness and the gift of privacy."

White's loneliness is also WOW's. It's not about solitary confinement but about having the freedom to live a lovely secret life, to populate a parallel universe as substantial as any other. Everyone at WOW went there seeking the secret New York. Some of us came from the other coast, from flyover country, Appalachian small towns, and some of us came from New York itself, the official city, in search of a place where a loud, wild yodel would be welcome, in search of a heavy unmarked door that would let us in while keeping the rest of the world out.

Now I follow the laughter up the stairs. The elevator works now, but I can't imagine using it. When we first moved here, there was an operator, a pleasant middle-aged man named Eddie. If there was a schedule, it didn't conform to any conventional division of a day; you never knew when Eddie would be there and when he wouldn't. Then one day he wasn't, and then another, and eventually I was told that Eddie had died. I was shocked. He didn't seem that old, and of course he probably wasn't that old, but my middle-class childhood had shielded me from the knowledge of the toll taken by manual work. I asked what he died of, and was told "He just died," in an impatient tone that suggested I was too stupid to be alive, which was, of course, exactly true. I walked by Eddie wearing the protective bubble of a private college education and regular dental care.

A few years later, during the strike of a show, a couple of WOW members dragged the remnants of a set out of the theatre and called the elevator. When the doors opened, one woman stepped backward into empty darkness. She survived the fall down a full story, but she had multiple injuries: broken bones, organ damage, brain damage. Like most of us, she had no insurance. She sued the city and won, but not until many years had passed. First, she had to suffer through trials, which focused more on her queerness and her gender presentation than on the city's negligence.

Inside, WOW looks like it always did. The floor looks like it needs to be painted, but I know that it was just painted and that's just the way the floor is. The ceiling is really too low for theater, but you don't notice that when you're working on the show or sitting in the audience. You only notice that after you have worked at other places and noticed that there is only the bare modicum of what it takes to be a theatre here. For thirty years, it's been enough.

There's a dressing room, and off the dressing room a curtain hides a toilet. No sink, just a toilet, with a tiny window on one side and a list on the opposite wall. How proud we were that we had a tiny place to pee for the performers; it was a cool thing we had and PS122 didn't. PS122 was the bigger gig, the place to get reviewed, the part of the iceberg that was visible above water, but it had no place for the performers to pee. And yet the entrance of PS122's building—a building ambitious enough to have an entrance, a foyer, some antechamber—this space between the theatre and the street, reeked of pee. WOW was better. Fuck them; who needs a gig at a place where you couldn't have a private place to pee?

In November 2010, that list by the toilet asked two questions. What is WOW for? What is WOW not for? According to the list, it's about community, it's about social change via resistance, and it's about hooking up. WOW is not for racism or any other form of prejudice. Nothing mentions success in the conventional sense. WOW's not about getting someone to come and offer you a gig on TV or even down the street at LaMama. Do the women at WOW have those desires, or is WOW for those who care about their own work regardless of what the rest of the world thinks? Or is a desire for traditional success taboo? Or just less important than changing the world and having sex?

I join the collective's meeting happening that night. I'm the only one there from the first ten years. No one from what I think of as "my generation" is an active member. Several generations have come and gone, taking their WOWs with them. Sharon Jane Smith says, "They have my number, and they call me if they get in trouble." I remember Sharon Jane and her mandolin, her painstaking freestyle tile work in the tiny public bathroom, the smooth angle of her jaw as she played both Trotsky and his sister, Frida Kahlo's lover in *Pickaxe*, her unswerving commitment to social justice, and her long fingers with their evidence of butch competence. I like to think of the various troubles she might be called on to fix.

After years of worrying about our mostly whiteness, WOW has evolved into a more diverse organization. Feel free to question that choice of verb. *Evolved* implies a force you can't control, something beyond the level of individual effort, somehow absent of struggle. Feel free to insert another word to describe the change from a mostly, but not entirely, white group, to the group I see in the room this night. Several women of color move with the confidence that this is their place. In the past, we invited women of color to do festivals, to use the space on specific nights. They were guests, with all that implied. At those infrequent moments when WOW had to act like it was a real organization in the world, we'd call on Alina Troyano and her sister Ela and designer Joni Wong to prove we were multicultural. We did so, I remember, with a sense of failure and shame. We didn't care if people came to WOW and couldn't deal with the campiness and sexiness; we didn't care if they left because they weren't willing to take out the trash. Good riddance. But we did mind the barrier of our whiteness. I'm happy to see the change, but I wonder what brought it about. A larger cultural shift? Did the move toward a more structured organization or some other policy shift make women of color feel they could claim WOW, too?

And it's no longer just women, a word that always begged quotes whenever we used it but still referred to biological women. Trans folk are welcome.

Mimi McGurl, a director and scholar, is facilitating the meeting. It falls to her to interrupt the flirtation, the gossip, the planning of the meetings that precede the meeting. While Mimi's not a founder, she's a sole representative of the demographic north of forty-five; she has the e-mails and phone numbers of myself, Peggy and Lois, Alina, and others. She's the institutional memory in the room. We go around what some might call a circle, but in fact is only a vague nod to that shape, a circle only when viewed from a distance. But inside the circle it's something else. A spinning, live thing, moving and rewriting itself, nothing as simple as a circle. The WOWettes offer their names.

I am uncomfortable here. This is not a place for spectators. You're supposed to make yourself useful, but I won't be in town long enough to see most of these shows, the simplest and yet most important way to be of use. I can't imagine sitting on the floor the way I used to do, and even sitting on the mauve folding chair feels like an example of Abramovician performance of the endurance sort. When did I come to judge a chair based on the adequacy of its lumbar support?

The jokes I hear don't make sense to me. They are all stories that grow out of sharing this space together, of many, many long nights, of bad coffee and too much beer. But being an outsider is the central WOW story. Woven into the scripts and stated again and again in the interviews I've collected is the story of being shut out, excluded. There's a stinging "no" at the dark center of everyone's tale. It's perhaps a deeper commonality than our queerness. There was no other place. But we were also rarely at home here, either. Again in the scripts and interviews I hear the sentence, "But I had to leave this part of me at the door." I hear how we were still outsiders even as we made this home; we had lost the ability to really be in a home, to be a part of a family. We were animals that lived on the edges of things, not wild, not domesticated; a feral world we made here.

So when it's my turn to say my name, I am not surprised it doesn't ring a bell. But Mimi's embarrassed. She jumps in to say, "Holly started the place!" This wins me no love. Yuck, history. It's like I've shown up demanding the rent. I'm the mother breaking up the party by flipping on the overhead light. A young woman sizes me up: "Who are you?"

She's right to be suspicious. She's right to worry that I'm coming to collect something she doesn't want to give, like her freedom in exchange for some sense of the past. A terrible deal. I'm glad that WOW is not haunted, that no one feels burdened by some sense of tradition or seniority. One of WOW's most abiding radical features is the absence of those gatekeepers who demand to see your aesthetic pedigree—time spent at a school, a relationship with someone on the inside. You don't have to know anyone to get your foot in this door. Other than yourself. Knowing that you are able to open your own doors. That you want more than one foot inside but your whole young self. And once inside this place, you are free to be fully young in that most American sort of way. To believe that you are the first one, the only one, to think this, to say this. In this room you enter with no one's help but that of your own body's work to climb the stairs. You are Adam; you get to name the animals. Time starts over; everything is new, starting with you.

An old and very American story of an artist's life, but not for the people in this room. This is freedom denied most women or "women" or those who skew to the feminine side of the equation. The freedom denied those of color, the freedom denied the unapologetically queer artist. The freedom that is not denied here. A small room with plenty of room to fail, to start over, to feel as though you were, at last, fully human, even as the knowledge that you are not fully human is what draws you here, night after night.

This is what she might lose to history. This is what she is afraid she is about to hear: she's doing it wrong, she's wrong. Whatever dreams she has have been dreamt before and better, and have now flown back to diminish her.

I want to offer in this book a different sort of history. Something she can use. I don't imagine I can offer her any light on her life today; perhaps that is not what she needs. Maybe her eyes are better than mine; perhaps I am bringing my darkness with me wherever I go. So this is not a light I'm offering. But perhaps you open the box you had forgotten about, and in it is a decoration, a string of lights that does nothing about the darkness but does help you see the room you are in differently. A string of lights that takes your ordinary day and makes it look like a party, a string of lights that sparkles more than illuminates, that calls for music. A string of fairy lights. Some bulbs missing, no replacements possible.

And if you were to insist that this string of lights is, instead, a book, it shouldn't be read as an account of ten years' time. It's partial, fragments that unfold in "lesbian time," a decade more or less, but when it starts and when it ends is the wrong question to ask. It's of an era, the golden age of the East Village art scene. The scripts offered within it are relics of a time between the moment feminism collapsed as a popular movement that could spin off songs on the radio like "We Are Family" and the emergence of queer theory as an academic discipline.

Perhaps this is a trunk of someone else's clothes, the scripts to be tried on as you might the garments of a forgotten relative. Of course, you'll notice how we reworked what we found, what we were given, what others threw out. The voices of TV shows that were old when we were young were in our ears as much as punk rock: Lucille Ball, the Honeymooners. Our sense of the absurd drifted ashore from Gilligan's Island, not from college seminars on Beckett.

This is a box of brightly colored, jury-rigged items for which no set of instructions is given. It is meant to be played with, it is meant to be enjoyed, to be handled, and even to be broken. Open it, use it, make this history work for you.

Introduction
Liberté, Egalité, Lesbianité

When Holly and I discussed doing a book about the first ten years of WOW, I was elated. Holly gave me one of my juiciest roles at WOW: Con Carne in *The Lady Dick*. It was at WOW that I'd found my voice and my tribe. If there hadn't been a WOW Café, I probably would not have become a performer or writer. That was true of many women who were part of WOW.

Over the years, that elation gives way to anxiety. We have the daunting task of being the curators. The word *curator* comes from the Latin *cur,* "to care for." How do we care for WOW's legacy and represent all the disparate voices, the cacophony and chaos, that made up WOW in the early years?

This is but one book. It includes interviews and photos, but its focus is on scripts, on the written word. We have had to choose from many deserving works. I feel like Meryl Streep in *Sophie's Choice*. And how ironic is that?! WOW was never about someone choosing work based on merit or its lack. WOW was based on sweat equity: if you worked box office, mopped floors, attended staff meetings, and were a woman (hopefully, a lesbian), you could put on a show. If it had been any other way, WOW would not have birthed so many thespians.

WOW became a safe place to learn by practice. Women could fail and succeed in theatre, but WOW was much more than that. It was an art salon and a social club. It was a place to meet girls that became girlfriends and then became friends or the other way around. It was a place that provided family to those whose families were far away or had disowned them. WOW was an instant community and, to quote cultural critic Alisa Solomon, a "force."

The WOW Café Theater came into existence in downtown New York

City in the 1980s. That's when our WOW revolution began, with an ethos that was scrappy DIY, a strictly under-the-radar, do-it-yourself operation without any licenses, permits, or grants, simply because we were driven. We believed in our mission to represent women like us—whatever that meant. Back then it was an easier time, a happy time for artists, playful, innocent. There was enough money for an artist to make art, survive, and hang out. Clubs and galleries flourished. Art was more about process than product, more about aesthetic edification than career, more about transgression than mainstream assimilation. And then those halcyon days ended. AIDS hit, clubs and galleries closed, the National Endowment for the Arts (NEA) started defunding, the culture wars began, and our revolution continued. Before *The L Word, Ellen, Will and Grace*, the Logo Channel, and *Glee,* there was WOW, making queer art, putting lesbians on the map, creating a culture that would one day seep into the mainstream.

I joined WOW when it first opened at the E. 11th Street storefront, well before it evolved into a full-fledged theatre. As a collective aiming for optimum democracy, the idea of leaders was anathema, but some of its women were more involved in the management of the space. Peggy Shaw and Lois Weaver, along with Jordy Marks and Pamela Cahme, created the WOW Festivals, which begat the WOW Café. Jordy and Pamela stayed after the Café opened but soon left. I remember an artsy American/European crowd at the Café for a brief stint, and when they left, Holly Hughes came in, followed by Susan Young. Maureen (Moe) Angelos, Alice Forrester, Lynn Hayes, and Diane Jeep Ries took on jobs of banking or accounting, and notably Sharon Jane Smith has acted as a link between the old and the new millennium WOW.

Moe disagrees with me over who was in charge at different times. To her the artsy American/European crowd was never in charge. And people have different recollections about how involved and for how long Pamela and Jordy were at WOW on 11th Street. But we all agree that Holly took over programming when many of the other members left on tour. She filled the space with activities. The brunches of melted brie sandwiches and beer continued, accompanied by fashion shows, art shows, and nighttime shows that included comedy, poetry, and music. Operating the Café was unpaid labor. Holly booked and staffed shows, designed flyers, picked up beer. The work took a toll. She took a break, and Susan stepped in. Susan moved into WOW, sleeping in the back and keeping quiet when robbers broke in and stole equipment. She was undeterred, but called the few of us active members worried that a crime wave had hit the neighborhood at the same time that rents were going up and the membership had dwindled.

WOW on 11th Street was always in crisis mode, but amid the controlled chaos problems got solved. When the box office could not cover the rent, WOW threw fabulous benefit parties with sets and costumes at Club 57 on St. Marks Place in a church basement. We threw a Xmas at Coney Island party, with game booths and a haunted house, and a Debutante Ball with femme girls parading in gowns, butches in tuxedoes, and a rose float that opened to reveal Moe as homecoming queen. The parties were huge fun and theatrical and a lot of work. The rose float for the Debutante Ball was hard to wheel through the streets in the middle of a blizzard. But the WOW girls were not discouraged; they partied like it was 1999 and the show must go on.

On E. 11th Street, we had two big problems: How to pay the high commercial rent, since we did not depend on grants, and how to keep a consistent working membership to run the space. Since WOW was a presenting space, many artists left once they had completed their shows. When members started presenting their own work, the focus shifted. And when Peggy and Lois and Moe and Alice came back from one of their tours, WOW was reenergized. Peggy and Lois conceived and directed big shows in which all the members participated, forming a kind of WOW repertory company. We performed *The Snow Queen*, a fairy tale adaptation, and *The Tennessee Waltz*, a piece with original monologues based on Tennessee Williams's characters.

Producing our own work got us all invested in the space, and that translated into a consistent, growing membership. The space was becoming a theatre. Lois spearheaded yearly retreats at which WOW's whole season was planned and members jockeyed for time slots. Those retreats, in pastoral settings upstate, were like a Fresh Air Fund for artists starved for nature. Business got done, along with moonlit swims, campfires, s'mores, breakups, and hookups.

After several years on E. 11th Street, Peggy Shaw solved a major part of our rent problem. She demanded that WOW be given a space in a city-owned building on E. 4th Street, where she lived, in a block full of theatres that included the New York Theater Workshop and LaMama. Not only was this prime real estate, but it also gave us more space and a permanent home. With a new space, we got busy. We began to produce big shows with as many WOW members as possible. Some of those people are not included in these pages, but their work was very much in keeping with the spirit of WOW: *Cinderella: The Real True Story; Hootenanny Night; Guitar Boy; Sex Lives and Rape; Tart City; Through These Walls;* and *Sex-travaganza*. WOW boasted in-house designers, composers, and musicians, along with house bands, and produced a film and video series.

WOW became a fertile playground. It was a theatre grounded in gender and sexual politics and a meeting place for like-minded individuals to create work with a social critique. We could not make money at WOW, but the opportunities were great. We were encouraged to do it all: write, direct, design, and act. Our work was irreverent, raunchy, part of the counterculture. We did not focus on coming-out stories because a lesbian identity was a given. We were then able to tackle other issues such as the impact of gentrification, the state of the economy, or the representation of lesbians in the arts. Our work was too edgy and raw to be "commercial," but we were professional and WOW was recognized with a prestigious Obie award.

As a collective, WOW was allergic to setting policy and writing rules. We were experimenting and making things up as we went along, and that could mean trouble. We had to grapple with issues of race, gender, and sexuality within the organization. Sexuality was the least problematic. As a women's space with a lesbian majority, we ruled, but we invited all women to participate. This was a departure from some '70s feminist groups, which did not want feminism to be identified with lesbianism. The straight and queer women who came knew the deal. It was up to each individual to navigate the waters, which may at times have had a gentle undercurrent of "try it, you'll like it." But it was mild. If they felt comfortable, these women stayed at WOW.

The role of men at WOW was always contentious and ran the spectrum. The artsy American/European crowd banned men altogether, even as audience members. Holly got in trouble after the fact for presenting David Cale's solo show. Peggy and Lois used a male actor in one of their shows, maintaining that acting was not as important a function as writing and directing. I went to the membership to get permission to collaborate with Uzi Parnes, but some women refused to work on the show on principle. Madeleine Olnek ran into problems when she wanted Dan Hurlin to direct her play. And there was the infamous Jack Smith incident. Jack was an important queer icon, renowned for his experimental theatre and avant-garde cinema. He was invited to perform in a sixties-style happening event at WOW. His performance consisted of standing quietly in a far corner of the stage with a lamp on his head as an installation. But when a couple of WOW members saw him, they were furious and unplugged his light. He was escorted to Darinka, another downtown club nearby, where he was replugged and illuminated the audience.

We may have not been of one mind when it came to gender, but we all wanted to have a racially and ethnically diverse WOW. There were few women of color. Some came and went. If my memory is correct, for the most part, there was one Asian American, two Latinas (I was one), and one African American. Unfortunately, at that time, WOW mirrored the segregated gay community and New York City at large. We had countless discussions about how to bring new women of color into the fold. We had festivals, where groups would come, and we'd hope some would stay and become members, but it never materialized. In the new millennium, WOW is finally diverse.

Other cultural groups and individuals have struggled for queer rights, but what makes WOW unique is its longevity. We thrived as a theatre because our loyal audiences needed to hear our stories as much as we needed to tell them. Audiences and artists were allies who imagined a world of possibilities. With the support of activists, critics, and academics, the word spread.

My personal narrative at WOW is as much a coming-out story as it is my initiation into a life in the arts. Although I had studied theatre, gone to Circle in the Square and HB Studio, I began my artistic life at WOW. At WOW we all had to negotiate who we were as individuals with our role as members of the group. As a Latina and woman of color, I was both a token and special, since there were few of us. WOW was not perfect, but it was there that I found a treasure trove of paramours, lifelong friends, and inspiring colleagues.

Many of the WOW women went on to pursue a life in the arts and academia. Their subsequent individual successes—Obies, Guggenheims, Tony award wins—were due to their talent, hard work, and luck, and to a collective that generously provided the necessary first leg of support. In the arts, women, lesbians, people of color, and transgendered folks still struggle to have their voices heard and their work recognized. In the '80s, WOW fought to level the playing field. Hopefully, as the scripts here attest, we fought with artistry. And, as we all know, the battle continues: "La lucha continua" . . . as does WOW.

WOW Women in Their Own Words

Brave New World

We start this collection with a group interview conducted by journalist Alisa Solomon, which took place on November 27, 1984, at the WOW Café at 330 E. 11th Street in the East Village between Second and First Avenues. WOW collective members Maureen (Moe) Angelos, Alice Forrester, Chris Henry, Debra Miller, Claire Moed, Peggy Shaw, Carmelita Tropicana (Alina Troyano), Lois Weaver, Susan Young, and others got together to discuss the history of their work and the founding of the Café.

What strikes us from this vantage point is the amount of performance and cultural work that was accomplished with so few resources. "Sweat equity," as they say, was the primary form of exchange, and the monthly rent on the Café was raised at the box office, through memberships, by selling food, and by hosting the occasional benefit party or performance. Most of the women involved lived in the neighborhood, near the Café; one woman lived at WOW. Thirty years later the high real estate values in New York and other big cities that often provide fertile cultural environments for new artists make it too expensive to create the kinds of imaginative venues that WOW was able to provide.

And already the difference between "downtown" work and "uptown" work—on Broadway and off—was stark in terms of gender differences, along with race and sexuality. WOW made possible a forum for women, women of color, and lesbians that existed in very few other places at the time—and since. —*Editors*

LOIS WEAVER: We produced two years of the [Women's One World] Festival, in 1980 and 1981. Peggy and I and Pamela Cami and Jordi Mark were the producers and called upon practically everyone else we could find. Peggy and I had been touring in Europe for years with different groups— Spiderwoman Theater and Hot Peaches—and had met a lot of theater companies who wanted to come to this country. We said that's impossible because the system just is not the same. We don't have the same kind of setup to invite you into a theater that could pay you a small fee or even accommodate you. You would have to produce yourselves, basically. That's how we do it. So we got the idea that if it was going to be done, we were going to be the ones to have to do it.

PEGGY SHAW: I don't know why we ever had that idea.

LOIS: And we said okay, we'd reciprocate.

PEGGY: We didn't think they'd really fall for it. We said, "We'll do it," and then all of a sudden, we had to do it.

LOIS: So we wanted to create not only an international women's theater festival so we could invite international groups, but also a festival that would highlight national and New York women performers, and mainly theater, because music had quite a circuit. Dance sort of had its own circuit, though we included all of those things in the festival. We also wanted to create a multimedia environment because in Europe you could go and pay one admission and see two or three shows, plus a movie, plus sit in a café and talk, plus dance afterwards. New York really didn't have anything like that. Theater in New York was so alienating and so isolating that we all wanted to create that European-style festival environment. So we did. God only knows how we did. We didn't have any money. We didn't apply for any funding because we decided in May to do it and we did it in October. We decided that the time could be spent trying to organize grants and probably not get them or we could just go to work and contribute our full-time salary. That was one of our philosophies.

PEGGY: That's still our philosophy. It's easier to get a job than a grant.

LOIS: We got a lot of in-kind contributions. We had space donated to us. We did benefits the whole summer of 1980, which was a really good thing because we not only got more exposure, and the festival got more exposure, but we got used to what it is like to produce and became acquainted with running a space. We didn't raise much money, but it did give us experience. And we also developed an audience.

PEGGY: The festival was at the All-Craft Center, the old Electric Circus on St. Mark's [*on E. 8th Street in the East Village*]. We had to break down the set and put it up and change the scenery and all that, because they had their own things going on, but they donated the space. They also donated space for benefits over the summer, plus about six months afterward, we kept going there with weekly events.

LOIS: The festival ran for two weeks, with two, sometimes three performances a night, and a couple of daytime performances. We did bring a lot of groups from Europe, who paid their own way and slept on our floors. We told them that that was our setup, but what we could do was give them a spot to perform in New York. That was a big deal for them. We could find them a place to stay and get them some press. Some actually got enough interest they could come back on their own later. There was a lot to be gained in terms of contacts. Also, because we were performers, we wanted to highlight it as a performers' festival. It worked well for them.

PEGGY: And we got a lot of them reviewed; having a review from New York was helpful for them.

LOIS: At the end of the festival, the woman who ran the space said, "Why don't you keep going?" And we said, "Why don't we what?" Then, as now, but not as bad, space was at a premium. We felt if someone was offering us a woman's performance space, we couldn't very well refuse. We stayed there until March.

PEGGY: Till she locked us out. But you don't want to say that.

LOIS: We continued to produce other people's work. . . . By then, we were starting to get lots of brochures and things from performers . . .

PEGGY: Glossy photos.

LOIS: I think we split the door, sharing some percentage with the performer, because we still didn't have any working capital.

PEGGY: The All-Craft Space was a women's education place that taught carpentry and other trades. Then we moved to University of the Streets.

LOIS: After we got locked out.

ALISA SOLOMON: You don't want to say why?

PEGGY: We had this event—it wasn't just a lesbian event, it was a black women's, very, very hot lesbian event—that was packed. And there was a fire next door. It was a little too hot for the woman who had the space.

LOIS: It was the Flamboyant Ladies. It was a very sensual and sexy show.

PEGGY: Beautiful, but a little too sexy for the center. And it just so happened that near the end of the show, there was a fire next door that had nothing to do with us, but she said there was fire damage. The next time we came, there were padlocks on the door and we were out. . . .

ALISA: Did you have a reputation for doing lesbian work there?

LOIS: We did have a reputation for it. We liked to create environments, so some of the time we might have kissing booths, when it went along with the theme, but we were open to all women. It wasn't just a lesbian festival. As long as it was either written by a woman or directed by a woman or had a woman's sensibility, that was the main criteria for a performance to be included.

PEGGY: You didn't have to be a lesbian to get in. But most people either came that way or ended up that way. . . .

PEGGY: We had to find a space because we had been locked out, but we had booked shows until March, which was three more months.

LOIS: First, we went to the Ukrainian Home. And we booked a month of Wednesdays there.

PEGGY: They were wonderful to us. It was an eighty-six-year-old theater. The only problem was that they had no electricity and it was gigantic. To create a mood in there was quite a trick. But we did it. We got chairs, and we got platforms. And had benefits there. Then we went to University of the Streets. They were very nice to us. They gave us space very cheap, like twenty dollars a show. And let us use the café space. . . . Then it was time to do another festival.

LOIS: This was around April '81.

PEGGY: We talked to a woman named Sadia, who ran University of the Streets, and she said she'd be willing to have a café space there during the festival. Plus, we could use her theater upstairs for "Pasta and Performance." We had an hour show, and then you'd eat downstairs in the café. We also booked the Ukrainian Home again every night for eleven nights.

LOIS: We planned this other festival for October '81, and again it was the same format, with us coordinating it. But by then we had assembled a really good technical crew, and we still hadn't raised any money, hadn't written any grants. We did get a couple of thousand-dollar donations right before we did the second festival. . . . We did main-stage shows at 8:00 and 10:00.

PEGGY: We had five shows a day at the Ukraine Home and at other venues.

LOIS: We had "Pasta and Performance" at University of the Streets at 6:00, shows at 8:00 and 10:00 at the Ukrainian Home, an 11:00 show at Theatre for the New City, and a 12:00 a.m. cabaret at the Centre Pub.

PEGGY: And films at the Millennium sometimes.

[. . .]

PEGGY: When the festival was over, there was no café, no place anymore, and there were all these people who said, "I want to keep working." And we had this huge production team. So we said, "Let's get a café."

LOIS: There was just this energy left over. We had a place where you knew if you just dropped by, someone you know would be there. So this arbitrary group of people came together and had brunches every Sunday, and some people organized some benefits at Club 57 [*another East Village perfor-*

mance club at the time] and said let's put this to work on at a café space. This is something we always hoped would happen. We worked with this performance artist who was making her living go-go dancing [*Diane Torr*], and she had organized a couple of other women into a performance piece for the second festival which was really—

PEGGY: Very controversial.

LOIS: Yes. The woman who organized that performance was one of the women who wanted to see things continue. She organized a party called "X-rated Xmas." And again brought her "girls" and did their performances, and we all got into doing—

PEGGY: X-rated things.

MOE ANGELOS: We had this kick line called the Tropicana Girls.

PEGGY: We also had a group called The Schlockettes. We had a chorus line. We don't ever stay out of the acts. Everyone is always in everything. While you're running the lights, people are still in the shows. Nobody ever stopped performing in order to produce. Club 57 was another wonderful place for us. Even after we got the café, we kept producing an event at that place every month. For seventy-five dollars, we got the whole night.

LOIS: It was in the basement of a church at 57 St. Marks Place. Again, we tried to create the craziest atmosphere.

PEGGY: We had a medical drag ball. People actually came with blood dripping or with IVs. People would dance with their IVs. We still have these parties. At the Club Chandalier on Avenue C between 7th and 8th . . . .

CARMELITA TROPICANA: A lot of new people came in through the festivals and parties. I saw one of these festivals, and I said, "Gee, these are people who have a sense of humor." That was one of the things that got me hooked, the sense of humor.

[. . .]

LOIS: All of a sudden we had five or six hundred dollars in our hands that had been raised for a café, and Peggy had been looking for spaces. One afternoon, we found this place [*330 E. 11th Street, the site of the first WOW Café*]. We talked the landlord into renting it to us.

PEGGY: We really talked him into it because he didn't really want any little lesbian theater. We told him it was a women's resource center.

LOIS: He immediately looked at us and said, "Oh, I have a son who's gay." We learned by then that you have to be up front right away because we weren't going to get our hearts into something and have another "situation." We rented the place. We talked about it. There were about twelve people then running it collectively. That's a loose term. It's always really been anarchy.

CARMELITA: There are people who come in, and who leave, who come in, and who leave, who come in, and who leave . . .

PEGGY: We have no idea how it's run. We have no idea.

LOIS: We just ran it with basically those twelve people collectively maintaining it the first year. And we did have a café.

PEGGY: We weren't sure what it was going to be when we opened. To pay the rent, we had to have some money. So we started serving sandwiches—

MOE: And because we had called it a café, we had to serve coffee.

LOIS: We really wanted a performance space. Everybody wanted that. We also wanted a hangout, a girls' social club.

MOE: Some artists also wanted gallery space.

PEGGY: We had fights over, should we have a pool table? [*Pool tables were, at the time, an icon of certain kinds of lesbian bars.*]

MOE: Or the ceiling. Every time you'd come in someone would have painted it another color.

PEGGY: We eventually learned that whatever you wanted to do you could do when nobody else was here.

CARMELITA: We got an art committee at one point. It was all set, people were chosen, and the next day somebody who was unaware there was an art committee came and hung her paintings.

MOE: The art committee was like, "How dare you do this to us?"

LOIS: We had a lot of support in the beginning because we sold memberships. For sixty dollars a year, you could get half off at the door.

PEGGY: That's how we survived. Food and membership.

LOIS: We had about 120 members in 1982. We opened March 27th. Memberships kept us going for a long time. There were fewer performances then. It was more of a hangout. One of the first things we did, though, was put up that platform and a curtain, because we were determined that at some point it was going to be a performance space as well as a café.

PEGGY: Then came Holly.

LOIS: Holly came in very early on. At a certain point, she basically took on management of the café and we started having more performances.

MOE: She did a lot of brunches.

LOIS: She managed it for almost a year.

PEGGY: That means booking, and being here, everything.

CARMELITA: She got a lot of good performers. Comedians came to perform, and she made a lot of contacts with performance artists.

PEGGY: She produced the Talking Slide Show, where artists would come in and show their slides and talk about their work. And she had brunches.

LOIS: We used to have Talent Night. We changed it to Variety Night, where a lot of people started doing new material. We started Tammy there, developing characters and material. [*This is Weaver's infamous Tammy Whynot, the country music star persona who parodies Tammy Wynette.*]

MOE: At one time, we did this collaborative effort with the Limbo Lounge called Cabaret BOW WOW—the Boys of Wow and the Women of Wow. [*Limbo Lounge was another East Village club space with a more gender-mixed clientele.*] We did this minifestival where we had performances here and performances there.

LOIS: Holly worked almost a year, and then she started to get very burned out, which is normal. What happens, unfortunately, when one person is in charge, is that the collective sort of vanishes and leaves all the little details up to one person. Right about that time, we decided to have a retreat, which was really a turning point for the café. We knew something had to change. We wanted to be serious about being a performance space. So we sat around a big table and everybody said what they'd like to see happen with the café.

CARMELITA: I think we wanted many things. We wanted to be an art space; we wanted to be a theater space. We wanted to have as much input from the community as possible. How do you maintain that? Is that feasible or not? If there are shows going on, do you hang pictures on the wall? Can they coexist?

LOIS: At the retreat, we drew up a chronological list of what we'd like to see happen each month, and we pretty much did it for the next year.

MOE: One of the big questions that came up was doing our own work, as opposed to only producing other people's work.

LOIS: We did Holly's play, *The Well of Horniness*; Split Britches' *Beauty and the Beast* [*the second production by Weaver, Shaw, and Deb Margolin*]; *Rosemary and Juliet*, directed by Alice Forrester; *Tennessee Waltz*, which was based on all the women in Tennessee Williams's plays. A lot of in-house productions. Some of these pieces we were working on independently. All these pieces were just ideas to shoot for. These were long-range projects that we could sort of go for and use the talent we had going in the café.

PEGGY: And Lois started teaching acting classes; we could also improve at the same time, which really drew everyone into more of a unit again. But also we realized in order for the next year to happen, we had to plan it. We didn't want the café to die. We realized if you don't think of the future, the future doesn't happen.

LOIS: We wanted to put all this talent that we had around us toward our own work. But we still left slots open where we could produce some other women. Because we had made this plan, each month just materialized into the next project. It wasn't as if anyone was there holding us to it; it just sort of happened because the calendar had to be filled in each month ahead of time. It was pretty magical.

CARMELITA: Then Susan came to us.

SUSAN YOUNG: I had just moved here. I didn't know any of these women; I hadn't seen any of the WOW Festivals. Or really knew that they existed. But I came here by myself and saw Split Britches perform and knew immediately that this was where I wanted to be. I had done theater since I was a teenager, old leftist, pseudo-feminist theater. I worked commercially as a designer. I came back to New York and met Peggy and Lois and decided that this is a place where women who have a lot of technical skill can really work. It's all very anarchic, but it's also very professional. There are a lot of very skilled women here, so it's fulfilling. It's not like you're just doing something as a dilettante. That's a real draw for me and for other women. [. . .]

LOIS: You happened to show up at a time when everything was falling apart. And Susan said, as Holly did, "I'll take on the booking." She saved us. She did. She booked it solid, she kept it going, she took in money, and she did all the work.

PEGGY: Because as anarchistic as you want to be, if you want to have other people in here, they have to speak to the same person all the time.

SUSAN: The goal was to maintain the café as a place for any woman in the community to come in and ask for a booking. . . . We've run into various problems, like performances being bad, talentwise, aestheticwise, censorshipwise. And there are always questions about what should we produce here and how we can judge. We don't really have any basis for censoring what women do here.

LOIS: It's been our policy, even in the festivals, that we never audition people.

PEGGY: And we're always criticized for it. We're told, "Now that you've been around, you have to have quality work." We feel the minute you start auditioning you become just like anyone else. Who says anything is good? Who says?

ALISA: Do you think there's a difference between censorship and deciding that there's something you want the space to stand for?

SUSAN: One thing is that it's work by women. It's sort of self-selecting. We say, okay, go ahead, Jane X, you supply the posters and we share the door. If she brings in eight dollars, the next time, we're not going to be that crazy about booking her again. Part of any kind of personal frustration I have is that we were still in the head set that we are producing as a service to the community, but women come in expecting a great deal and do not give anything back to the space. A lot of women who aren't regulars here come in and perform; they put holes in the wall, break our light board, and split and don't think of ever coming to a staff meeting or to a performance of anyone else's work. Since last spring, we formulated this idea of producing our own work. So far this means producing Split Britches and Alice's plays. Different women have said, "Okay, I'm going to produce a play in this next season." Peggy and Lois are directing *Snow Queen*. I'm going to be directing something in the spring with Sarah Schulman. These are things we set out in the summer, and they take priority over performances by other women.

LOIS: We saw last year that by feeding ourselves, essentially, we are able on other occasions to produce other people's work.

SUSAN: Because of that decision, there was an economic exigency. If we're not going to be booking other women, we have to take this seriously, because we have to come up with seven hundred dollars per month rent. It has to be serious work. Also I planned this film series curated and directed by the Asian Lesbians of the East Coast that has been going on for three months. They use the space during the time that they are here. We decided that that's a project that's important for the café because we don't always represent a wide group, a multiracial experience. The outcome has been incredible. They've done video, film, poetry readings. The place just rocks on Sunday nights.

PEGGY: It's like church. It's fabulous. I was trying to get third world women and women of color here, but it just doesn't happen unless it's their own thing.

SUSAN: Another group we wanted to get to use the space is visual artists from the Limbo Lounge, Women in Limbo. And Reno. She does a monthly show here. She's a very funny stand-up comic.

LOIS: . . . The fact that we might possibly lose the space in March forced us to redefine ourselves in such a way that were we to be without a space we would still have definition. We had WOW as an umbrella, and we had WOW productions. We now have Working Girls Repertory, which *Snow Queen* has come out of, and it's my dream and Peggy's dream to create an in-house and ongoing women's repertory. A Lower East Side girl's chorus, which is sort of waiting for a director.

PEGGY: It used to work, but now it's resting. . . . But women do get jobs in the real theater world from here. People call here and say, "We need a stage manager in an hour!" And they get them. It is a resource center.

MOE: And a dating service.

PEGGY: We're a club for the politically incorrect, for people who don't fit in anywhere else, people wandering around here because they have nowhere else to go.

LOIS: We called it "WOW at 330" because that was the address, but also because we had this sense of what happens to girls when they get out of school—3:30 is the time you get out of school and girls go out on the prowl looking for fun.

PEGGY: We're open from 3:30 till 11:00. We're asked, "How do you stay open all those hours?" Everyone has a key! There are at least thirty thousand keys.

ALISA: Does Susan get paid? How many hours does she work?

SUSAN: No, I don't get paid. I don't want you to publish this, but I live here, so it all meshes into each other. [*Because time has passed and this is no longer the case, we included this story to give people a sense of how lesbians used to make these spaces run, back in the day.*] I work full-time during the day at a straight job. I'm a production manager at a printing plant, just to give you an idea of the mixed lives we all have. I pretty much work all the time. I don't think of it as work so much as just my art. I do set design, I do costume design. I can't count the hours.

PEGGY: Susan's come home to twenty-five women sometimes. She's been sick when there have been shows going on, lying back there.

SUSAN: I find it easier than trying to keep an apartment and keep this space. It's perfect, because I can use it as a studio. There are times, believe it or not, when I'm the only one here. It's a very productive space. The other expenses we have are rent, utilities, and production costs for shows, which are generally covered by box office.

LOIS: We've made the rents. And when we haven't, we've gotten together a rent party.

CARMELITA: Or we throw a benefit and everyone has to put in.

PEGGY: Carmelita will do a dance for sixty dollars.

LOIS: And Peggy's been known to sit outside and beg from people who walk down the street.

ALISA: So you never applied for grants? Is that a philosophical or political choice?

LOIS: We've had meetings where we've talked about it.

CARMELITA: But you know the problem, people really have to sit down and write them, and no one wants to do that.

PEGGY: And besides that, it changes you.

LOIS: We did get some small grants from poets and writers.

PEGGY: And you know what, we have books for three years, five years. We have books! We have kept books.

MOE: What kind of books, encyclopedias?

LOIS: We don't pay taxes. We have the Experimental Theater Project as our umbrella, and so we get tax exemption from that. We have had many philosophical and political discussions about grants and how they affect people, how they might change things. We've talked about paying people, too. No one has ever gotten paid.

CARMELITA: Another one of our disagreements has been, should we pay people?

LOIS: Will it change the work?

PEGGY: Because we can't pay everybody.

LOIS: And how would grants change content? It's pretty free here; people say what they want in their work. How would that change when you start having auditors come in?

PEGGY: You get grants and all of these people come in and judge things. They come in and they cut your grant for the next year.

MOE: A big part of it was that the kind of things that you get grants for were not the kinds of projects that we particularly wanted to put energy into. I remember trying to research how we could get money. The kinds of things I thought we might be able to get money for were not really the kinds of things that we wanted. Ideally, it would be nice to get somebody to just give us twelve thousand dollars a year to pay a manager to work here. Or to pay the rent.

LOIS: We're terrible at things like yearly reports.

MOE: And it's hard to get an operating grant.

CARMELITA: We start with systems, but they sort of degenerate. We have so many people coming through.

ALISA: Do you have any aesthetic philosophy? You have a reputation as a feminist space, at the very least.

MOE: Oh, no, how did we do that?

PEGGY: New works and revivals.

CARMELITA: I think there are a lot of strands of feminism here—

MOE: Sometimes we do things about, you know, lesbians.

SUSAN: If there's an artistic strain, you could say it's to invent from what we have. We don't go out and buy things.

LOIS: Our material too. It's all made from our lives.

SUSAN: Our work is made from our own lives through self-scripting, through Lois's workshops. And even if it references something else, like *Romeo and*

Juliet, it's very much material from our own lives. The materials for our sets and costumes are all invented, all made from found objects.

MOE: And in the same sense, our stuff is made from the space, which is very tiny. This space has changed so many times, but that confinement makes your imagination go someplace.

SUSAN: Our aesthetic would be "creative within our limitations."

LOIS: We enjoy that. We don't resent it. For me it's reflected in a sense of detail. I see it a lot in Susan's designs, in Holly's writing, the little particulars. Attention to detail is something that could be called a "feminine aesthetic" because it's details that are often forgotten or stepped over in male-dominated work. Little parts of our lives are as important as the big climactic events. Moments, relationships.

MOE: The simple things sometimes tell a lot, a big story.

PEGGY: Life, death, murder, wars. All those climactic events.

LOIS: One of the things that we work from is just a simple image, say a day of a woman's life, sitting down and having a cup of tea. There is something of value in that, in her relationship to her teacup, or to her friend. I see that a lot in Susan's work. And Holly has that sense of detail in her language and in her relationship to pop culture.

SUSAN: The detail of humor in her work, in her puns. Not many people can pull that much out of their heads.

PEGGY: Most don't notice those things.

LOIS: A sense of humor is another big thing.

MOE: We laugh at ourselves.

CARMELITA: It's not Serious Theater. We take it lightly.

PEGGY: Because this is a safe place. Not in the sense that our work is safe—

SUSAN: I worked in the theater before, and I had a lot of humiliating experiences. I felt very inhibited and didn't want to perform in front of people. It took about a year, but gradually I began to feel secure enough to perform at WOW. Now they can't get me offstage.

LOIS: Anyone who has anything to say should have the space to get up and say it. That encouragement creates a freedom to express yourself onstage. And then you can train. Once you feel safe.

CLAIRE MOED: And also realizing you can write your own stuff. When we did *Tennessee Waltz*, we all wrote our own stuff and it was good writing. I found it really exciting because I didn't know I could do that.

CHRIS HENRY: Along the same lines for the technicians, 'cause I don't do any acting. As I said, I just walked in, a couple of weeks ago. I'd only been in New York for a month. I'd only done stuff in L.A. I was really intimidated by the idea of New York theater. But when I got in here, everybody encourages you to do stuff.

LOIS: It's community theater. It's creating theater of, for, and by the community. Whatever the community is, and it's not particularly defined. If we have a big show to put on, we don't go outside to find a more talented actress, for instance, or a more talented and expensive lighting designer. But we pull the resources in and work in the community as it forms itself.

ALISA: How would you define your community? Who comes here mostly?

PEGGY: It's difficult to say. It depends on the show.

CARMELITA: Each show brings its own audience.

SUSAN: For the first couple of weeks, we had all women for Split Britches, the Split Britches following. Then, all of a sudden, we started getting all these couples in, men with moustaches and sports coats. I couldn't believe it.

SUSAN: Bianca Jagger came once. She had a hundred-dollar bill and it was like three dollars to get in.

PEGGY: We had to run out and get change. And nobody knew who she was. Reno told people who she was.

CARMELITA: And she did not pay for her tea, if you want to include that in your article.

DEBRA MILLER: This wasn't Reno's fantasy was it? She seemed to be the only one who recognized her.

ALISA: Does anyone charge you with being separatist?

DEBRA: We've had complaints from women about allowing men to come. I've had women at the door say, "Oh, you have men coming here? I thought this was a women's space." And I say, "Yeah, it's a women's space to perform."

PEGGY: If they pay five dollars they can come in, unless the performers designate otherwise and advertise women only.

DEBRA: Most of the men are friends of the performers or they're just interested. They're pretty cool. More of the criticism is about our being separatist. We're not separatist enough.

[. . .]

ALISA: You've said a few times you go out to that "other world," or earlier, Peggy referred to the "real theater world." Do you see yourselves as that separate an entity?

CARMELITA: It's because when you're here, you know you're gonna get the support. You know as a performer when you're not very good, you know deep down that you stink. In this situation, people will be critical. But where the audience doesn't know you and it's just a bunch of strangers looking at you—that's challenging. We did a fashion show at the Limelight [*a performance/dance space on Fifth Avenue in the West Village at the time*] and people thought I was really weird. It's a straighter world, but that's an exciting challenge. It's positive.

LOIS: We want criticism. We don't want to be ghettoized. We want to be validated. But we also like the safe, growing atmosphere.

CLAIRE: I'm in school, where I study traditional technique. That technique only makes sense because of the work I do here, not the other way around.

DEBRA: I work as a stage manager for an Equity showcase, and that feels like it's out there. I was sitting at Barrymore's the other day [*a restaurant in the Theater District*] with the boys, and the only difference was that they have the money.

CLAIRE: And what do they do with it? They create shit.

Lynn Hayes and Debra Miller's band, the Useless Fems

Song
"It's Hard to Be a Dyke in NYC"

Chorus:
Well it's hard to be a dyke in NYC
To go around just trying to be true
To the one that you've pledged undying devotion
When there's so many other gals looking at you

Well to walk arm and arm down the sidewalk
In your feathers or your leather or your furs
And be jeered at by the assholes with the names on their pants
And the drunks on the corner askin' for booze

Yes it's hard to be a dyke in NYC
(*Rest of Chorus*)

Then you come home from workin' late one evening
To the gal that you thought would be forever true
And she's lyin' on your couch with some street lookin' gal
And you thought you had nothin' to lose

Well my friends, my suggestion to you couples
Is to run to a town where dykes are few
Then you know that the one that you're pledged to
Will be by your own side forever true

(*Chorus, twice*)

Lesbian Camp:
Redressing the Canon of 1950s Television

I loved that we thought we were actually a café back at the old
E. 11th Street space, one that served up food and drink to the
masses. I loved that we had visual art back then on our tall walls
in the skinny storefront. I liked that we had a clubhouse feel. There
were many barbeques in the backyard. We would grill on old
refrigerator wire shelves salvaged from the 'hood and propped up
by a couple of bricks, right on the pavement out back. We drank a
lot of beer.

—Moe Angelos

In her groundbreaking 1997 book *Redressing the Canon: Essays on Theatre and Gender,* scholar and WOW booster Alisa Solomon explored how theatre companies ranging from avant-garde stalwarts Mabou Mines and Split Britches to the Yiddish theatre, the Ridiculous Theater, and the Bloolips troupe, reworked the canon of western theatre from Aristophanes to Shakespeare and Tennessee Williams, tearing down not only the fourth wall but oppressive notions of gender and sexuality in the process. Solomon argued that radical troupes or artists from stigmatized groups might use traditional material for radical, liberatory purposes.

The first generation of WOW artists often pursued a similar strategy—but we had a different canon in mind. Although Deb Margolin, Lois Weaver, and Peggy Shaw were interested in Williams and Shakespeare, many of us wouldn't have known Hamlet if he'd gotten in bed with us. Our canon was pop culture, more *Gilligan's Island* than *Waiting for Godot.* Most of us were children in the '60s, when the country was ripped apart by racial tensions, assassinations, and the Vietnam War and then put back together by social justice movements of that time. Most of us were too young to play a part in the radical rebuilding. We ducked and covered as we were told.

And we watched a lot of TV. We couldn't escape the way this new medium was teaching us how to be American, how to be girls. In the midst of that turbulent era, a stream of shows told the same story. White fathers know best. Make room for daddy. When I hear the phrase "heteronormative," scenes from these shows flash through my mind forty years later. But a few shows had a hint of complexity. The couple in *I Love Lucy* was biracial; the wife chafed at the limitations of being a housewife and almost every show revolved around Lucy's schemes to break into show business. No one had to tell you this was a terrible idea. *The Honeymooners* gave a glimpse of urban blue-collar life.

Some of the silliest comedies pulsed with undercurrents of subversion. *The Addams Family, Gilligan's Island, Green Acres, Petticoat Junction*, and even *Hogan's Heroes* were about groups of people who were not necessarily biologically related. If they were—as in *The Addams Family*—they inhabited a different neighborhood than that of the Cleaver clan. They were weird, but weird was cool.

Weird was better than normal. We learned that not in performance studies or even in feminist groups—we got that from bad TV. Those shows were set in absurd, obviously unreal, sanitized places, from deserted isles to concentration camps to farms or small towns. Each week's show hinged on attempts to break out and return to "real life," but, of course, they never did. Thank god! Life was so much better with the Professor, the movie star, and, of course, Gilligan in their version of a family. What perverse person dared to suggest that life as German prisoners of war was such an endless laugh riot?

These shows' sensibilities were deeply queer. They suggested that life could be organized around something other than a patriarchal family, and their ridiculous comedy implied a critique of white heterosexuality. Perhaps no show punctured the myths of midcentury normal with vivid evocations of anxiety better than *The Twilight Zone*. Every episode involved a moment when the everyday cracked open to reveal another shadowy, adjacent universe. Sometimes characters leaped into the zone, sometimes they fell; you couldn't always get back to the other side.

WOW artists, like many East Villagers, referenced these shows over and over again to conjure up family values that were subsequently spoofed or smashed, often to the theme of *The Twilight Zone*, which you could assume everyone knew. We valued humor above all; we loved cheap jokes best of all. We were not interested in merely breaking silence and certainly not in creating positive images of women. We wanted to insert ourselves into the lowliest forms of pop culture and bust up the joint with our messy, undomesticated sexy selves, always entering, always laughing. *—Holly Hughes*

Lois Weaver, Peggy Shaw, and Deb Margolin

Split Britches (1981)

One of the most important plays to come out of the 1981 WOW Festival was *Split Britches*, a collaboration by Deb Margolin, Peggy Shaw, and Lois Weaver, who later formed a theatre company by that name. Rooted in feminist politics, Split Britches is one of the most renowned theatre companies in the United States and has long had a global reach, presenting work and leading workshops from Europe to the Far East. Both collectively and as individuals, the company has received numerous awards, including multiple *Village Voice* Obies.

As a trio, Split Britches presented *Beauty and the Beast* and *Upwardly Mobile Home* at WOW, as well as solo pieces and work with other collaborators. As senior members of WOW, they acted as mentors and teachers to many of us fledgling thespians and lent their expertise to WOW productions in many ways, most often Lois as director, Deb as writer, and Peggy as performer.

Their signature show, *Split Britches*, begins with Lois Weaver/Narrator/Cora dressed in layers of clothing on top of her "split britches," explaining that she started this project years ago, basing the story on her relatives, who lived in the Blue Ridge Mountains of Virginia. We then hear the sound of a slide projector, and the women pose to create a tableau vivant, as if the images they create are being projected. The play is a portrait of three poor, older women: Cora (Weaver), the slow one who's never left the farm; Della (Shaw), the lesbian and caretaker; and Emma (Margolin), the philosopher—and possibly senile—third wheel. The play offers a rich portrait of three women living in rural poverty. The characters are eccentric and isolated; the relationships between them defy categories as they create one another's worlds.

In the following excerpt, the troupe uses vaudeville techniques, songs, monologues, and masterful appropriations of coded language to transform the mundane details of these women's lives into vivid theatre. Although the entire script is available in the collection *Split Britches: Lesbian Practice/ Feminist Performance*, which won the 1997 Lambda award in the Theatre and Drama category, the play represents the abiding spirit of WOW and is essential to include here. Many WOW artists note the importance of seeing the play as an inspiration for their own writing.

When I, Carmelita Tropicana, first saw *Split Britches*, I thought it was *Waiting for Godot* for women: a terrifically funny play aching with humor, a slice of Americana so foreign and yet so familiar. The final monologue, written by Margolin and delivered by an impassioned Peggy Shaw, about "the fire in my pocket," ignited many a fire in the women in the audience. We may not have known what to do with the fire, but were about to find out at WOW.
—*Carmelita Tropicana*

SPLIT BRITCHES
Written and performed by
Peggy Shaw, Deb Margolin, and Lois Weaver
Conceived and directed by Lois Weaver
with original contributions by Naja Bey, Cathey Gollner, and Pam Verge
Costumes designed by Cathy Gollner
Set design by Lois Weaver
Workshop production with Peggy Shaw, Lois Weaver, Cathy Gollner,
    and Naja Bey
WOW Festival
October 1980
Final version with Peggy Shaw, Deb Margolin, and Lois Weaver
WOW Festival
October 1981

CAST
Cora: Lois Weaver
Della: Peggy Shaw
Emma: Deborah Margolin

DELLA: Where you goin', Cora? Where you goin', Emma? Cora Cora!

(*Slide 20 appears.*)

EMMA AS NARRATOR: In her youth, Della Mae was a handsome woman, and a stylish dresser. She had a job in town, and she drove a horse and buggy to and from her house, also in town. I heard it was an unfortunate love affair that brought her back to the farm.

(*Slide goes off.*)

DELLA: Go on. Go ahead and leave me here by myself. Go on Emma! Go get your wood. Don't make no difference to me if you're here or if you're not here. I'm the same woman if you're here or not here. I'm a free woman. I do everything anyway. If you were here, I'd have to pick you up and clean under you. Don't make no difference. It gets cold here in the winter. A draft comes through the kitchen and you gotta keep warm. You can't keep the fire too high or it'll burn down the whole house. I got to have my protection. I didn't always dress like this. I didn't always live like this, you know. I got to have my protection. This here (*she takes off her coat*), this is for the North Wind (*she throws it downstage*). This here (*she removes her apron, and throws it downstage*) is for the fog that comes in over the mountain. (*She starts unbuttoning her dress.*) This is for all the mothers that thought I was after their little girls. (*She takes off her dress.*) This is for all the little girls my Mother broke me up with because they was . . . Catholic! (*She throws the dress at Emma's chair and starts removing next layer.*) This is for the time in church my brother was embarrassed because he said I look like a boy. (*Finishing the clothing removal.*) And this is for the $25 I saved up to go to the prostitute and I walked back and forth all day trying to get up the nerve. (*She throws the dress at Cora's cot and removes the last night shirt.*) And this is for all the nights I cried myself to sleep. (*She throws the shirt, standing only in her long underwear. She goes over to her secret stash of whiskey and takes a long, luxurious slug.*) And this is for Amelia. AMELIA! (*She sings several verses of a blues song from that period, "Bull Dyke Women," originally sung by Besse Jackson, until Emma interrupts.*)

EMMA: Well now! There was an old, blind turkey! I know, because I saw him! I used to know him. And all the animals used to squabble for a place to sleep. Inside. (*She pulls an old chair and drags it over to the woodpile.*) But he was blind. He couldn't squabble. So he had to sleep outside and the weather was bad. First it rain. And after it rain, it shiver. And after it shiver, it got cold, huh! And when it got cold, he got mad, because . . . I know why! Because the cold don't make no noise. Well. He started a singin'. Because the singin' made him less mad. And the singin' attracted all the birds to him. Because. I know why. Because birds is attracted to singin'. Even if it's comin' from an old blind-up old turkey.

(*Slide 21 appears.*)

(*Slide 22 appears, catching Emma between the woodpile and the outdoor wood, from where she will procure a huge tree trunk to drag across the stage.*)

(*Slide goes off.*)

EMMA: Well he heard it. And he thought he had made the stars squeak. How'd he know there were stars? (*She thinks.*) Well. Everybody knows that. Well, the birds. They started peckin' on him. And he felt it. And he thought it was time for the dancin' to begin. (*She begins a long peregrination across the stage with the tree trunk.*) And it went that way. He was singin' so they were peckin' and he was dancin'. So they were peckin' and they were dancin' and he was singin' and they were dancin', so he was peckin' and they were singin' and he was dancin' and he was peckin' so they were singin' and they were dancin' . . . what the hell was I talkin' about? Oh. There was an old blind turkey. I know, because I saw him. I used to know him. Well, it come to Thanksgivin' one time, and the cook come after him with a knife. And he felt it. And he thought it was time for the dancin' to start. But they killed him. And they opened him up. And when they opened him up there was . . . (*she sees the bed*) a place to live in there. With a bed. With the feathers of two hundred ducks in there. (*She faces the table.*) And there was a table. With bread. And wine. And 50 turkeys. And 200 country ham. (*She sees the chair.*) And there was a chair by a window. In the dust. In the light. The dust dancin' in the light. Like in church. The clean dust. Like in church. And there wasn't no bugs. And there were two hundred girls there swattin' the bugs there. Feel my muscle. I built this wall myself. Take a trip to California. Walk on your fingers.

DELLA: (*Dressed again.*) Emma! You seen Cora?

EMMA: Of course I seen Cora. Who do you think I see around here? I see you. And I see Cora Jane.

DELLA: Cora! Cora!

CORA: (*Echoing from the audience.*) Cora! Cora!

DELLA: I hear you, Cora! You better get in this house, Cora.

CORA: You better get in this house, Cora!

DELLA: You want me to get the fly swat, Cora? Cora Jane, where are you? You better get up on this porch. Show yourself!

CORA: Show yourself!

DELLA: Cora Jane, I'm going to count to three and you better be up on this porch. One.

CORA: Two!

DELLA: Two.

CORA: Two!

DELLA: Three! (*CORA enters from house left and DELLA grabs her by the shirt collar and holds her close.*) Where you been Cora?

CORA: I was at the store!

(*Slide 23 appears.*)

EMMA AS NARRATOR: Cora Jane was considered mentally retarded.

(*Slide 24 appears.*)

EMMA AS NARRATOR: She was good at needlework, and easy to handle . . .

(*Slide 25 appears.*)

EMMA AS NARRATOR: Until she got into one of her moods.

(*Slide goes off.*)

CORA: I was at the store!

DELLA: You're too stupid to go to the store!

CORA: I WAS AT THE STORE! It's Thursday. I always go to the store on Thursday. I go to the store on Thursday because Wednesday they deliver the kind of tobacco I always buy on Thursday! I go to the store and I buy two kinds of tobacco! I buy one for Emma and if I have enough money left over I always buy a little candy for myself. I have money to go to the store because when I collect all the eggs and I give Della twelve eggs and I keep one egg until I have my own dozen eggs. And then I go to the store. And I buy two kinds of tobacco. I buy one for Emma and I buy one for me if I have enough money left over I always buy a little candy for myself. And I buy a special kind of tobacco. The kind that's got those little red tags on it. And if I go to the store three more times and I buy two tins of tobacco I'll have enough little red tags to send away and get a cup and saucer like the one I took over to Blanche's house. And I go early to the store on Thursday because I can stop by and visit people. I visit Virginia and I visit Miss Clayter and they give me things. They give me coffee. And they give me cigarettes . . . and they give me white bread. And they save me things. They save me the coupons off the evaporated milk container. And if I go to the store two more Thursdays and they give me one coupon I'm gonna have enough coupons to send away and get a salt and pepper shaker made out of a chicken! Just like the teapot is made out of a chicken!

[. . .]

(*Slide 27 appears.*)

CORA: (*Speaking within the slide.*) That's one way that Della could get Cora was through her little treasures.
EMMA: (*Simultaneously.*) They all used to get up there and play dolls together. Cora and Emma . . . and Della too.
DELLA: (*Simultaneously.*) Della told me she had cash money in the bank for both their funerals . . . and she did.

(*During these recitations CORA goes and sits on the floor at EMMA's feet and EMMA, seated in chair, puts her hand on Cora's shoulder. DELLA is standing behind the chair, stage left slightly of the other two. The next slide catches this final portrait.*)

(*Slide 28 appears.*)

CORA: Cora Jane Gearheart. Born in 1890, died in 1949. Emma Gay Gearheart. Born 1863, died 1952.
DELLA: Fire ain't just a thing, it's a person, I mean, it ain't a person, it's a livin' thing. Got a mind of its own.
CORA: There was a brushfire there on the hill and they all got out there fightin' it . . . I guess Cora Jane just got too excited . . . she started peein' and she couldn't stop. She died the next day of kidney failure.
DELLA: I seen fires. I've felt them on my skin. I heard them cracklin' in my ear, even in the rain. Fires think. They got purposes.
EMMA: Emma Gay had a peaceful death. She died one morning in bed.
DELLA: Once I saw a whole farm burn down. And all the cows and chickens. And the fire went out and brought in other creatures from miles around . . . big black birds that flew upside down next to the fire. And the fire held them there with a string tied to their wings in order to scare all the animals to death. I seen a chicken fall over and the fire went up and ate up its whole body and burped out a big white smoke! I heard dogs barkin' but there wasn't no dogs. And I got fire eatin' inside of me. I can feel it but you can't see it. And that makes me be a person with a secret. I can feel it in my eyes. I can feel it in my chest. And I can feel it in other places.

CORA: Della Mae lived for 15 years alone on that farm, and then she finally sold it. To a stranger. And the very next Halloween that farmhouse burned down.

DELLA: I feel like that farmhouse . . . and dry. And that fire can make ashes out of me if I ain't careful. Once I had fire in my pocket. I put my hand in and pulled it out real quick, and I said, why'd I do that? And I looked in my pocket, and there was the fire, lookin' up at me just cute and sweet as a pretty girl. (*She leans over Emma.*) That ain't even funny, Della! But then it starts to hurt. So you got to beat it. You got to put it out, Emma. Cora!

CORA: She spent the rest of her years in a rooming house in town, and in 1974 Della Mae was buried right between Emma Gay and Cora Jane . . . and to this day not a blade of grass is growin' on her grave.

DELLA: Sometimes I think the fire waits until the whole world is bored, and then it comes along to entertain 'em. But it hurts to laugh. Do you know . . . by the time the men got there, there was nothin' left. It was burned right down to the ground. It's fire steals the land for real.

(*Slide 29 appears.*)

(*Slide goes off.*)

END OF EXCERPT

Alice Forrester

Fear of Laughing on the Lower East Side (1984)

Alice Forrester was involved in the first WOW Festivals and was a constant, welcoming presence at the Café. A femme who often wore little ties and men's suits, Alice could flirt, make newcomers feel welcome, and build an elaborate set out of what she found lying on the street. She worked as a designer on many shows and regularly performed at Variety Nights. *Fear of Laughing on the Lower East Side* was, like most of her work, a spectacle. As the cast list makes evident, the play referred to many television shows, from *The Honeymooners* to *Leave it to Beaver* and *Mayberry, RFD*, with each scenario riddled with holes that led to the Twilight Zone. Like much camp humor, the show relied on incongruity and revealing the absurdity of the normal; it delighted in showing us the seams and the mistakes, and it called attention to the elaborate construction of the normal. In one memorable moment, a set piece collapses and the entire cast is caught (literally) with their pants down. At the same time, *Fear* demonstrated the acting chops of many of WOW's untrained performers, who paid careful homage to great comic performers, even as we snickered at old, rickety plots that reeked of stale bigotries. —*Holly Hughes*

FEAR OF LAUGHING ON THE LOWER EAST SIDE
CAST
Debra Miller: June Cleaver, Useless Femme, "Singer" Sister, Lustre Crème Girl, Townie in *Mayberry, RFD*, Johnnie Olsen.
Lynn Hayes: "Singer" Sister, Rod Serling, June Taylor, Useless Femme.
Susan Young: June Taylor Dancer, Lucy, Martian, Townie in *Mayberry, RFD*.

Peggy Shaw: Norton, June Taylor Dancer, comedienne with Lois, Wally, "Singer" Sister, Townie in *Mayberry, RFD*.

Lois Weaver: Alice, Comedienne with Peggy Shaw, late actress, June Taylor, Townie in *Mayberry, RFD*, "Singer" Sister.

Deb Margolin: Trixie, Comedienne with Peg Healey and Lisa Kron, Townie in *Mayberry, RFD*, June Taylor Dancer, Purina Dog Chow Girl, one of Jackie's girls, "Singer" Sister.

Lisa Kron: Aunt Bea, Joe the bartender, June Taylor Dancer, "Singer" Sister, comedienne with Deb Margolin and Peg Healey.

Diane Jeep Ries: Eddie Haskell, Barney, June Taylor Dancer, "Singer" Sister, Jackie's girl.

Julia Dare: Crazy Guggenheim, "Singer" Sister, June Taylor Dancer, Marlboro Girl, Ricky Ricardo, Martian.

Peg Healey: Ward Cleaver, Andy Griffith, Comedienne with Lisa Kron and Deb Margolin, Warren, June Taylor Dancer, "Singer" Sister.

Shara Antonia: Beaver, Opie, "Singer" Sister, June Taylor Dancer, Martian.

Alice Forrester: Jackie Gleason.

LEAVE IT TO BEAVER
Ward: Peg Healey
June: Debra Miller
Wally: Shara Antonia
Eddie Haskell: Diane Jeep Ries

Setting: It is morning at the Cleaver household . . . JUNE is fixing cucumber sandwiches for the boys. WARD is reading the paper.

WARD: June, Dear, it says here that mothers who stay home all day and do housework have a 90% (greater) chance of becoming mentally ill or schizophrenic than a woman who teaches archeology in colleges. Now I think that's very interesting, don't you?

JUNE: Yes, dear.

WARD: Has Wally come down yet? I have to talk to her. Last night I saw her on the front lawn with that Smith girl rolling around for the whole neighborhood to see. What am I going to do with her? I told her if she wants to do this sort of thing she'll have to use the family car like other normal teenagers. I'm not sure if she even uses a safe contraceptive. I'll have to have a talk about the birds and the bees with her again.

JUNE: Yes, dear. (JUNE *has made a lot of cucumber sandwiches.*)

(*Knock at the door. It is* EDDIE HASKELL *for* WALLY. *The audience sees her outside the house, at the door. She is a leather butch done up as Elvis.*)

EDDIE: (*Outside the door.*) Oh, yeah, well your father sucks eggs at the A&P. Go to hell you prick. Stick it where it will do some good like in a Waring blender . . . (*She knocks on the door.* JUNE *answers.*) Good morning, Mrs. Cleaver, how beautiful you look today as always I must say.

JUNE: Why thank you, Eddie.

EDDIE: Good morning, Mr. Cleaver. I was just saying to your lovely wife how beautiful she looks today. You are very lucky to have such a beauty over breakfast.

WARD: Yes, sit down, Eddie.

JUNE: Did you eat, Eddie?

EDDIE: Well, my mother, God bless her, did manage to get up from her sick bed and make me a piece of dry toast.

JUNE: Oh, you poor thing, I'll make you something.

EDDIE: Thank you, Mrs. Cleaver.

(WALLY *enters, very monotone and stupid.*)

WALLY: Hi Mom, Dad. Oh hi, Eddie. What are you doing here? I thought you were in juvenile hall for that sodomy case with that 16-year-old?

JUNE AND WARD: What?

EDDIE: Oh, what poor young Wallace means is that I am helping a poor young friend of ours who is in unfortunate circumstances. Sad story, really.

JUNE: Oh, Wally. Did you pick up your room?

WALLY: Oh, Mom, I'll do it when I get home from school. Oh, yeah, Mom. I forgot to tell you that some lady called yesterday and said something about meeting you at 3:00 at the Last Lick Motel. Something like that.

WARD: June . . . what does that mean?

JUNE: Oh, oh, that is where our bridge club is meeting this afternoon. Thank you, Wally, for the messages. So, what is new in school, girls?

WALLY: Oh, nothing much. Except Donna Petti fainted in the lunch room yesterday.

JUNE: Oh, how terrible, what did you girls do?

WALLY: Eddie pulled her skirt over her head.

WARD: June, I can't believe that the bridge club is meeting at the Last Lick. Why I was just over there the other day . . . (*Gets embarrassed;* EDDIE *guffaws and hits* WALLY.)

JUNE: (*Missing it, spacey. She is still making sandwiches.*) Yes, dear. Wally, have you seen the Beaver?

WALLY: Oh, yeah. He was in the bathroom doing something stupid like counting his teeth or something like that.

JUNE: Beaver, come down or you'll be late for school.

BEAVER: Hi, Mom. (*Everyone freezes.*)

ROD SERLING: This, as you may recognize, is a little town on a big map of the United States. On a given morning, not too long ago, the rest of the world disappeared and—was left all alone. Its inhabitants were never sure whether the world was destroyed and only—was left untouched, or whether the village had somehow been taken away. They were on the other hand sure of one thing—the cause. A monster had arrived in the village. Just by using her mind, she took away all the automobiles, the electricity, the machines. (BEAVER *looks out the window. The lights all go off except for the one on* ROD—*the appliances disappear or fall down.*) Because they displeased her and she sent them back to the dark ages. Just by using her mind, you'll note that the people in—USA have to smile, they have to think happy thoughts, say happy things because once displeased, the monster can wish them into a cornfield, or change them into a grotesque walking horror. This particular monster can read minds, you see. Yes, I did forget something didn't I? I forgot to introduce you to the monster. Her name is Theodore Cleaver, alias the Beaver. She is six-years-old with a cute little girl face and blue guileless eyes. But when those eyes look at you, you better start thinking happy thoughts, because the mind behind them is absolutely in charge. This is the Twilight Zone.

BEAVER: Hi, Dad. Dad, how many teeth do people have? I tried counting but I couldn't tell.

WALLY: As many as you want, Beaver. Whatever you say.

ROD: No comment here, no comment at all. We only wanted to introduce you to one of our special citizens, little Leave it to Beaver. And if by some strange chance you should run across her, you had best only think good thoughts. Anything less than that is handled at your own risk because if you meet the Beaver you can be sure of one thing: You have entered the Twilight Zone.

END OF EXCERPT

Alice Forrester

WOW Women in Their Own Words

I lied my way into WOW by telling Lois Weaver at the 1980 Boston Women's Festival that I was moving to New York and they should call me if they ever needed anyone to sweep their floors for their show. They called, I swept their floors, and they asked if I wanted to stage-manage at the second WOW Festival. Of course, I agreed. I went there on day one of the festival. Peggy put me in charge of the University of the Streets Theater. I told my boyfriend in New Jersey that first morning I went to work at WOW that I would be back late, and never returned.

I lived and breathed WOW from 1981 to about 1988, hardly went above 14th Street, sublet on almost every street in the East Village, stage-managed for Split Britches, did a few shows, toured in Europe and the States.

At WOW I served a lot of brie and Rolling Rock, was one of the gals who thought the walls of WOW at 330 E. 11th Street should be pink, worked the door, changed a hundred-dollar bill for Bianca Jagger's crew when they came to a Reno Comedy Night [*Reno was one of the WOW performers.*], swept sand down the heating pipe into the basement after gentrifiers bought 330 E. 11th, put in the wood floor at the new WOW on E. 4th Street with my then honey, Lynn Hayes, directed, wrote, designed, and acted in too many shows to count. Grew up there.

How did WOW work? We worked hard.

I remember the fund-raising for opening the WOW space. It's the 1981 WOW Festival. It's almost over. Cleanup day. Maybe a Sunday or a Monday. We wake up Moe Angelos from under the piano, clean up, eat, drink some beer. Peggy says that we need to get our own space. We meet over the next few weeks. Where? Oh, yeah, University of the Streets. A lot of gals are left over from the festival, hanging out at the little café we had put together there. Lots of beautiful Italian, German, and Dutch women, Americans, just a lot of women with a lot of energy.

We threw a lot of parties. "Erotic Underwear" . . . Individuals produced the parties. Lots of women with red lipstick and wearing black. We had a Halloween party. I decided to organize a haunted house, just like I did when I was eight years old in New Jersey. Moe helped me. I had a bowl of cold pasta, Day-Glo lips, screams, lots of scary things. The energy was really high. Fun, sexy, irreverent parties that were a lot of work. The work was contagious. The work brought us together, provided a community. You could volunteer, have creative freedom, and feel instantly like you belonged. Prepare, decorate, hang flyers in the middle of the night, worry you're going to get arrested, sell tickets at the door, bartend, dance, provide the entertainment, clean up, go out after, wake up the next morning with another project in the works, have breakfast at Leshkos, and do another show.

My favorite show? All of them. My images from shows? All the women lined up on the brick wall in slips in *Tennessee Waltz*. *The Snow Queen*'s costumes. Meeting Susan Young for the first time and going home with her and sleeping on her floor. The phone ringing during "WOW at 330" shows. The beautiful tile floor at 330. The tiny little stage and the purple velvet curtains Peggy found in the garbage.

Staff meetings in the backyard. The fight over whether men can use the bathroom in the back. We lost some very beautiful women over that one.

The kitchen at WOW 330, during one of my first shows, *Rosemary and Juliet*. Claire Moed as the nurse, cooking bacon. Deb Margolin as Juliet, under the gauze of the bed attached to the wall. I thought she wasn't there, that she left the show, and I ran down 11th Street looking for her. Adrienne Collins coming in as some character, late and drinking, as Cleopatra, interrupting the show, and everyone thinking she just walked in off the street.

Another show at 330: *The Heart of the Scorpion*. My girlfriend, Denise, who was the star of the show, got Bell's palsy. She couldn't act. Susan Young, Shara Antonia, Moe Angelos, and I tried to figure out what to do. We solved it by taping me on video and attaching the TV monitor to the chair's headrest. Then I acted with myself. Kate Davy published a review of the show in *The Drama Review* that said it was a very clever and intellectual reflection of lesbian love. Happenstance and personal lives always interfered and were fodder for productions at WOW.

Designing Holly's plays . . . *The Lady Dick* . . . Holly's beautiful words strumming from a very cool dick. I remember Sharon Jane [Smith]'s first performance at WOW. She came and played her mandolin at a variety show.

Becky, her girlfriend, sitting proudly, telling us that Sharon Jane was shy but very talented.

St. Joan of Avenue C. Our first play in the new space on E. 4th Street. Anyone who hung out at WOW was in that show. Alina starred in it; she had just quit her real job to work in the theatre full time. Rehearsals were long and really hard.

Variety shows. I used to prepare for my character, Blanche, by dressing in costume and getting into my role as I walked down the street to WOW. The East Village felt like a large backstage at that time. Everyone was doing some sort of performance theatre. In the variety shows, we could introduce characters or try out new work. I remember sitting together after a Variety Night, or after a staff meeting, and Moe doing imitations of everyone, especially of Holly.

Butch/Fem Nights. Butch Nights were always better attended and more fun. The fems had a lot of difficulty finding something funny if they weren't working off the butches. Joy Tompkins rode her motorcycle into the space for Butch Night. Jeep handcuffed me to the chair as the fem emcee to make her point as a butch.

Staff meetings. We would have big meetings occasionally during the year where we would sit in a big circle and try to hash out personality problems or value differences.

Those were some tense moments. We had to agree on how to run the space as a large group. And there were a lot of differences. We had to work on each other's shows for the space to keep going, and that was difficult when some people didn't keep up their end of the bargain.

I kept coming to WOW because of the women, the people, and the creative energy. There was always something to do. And as I continued, I became able to articulate my own creative voice. There was a buzz, an energy, a dedication to performance. It was like a very long theater training program where you learned how to perform, how to create. It was my family. I was growing up there. I learned how to work hard there. I learned how to support others. I learned how to get along with others, too.

I didn't leave there for almost eight years. I did everything: house-manage, stage-manage, act, direct, write, install the floor, manage the books, pay the bills, clean the bathrooms, make the monthly calendar, serve beer, and fall in love.

For a long time Peggy and Lois were the leaders, even though they denied and rejected the role. Everyone had their own issues with leadership. Others could assume the role of leader, but when the shit hit the fan it was Peggy and Lois who would come through and try to iron out the problems.

I believe it was Peggy Shaw's Protestant work ethic that WOW was founded on. There was a very strong work ethic at the space. Believe me, you were watched. If you didn't come to strike night [*the moment when the set is taken apart after a production and the theatre is returned to a neutral state*] and carry the wood up and down the stairs, or if you didn't break your fanny doing something for someone else, the group knew, and you would feel out of the crowd, unaccepted. I believe the people who felt most estranged were the ones who worked the least for another person's show.

Decisions were made by the group, but it was the people who had the loudest voice, the loudest and strongest opinion, who swayed the group. If you were loud, and believed in what you were saying, you usually got your way. People also left each other alone. No one had opinions about each other's creative work. We stayed away from critique. That was one of the best things about WOW. People did not judge each other by the quality of their work but rather by the quantity of their work.

WOW was a mix of people. Most of them lived in the East Village in the '80s and '90s. That's what they had in common. We didn't have a lot of personal information about people (unless you were sleeping with them, and even then, it could be minimal). Their past lives weren't important. Their present lives were important. It was like they just arrived on this planet when they walked into WOW, and that was who they were then, at that moment, rather than what they had done in the past.

Most of us had little money at that time. There were real class differences between the women who worked at WOW and the ones who came to see the shows. A lot of the audience was women who worked nine-to-five jobs. There were a few women's groups organizing social activities in the early '90s, like at Shescape [*a rather well-heeled dance bar on the Upper East Side*]. Some of us would go to parties, and I would feel really different from these women who were choosing a career in finance or advertising and who had to wear suits. Thinking about those who choose to work in the system and those who lived in the East Village with no money and produced art—that was a big theme in my life then.

WOW was a lesbian space. Bisexuality was hardly accepted, and heterosexuality was tolerated. We used to joke and say that straight people had to pay double at the door, so everyone had to say they were queer to get in at regular price. In my opinion, that wasn't feminist politics, it was queer politics. We explored butch and fem themes, we explored queer relationships . . . WOW was a place where sex, fashion, art, and drama were the focus.

Were there men at WOW? Uzi Parnes was the only guy who really had any creative say at the space, and that was only when Alina or Ela asked him to be there. [*Uzi was a performance studies graduate student at NYU, who was dating Alina Troyano's sister, Ela, at the time.*] Men would visit. The boys at Limbo Lounge came for a festival Holly arranged in the summer one year, and they came to see the shows. [*Limbo Lounge was another bar/performance space in the East Village at the time, which attracted a more gender-mixed crowd.*] That was fun—it was like the guys from the camp across the lake were coming over to visit. Men were in the audience. We took their money. But they were not our focus at all.

WOW was an ugly stepsister in the theatre world at large. We worked hard, but we were barely recognized or valued. We didn't choose to compete there either. Our community had an antitheatrical bug. We drew audiences from the club scene rather than the theater world. We put up a lot of flyers and had a listing in the *Voice* and occasionally we would try to get listed in the *New Yorker* and things, but really, we would advertise with women who wanted to be with women.

We were doing performance art at 330. It was a very lively time in the East Village for performance, and that's where we fit. We were exploring the boundaries of theatre, the edges, and producing work that came from the organic center of a lesbian community. We were giving voice to queer politics through theatre.

Of course, we all were interested in the theatre. We took acting lessons from Lois, and as we moved into a larger space we produced more theatrical shows. As we got older, fitting into the larger theatre world became more important.

Sadly, I have not been to WOW in many years. I moved on to become a drama therapist, an interest that I believe came out of working at WOW.

Alison Rooney

Waaay Beyond the Valley of the Dolls (1986)

I first arrived at WOW a few years before this production. Unlike the majority of women who arrived at WOW in a migratory pattern from far afield, I grew up in the City and never felt that I meshed well with any particular group of people. Neither rebel nor conformist, what led me most was language and irreverent humor and a theatricality not at home in the "I am deadly serious about my craft" world of the HB Studio crowd.

I was introduced to downtown performance by my friend David Cale, who told me breathlessly one day, "You've got to meet this woman I've just met. She's right up your alley—you two will love each other—she has Petula Clark on her answering machine." By that time, I had started writing and performing short, odd, language-based monologues on themes ranging from terriers to the witness protection program. I called the Petula person, in hopes of booking a performance at the café she programmed. Her name was Holly Hughes, and she told me that there were a lot of "ad hoc" performances that took place at the WOW Café, and that I should talk to Susan Young, "who lives just behind the stage," and get put on the calendar. No audition, no "Send us your script," just a "Let's find a free date and slot you in."

What followed were several years of feeling completely welcomed, despite dubious credentials as an uptown straight chick. I worked and played all the time at WOW, as a writer-performer in my own work and as an actress in shows by many of WOW's luminaries. The culmination of my WOW time was the production of my first full-length play, *Rabbit Plantation*.

I remember a great deal of licking-the-chops eagerness about *Waaay Beyond the Valley of the Dolls* from both cast and audience. The audiences did eat it up—in particular the "doll dance" sequence and Helen Frankenthal's sublime performance as the deranged diva. Earlier, I had performed a piece at Avant-Garde-arama at PS122 to an awkward reception. I was later told that "the audience didn't really know what to make of it." Both nights, same reaction. My oddness had struck again. My disappointment in that experience was erased the moment I walked into WOW and felt the great good fortune of supplying a yuck-a-thon to the completely receptive audience there. —*Alison Rooney*

WAAAY BEYOND THE VALLEY OF THE DOLLS

(*Tape on with voice-over leading into "Theme from Valley of the Dolls." Lights up one by one on each of the starlets, as she sings her verse. Starlets are seated together in a row on three stools with Jennifer in the middle.*)

ANNOUNCER: The Year: 1967. The Place: The United States of America. (*To music.*) The Story: A sordid one, dark and ugly, ridden with sin and sequins, One that Needs Telling! As our nation grapples with war, social upheaval, race riots, student demonstrations, and love beads, three young ladies, each from a different sociosexual stratum (*Girls look at each other snidely.*) battle their own personal demons in their own private hells, in their quest for that elusive jewel, FAME (*Girls repeat softly, "Fame, fame, fame . . ."*)

(*Music fades, lights fade out and up again.*)

Ladies and Gentlemen, in a little hamlet in sleepy Northern California we find the town thespian—the driven, the intense, the some say ultra bitchy star of Calabasas High's senior production of *The Pajama Game*—at nineteen she's already fighting weight gain and violent mood swings, but a true talent nonetheless, we are proud to present Miss Patty Duke—yep, that little blind girl has grown up and out—as Neely O'Hara.

NEELY: (*Takes bite of Mallomar and then stuffs her lit cigarette into the remains. Speaks with mouth full.*) I'm gonna make it, no matter who I have to trod upon or sleep with. I want, correction, I *need* adulation, Golden Globe awards, and all the other trappings of success. (*Looks down at silver "reducing" wrap on her thighs.*) Burn, baby, burn!!!

ANNOUNCER: Oh, she is exhausting, but exciting!! (NEELY *freezes into a manic smile on "exciting" and holds the pose during the other intros.*) Meanwhile, in wintry Vermont, land of maple syrup, quaint bed-and-breakfast inns, and the great urban metropolis of Montpelier, a pensive young lady sits by her bay window, reflecting on the snowflakes and her intellectual prowess. It's with great pleasure that I introduce, fresh from her triumph in *Peyton Place*, Miss Barbara Parkins, as Ann.

ANN: Like Edith Wharton, Ann Beatty and Steven King, I will become one of New England's finest scribes, known for my terse, elliptical style. I will then build a publishing empire, second only to Random House. The first step, an Adirondack Trailways 35-seater coach to New York City via Saugerties. So what if I'm frigid?

ANNOUNCER: My, she's brainy, but a wee bit repressed . . . And, finally, from 'neath the sunny skies of the corn-belt, a young and comely maiden (JEN-NIFER *runs comb through her hair and tosses it into the air.*) blessed with an ample bosom, a giving heart, and a brain that's been sitting in a silo for 18 years. In her silver screen debut, the beautiful and marginally talented Miss Sharon Tate, as Jennifer.

JENNIFER: When that producer with those groovy aviator shades came to Davenport and singled me out for mega-stardom, I thought he was joshing—after all, I didn't know the ways of the world, much less a zoom lens—but here I am, ensconced in a Beverly Hills manse—the world is my oyster and I'm just ripe to be taken advantage of.

ANNOUNCER: One more time, Sharon, with more inner motivation, please.

JENNIFER: The oyster is my world and I'm just ripe to be taken advantage of.

ANNOUNCER: Thank you, Sharon. We'll call you. There you have them— three young lovelies teetering at the brink of womanhood (*Girls stand uneasily on their toes as announcer flashes sign saying "womanhood—five miles."*) whose paths are destined to cross (*Girls turn and cross each other, giving each other looks of lust crossed with hatred!*). There they sit, each at the gateway of their lives. Who can predict their futures? Will it be lucrative contracts (NEELY *mimes signing a contract dismissively*), whirlwind romances (ANN *takes off her glasses and gazes upwards longingly*), hernias, drug-induced depravity, or simply oblivion? (JENNIFER *looks befuddled.*) This is the story we are here to tell tonight!!!

(*Girls run off. Music starts up and one by one, each girl's story is silently en-acted to the music—rapid fire—while ANNOUNCER describes the events rap-turously!!!*)

ANNOUNCER: NEELY! PACKS SUITCASE . . . STORMS OUT OF HOUSE WITH GOOD RIDDANCE LOOK . . . GETS SCRIPT THRUST IN HAND . . . AUDITIONS . . . SIGNS CONTRACT . . . SMOKES CIGA-RETTE . . . MAKES THE NEWSPAPERS . . .

(*Holds out signs which say, in block letters, "Newcomer* NEELY O'Hara *signed for lead in "Pointless" and "O'Hara tapped to co-star with Peter Fonda."*)

SMOKES JOINT . . . LOVER COMES IN BEARING FLOWERS—THEY KISS . . .

THEY SQUABBLE . . . LOVER STORMS OUT, NEELY HANGS ON TO LOVER'S CLOTHING . . . HAS TANTRUM . . . SHOVES FOOD IN MOUTH . . . HOLDS UP PILLS WITH GLEE . . . ANN! . . . HUGS SOMEONE WEARING A SIGN SAYING MOM, WIPING AWAY TEARS . . . WALKS UNDER SIGN SAYING, "PUBLISHERS CLEARING HOUSE, NEW YORK CITY." (*Holds out sign.*) LOOKS NERVOUS . . . HANDS OVER A MANUSCRIPT TO AN EDITOR . . . EDITOR SHAKES HEAD "NO" . . . HANDS OVER MANUSCRIPT TO SECOND EDITOR . . . SHAKES EDITOR'S HANDS OVER "YES" . . . MAKES NEW YORK TIMES BESTSELLER LIST FOR SIX STRAIGHT WEEKS . . . LOVER COMES IN BEARING FLOWERS . . . ATTEMPTS TO KISS ANN WHO CROSSES LEGS . . . LOVER LEAVES . . . ANN LOOKS DEJECTED . . . ANN HOLDS UP ONE PILL TO THE LIGHT, CONTEMPLATES TAKING IT . . . JENNIFER! . . . PULLS STRAW OUT OF HAIR . . . PACKS GRANNY NIGHTGOWN AND HUGE BRA IN BAG . . . SIGHS . . . BITES LIP AND RAISES EYEBROWS . . . MOVES TO HOLLYWOOD AND VINE . . . ENTERS OFFICE OF BIG PRODUCER . . . PRODUCER MIMES, "TURN AROUND AND SHOW ME YOUR STUFF" . . . SHE DOES . . . SIGHS . . . LIES DOWN ON THE FLOOR, HEAD OUT TOWARDS AUDIENCE . . . LEGS SPREAD . . . PRODUCER MIMES A THRUST OR TWO . . . GETS UP . . . BITES LIP . . . PRODUCER MIMES, "GET OUT" . . . TEARS . . . SIGN: "OPEN AUDITION FOR *LET'S MAKE A DEAL* HOSTESS." (*Holds out sign.*) . . . LOOKS AT SIGN . . . HAS A LOOK OF RESOLVE . . . TAKES ONE PILL . . .

ANNOUNCER: Meanwhile, in a somewhat ritzier section of the City of the Angels, the famous chanteuse slash pin-up queen Lola Lawson reflects on her past glory for an interviewer. We are honored with a very special comeback appearance here tonight, Ladies and Gentlemen, Miss Susan Hayward as Lola Lawson!!

(INTERVIEWER *sits with steno pad, silent and writing throughout.*)

LOLA: Yes, those were the champagne years, when it was all corsages, limousines and stage door Jennies, er Johnnies. I dated Eddie Fisher. That was a barrel of laughs. I was on the cover of *McCalls* six times wearing the trademark "Lawson snood." I belted with the best of them honey, and don't you forget it. Marriage? Oh, I never had time for that nonsense. I brushed up against some fabulous men, honey, but I couldn't stand the lint. Get my drift? Rumors? What rumors? Oh, I think that's the oven timer now, I'd better go baste the bird. Have you got enough material, honey? Just pad it with lots of photos—call my rep.

(*As* INTERVIEWER *leaves*)

Ciao, you little varmint. Yet another minion trying to usurp my position. Why do I agree to these things? I know why I agree. Why am I kidding myself? I'll do anything to keep myself in the public spotlight. I know, I'm just another glamour gal gone slightly to seed, but I'll show 'em yet. No bus and truck tours of *Sugar Babies* for me. This town hasn't heard the last of Lola Lawson. Now if only I could get some action, enough to last me till I get hot again at the wickets and it doesn't matter how decrepit I look. Till I can lure those beautiful young starlets with just the promise of an introduction to a mogul or two. Oh why am I worrying? With my talent it's a cinch.

ANNOUNCER: Over in Stockholm . . .

ANN: Dr. and Mrs. Nobel, members of the nominating committee, assorted international eggheads: Thanks. Thanks a million. The Nobel Peace Prize. It's more than a statuette. I think we all know that. Peace, peace, what is peace? There are many peaces, a piece of pie, a piece of the action, yes, a piece of ass—I know, it makes me shudder too. Luckily, I was able to put all the pieces together in *The Other Side of Afternoon.* (*Waits for the sound of applause.*) Thank you. Thank you a million. To think that through my craft I have brought the ultimate summer beach reading into the lives of millions of dull people moves me more than I can describe. Though my descriptive powers are by now legendary, of course.

When I started, with quill in hand in my lonely garret—and you know a quill can come in handy in a lonely garret—the feathers, ever so lightly, along the inner thigh (*Someone taps her on the shoulder.*) DON'T TOUCH ME! When I started I never dreamed that *The Other Side of Afternoon,* with its turmoil and epic sweep, would soothe all the world's woes. Well, except for the Peruvian/Equadorian border skirmish it has. And that's a hoot. Gratifying, too. All I had hoped for, even as little as a year ago, was maybe a publishing war over the softcover rights, perhaps a lucrative mini-series deal, maybe mass merchandising and an appearance on *Hour Magazine.* Well, I got those things—and a Nobel to boot. Sure it's just the icing on the cake, but that's my favorite part to lick. Although I don't do that sort of thing. Often.

MRS. NOBEL: Miss Welles, Miss Welles, I beg your pardon. You haven't won the peace prize. That honor went to Dag Hammarskjold.

ANN: (*Softly, as if trying to calm someone down.*) Yes, yes, dear. Sure, he did. Dag Hammarskjold's a plaza near the UN in New York. (*Suddenly shrieks.*) How can a plaza win a peace prize? This woman is obviously bonkers. There's one at every awards show. Personally, I'd rather see a streaker. Honey, take off all your clothes and start running the bell lap and you can have me at your finish line any time. You are Finnish, aren't you?

NOBEL: I most certainly am not finished. I must repeat, Miss Welles, you have received the supreme honor of copping the Nobel Prize for literature.

ANN: Literature? Oh. Literature, literature, what is literature? How the hell should I know? It took me six months to research peace. Anybody got any vodka? (*Bottle handed over.*) Thanks. Thanks a bundle.

(*Blackout.*)

JENNIFER: Hi, I'm here for the "Let's Name That Tune" audition.

CAROL: Let's Make A Deal then. Step right down here. I am Carol Merrill and they are replacing me, as I have experienced some small hair growth about my upper lip and those squares in Hollywood have decided that middle America is not quite ready for me yet. What is your name?

JENNIFER: Who is Jennifer North for 25.

CAROL: Very good. Now let's see your arm motions.

JENNIFER: I've got polio and tetanus.

CAROL: (*Puzzled.*) Yes . . . Like this, ah one and two and one and two. Now you try it.

(JENNIFER *slugs* CAROL.)

CAROL: Tremendous. I can see you're willing to take a gambit.

JENNIFER: I didn't put you in any kind of jeopardy, did I?

CAROL: No, I like that kind of stuff. You hit the bull's-eye.

JENNIFER: I can do it for you privately if the price is right.

CAROL: Well, to tell the truth I'm sort of tied up most evenings.

JENNIFER: Well, don't make any snap judgments.

CAROL: Yes. Now, let's try the pointers. Now, indicate to your right and repeat after me. Spiegel Catalogue, Chicago 60609.

JENNIFER: Siegel Catalogue, Chicago 60609.

CAROL: Spiegel.

JENNIFER: Spwiegel.

CAROL: Spiegel.

JENNIFER: I have trouble with my p's.

CAROL: I think I'm going to have to let the producers know about this.

JENNIFER: Tattletale.

CAROL: Look, it's the truth or consequences around here.

JENNIFER: I guess I'm just not cut out for this type of work.

CAROL: Look, sweetheart, you're not alone. I haven't a clue as to what's my line either.

(*Lola enters.*)

JENNIFER: Oh, excuse me. Do you know the way out of this soundstage?

LOLA: All too well.

JENNIFER: Pardon?

LOLA: Nothing. Who are you, you cherubic naif?

JENNIFER: My name's mud, it seems. I'm just another young hopeful on a wayward path.

LOLA: My favorite kind of walkway. In need of a little consoling are you? How about we discuss your minor problems over a tête-à-tête chez moi?

JENNIFER: Huh?

LOLA: If you sleep with me I'll open a lot of doors for you.

JENNIFER: Super, I haven't had a lotta luck with doors lately.

LOLA: It's a cinch.

JENNIFER: You're swell.

LOLA: And you're a cute kid.

[. . .]

(*Blackout.*)

(*Sign reads, "Somewhere on the Sunset Strip." Lights up on* NEELY *and* AGENT, *both on the phone, both wearing caftans.*)

AGENT: Neely, baby, I've got big news for you. I'm just off the phone with William Morris, and, you're not going to believe this—Ingmar Bergman wants you for the lead in his next opus.

NEELY: Huh—I believe it. In fact, I've been waiting for the call. Ingy's been sending me mash notes for years.

AGENT: Look, this is not going to be boffo box-office but it's prestige. And you could sure use some of that honey, especially after that frying pan episode. There's one catch though, Bibi Anderson was caught in a snowdrift and eaten by some starving Laplanders, so he's signed Helen Lawson to co-star.

NEELY: That battle-ax? What's this turkey called?

AGENT: *Persona non grata.*

NEELY: No, what's the English title?

AGENT: I don't know, probably *Shame through a Dark Glass Fanny.*

NEELY: Sounds really upbeat.

AGENT: Shooting begins in Stockholm next month.

NEELY: Great, maybe I can score a Swede.

[. . .]

INGMAR: (*To offstage actresses.*) Now, dahlinks, I vant you to understand that what we are making here is a mood piece. Think of yourself as lava lamps, bubbling upwards and downwards in different shades of light.

(*Enter* NEELY *and* HELEN *wearing sheets, white powder makeup, barefoot.*)

HELEN: No sweat. Bergdorf dear, what side am I going to be shot from?

NEELY: As far away and as gauzy as possible would be best for the old career, wouldn't it now?

HELEN: Get this bitch off my tail.

NEELY: I have no desire to get on your tail, or your horns.

INGMAR: Ladies, ladies, this bantering is all very amusing, but we have oppressively serious work to do. Shall we begin?

NEELY: The forest is dark, still, like my heart. I am like the trees: barren, leafless. I am Leafless Ullmann. I was once a very famous actress, pale skin, fair hair, worked in quality pictures which no one understood. Now I sit in contemplation of the woods and think about death, dying, and why I made *Forty Carats.*

HELEN: I am Nurse Goneril, here to bring you back to health.

NEELY: Goneril? You sound like a social disease. Anyway, I do not deserve to be healthy. I am content only with phlegm rising in my wretched mouth.

HELEN: Hey, is this for real? This is a real downer. And I don't like this no makeup look.

NEELY: You're ruining my moment, you has-been.

INGMAR: Ladies, ladies, you have lost sight of your characters. Remember our theme—that little by little, the two of you absorb each other's personality so that you turn into each other's personality so that you turn into each other and (*Turns to* NEELY) you wind up mute.

END OF EXCERPT

Lisa Kron for the Five Lesbian Brothers

Paradykes Lost (1988)

Before she was a Tony-Award-winning playwright and performer, Lisa Kron was a WOW regular. She was one of the few at the Café with any formal training—she studied theater at a liberal arts college and had a stint touring in professional companies. Not long after arriving in 1984, she was cracking us up with stories about her lovable but highly eccentric family and working with directors and teachers who recognized her talent but were flummoxed by her queer Jewish body. She had a way of crafting her personal stories so that we could read ourselves into them. Some of this earliest work seeded her solo show, *101 Humiliating Stories*.

Before cofounding the Five Lesbian Brothers, Lisa collaborated on and performed in two epic comedies at WOW: *Paradykes Alley*, set, of course, in a bowling alley, and *Paradykes Lost*, a queered-up murder mystery reminiscent of Agatha Christie. This work makes no attempt to deconstruct genre or inject metanarrative technique. In fact, part of what makes it so much fun is its gleeful embrace of genre conventions: a country manor house, an improbable cast of characters, amnesia, evil twins, romantic triangles, and secret identities. A predictable distraction ends with the discovery of a body. And of course everyone concerned had not just a motive but just cause to want that body dead. *Paradykes Lost* makes us less interested in whodunit than in rediscovering just how much fun it is to play with conventional entertainments.

Like so many of the WOW shows, heterosexuality is entirely absent here. No one plays a man in drag; they play butch lesbians. This is an entirely lesbian world, where one woman can knock up another without resorting to a turkey baster.

We've excerpted this play (the cuts are indicated by ellipses in brackets), but the plot should be familiar to anyone who has seen an Agatha Christie–type murder mystery, the genre it lampoons. A group of eccentrics assemble at an estate. They are gradually introduced, with hints about the skeletons in each of their closets. Suddenly, the power fails. When the lights come on, the disagreeable lady of the manor is dead. A handsome detective shows up and begins to detect.

As always, we're less interested in "whodunit"; it's established early that any person would want Lucretia Owner six feet under. What's more intriguing is the play's queer feminist take on otherwise stock characters. —*Holly Hughes*

PARADYKES LOST
Written by Lisa Kron in collaboration with the cast
Directed by Lisa Kron
Set design and costumes by Susan Young
Lighting design by Amy Meadow
Sound design by Lisa Kron and Tommy Hawk
Stage manager, Dominique Dibbell
Photos by Eva Weiss
Poster and program design by Donna Evans

CAST
(In order of appearance)
The Doomed Waitress: Susan Young
Amelia Harris, the Heiress: Peg Healey
Doctor Constance Boswell, M.D., Ph.D., D.D.S., M.S.W.: Babs Davy
Chalmers, the Butler: Betsey Crenshaw
Lucretia Owner: Lisa Kron
Cecily Wainscotting: Maureen Angelos
Gwendolyn Woodwork: Carolyn Patierno
Madame St. Vincent Millay: Imogen Pipp
Dashiel O'Shaughnessy: Kate Stafford
Linda Owner, Lucretia's twin sister: Lisa Kron

Act 1, Scene 1

(*In a greasy spoon somewhere in the Catskills.*)

DOOMED WAITRESS: So, uh, Mack. Oh, sorry, Mabel. What can I get for you? I got some nice looking chops gettin' all lonesome in the back. Okay. Adam and Eve on a raft, wreck 'em! So where you headin' to, anyway? Oh, the big city—Buffalo. And right next to Niagara. I bet them falls is somethin'. The lady sittin' right next to you's goin' up there today, too. But she's got a rig with her. Lavidia! More fire on that burger! I said well! That girl don't listen to me. I think she's a little naturally rare herself, you know? Like some people's is naturally colorblind? So what can I get for you? Yeah, the beef's usually pretty good. Okay. Lavidia! Beef Special! Corn! Mashed! I bet you been up here in the Catskills before. I can tell just by lookin' at cha. Huh? Lucretia Owner? Yeah, she lives up here all right. Her estate's just down the road. To tell you the truth, though, I ain't seen hide nor hair of her for years. I figure she's still up there, though, 'cause there's this young girl, friend of the family, and her nanny type who go up there every so often. Somethin' strange though, I tell ya. I'd like to be a fly on the wall. Lavidia! Lavidia! Will you stop slamming the damn bell! I hear ya! You know all those rich ladies don't have to work. That's what makes them so crazy. Like in Chekov. You know, you look really familiar to me. Hey! Wait a minute! Don't get all hot under that collar. I just said you looked a little familiar. Jesus! Cool down, cool down. Forget I mentioned it. Get her! Some people's children. Hey! How's your girlfriend?

(*Lights go out. They come back up on dead waitress with a knife in her gut.*)

Act 1, Scene 2

Setting: *The library of the manor house of Lucretia Owner (located somewhere in the Catskills). Lucretia's niece, Amelia, sits at the piano playing "Tubular Bells" (the theme from* The Exorcist*) with great feeling. Dr. Constance Boswell, the chemically-dependent family physician, sits reading Dickens' Bleakhouse or something, while sneaking sips from the flask she has hidden in the couch. Amelia stops playing the piano and sighs.*

DR. CONSTANCE BOSWELL: Oh don't stop playing, dear. That was lovely.

AMELIA: Do you think so, Doctor? I can't tell. Nothing sounds very pretty to me these days.

DR. CONSTANCE BOSWELL: Oh nonsense, Amelia. You're quite a natural talent. Another Stanislavski, I'd say.

AMELIA: Oh, Doctor. I do love the piano. But I also love dancing and painting and poetry and horseback riding and badminton and cricket and Jai'alai.

Oh, Doctor, there's so much to see and feel in the world. Sometimes I feel I could just choke and die from it.

DR. CONSTANCE BOSWELL: Yes, I see your point. So, tell me. How was Paris?

AMELIA: Paris? Oh! Paris is ever so gay! It was everything I could have hoped my first trip abroad would be. Did you know that I actually had a room to myself?

DR. CONSTANCE BOSWELL: No!

AMELIA: Yes! It took some coaxing because Madame wanted to stay in a hotel. But I put my foot down and convinced her that when in Paris one should do as the Parisian do. And so we took up residence in a little pension near the Rue de Claudine Longet. I adopted for myself a somewhat meager lifestyle. Nobody had the slightest idea of who I might be and I believe they must have thought I was a poor poet or a painter because I led such an austere existence. Oh, dear Doctor, I'm afraid my heart is still in that little room. Isn't it ironic, Doctor, how love can sometimes make you the saddest person in the world!

DR. CONSTANCE BOSWELL: Ah! I understand now.

AMELIA: Oh Doctor! You knew it all along, didn't you?

DR. CONSTANCE BOSWELL: Amelia, I brought you into this world. Give the old doctor some credit, would you?

AMELIA: (*"Spring in Paris" type music up.*) I remember it as though it were yesterday. I was lying on my bed in my tiny room watching the warm Parisian spring air blow the curtains about when I was called to the window by the most divine song. A flower girl peddling her bouquets. Doctor, she took my breath away at a glance. And I just had to meet her. You know how that can be? So I threw some franks down to her and asked her for some of the redder flowers. She must have been very hungry because she devoured the franks immediately. Then she told me if I wanted a flower I could just come down and get it myself. Only she said it in the dearest French fashion. I understood then why they call it a romance language. The defiance in her eyes sparked me and I on a whim told her I would love nothing more than to come down, but that I had been crippled in a dreadful childhood accident and would she take pity on me?

DR. CONSTANCE BOSWELL: You didn't!

AMELIA: Doctor, I did! It worked like a charm, as I can be quite the actress when I like. I felt just like Heidi. She was at my door in an instant. In my excitement to see her, I had forgotten all about my tale, and I rushed to open the door. Her expression at seeing me standing there on my own two legs, which I had just told her were dreadfully crushed, was priceless. In that instant, I fell madly and passionately in love with her and took a silent vow that I should never again move beyond her, Violette's, grasp. It took a little coaxing to get her to pledge the same. But of course I did. And we were so happy together. Then I got Aunt's telegram telling me she needed me and that I must come home. And as far as I can see, she's just the same as she ever was and I could just kill Aunt for making me leave my beloved Violette!

DR. CONSTANCE BOSWELL: Yes. It's a shame. Someone ought to pay for that.

AMELIA: Oh, listen. Now I've gone and spoken harshly of Aunt and I didn't mean to at all. It's just that I . . . Oh, there I go, thinking of myself again when perhaps Aunt really does need me here. Tell me, Doctor, is she alright?

DR. CONSTANCE BOSWELL: She's fine. I've prescribed a mild sedative to keep her calm.

AMELIA: Sedative. Oh, you see Doctor! She is ill.

DR. CONSTANCE BOSWELL: Oh, no, no. That's not it at all. It's just to keep her clam so she doesn't have any accidents or anything. Who knows what could happen to her? She could fall down the stairs or choke on a peach pit or get her fingers stuck in the door of the Bentley or stab herself with knitting needles or poison herself on very, very bad pate or—

AMELIA: Please, Doctor! Let's not talk of such morbid things. If Aunt needs me, or thinks she needs me, then I'm glad to be here for her. I do love her. I dare say I love her quite as much as I would if she really were my Aunt and not just a dear, dear friend of the family. And there are some cheery things about being home. Tomorrow, after the dinner party, Madame St. Vincent Millay and I are going home to Two-Towns-on-Croton. My parents won't be there, of course. They're off someplace, the Orient this time, I believe. But I will get to see my horse, Champ.

DR. CONSTANCE BOSWELL: Yes, another one of your Aunt's dinner parties . . . you and me and Madame St. Vincent Millay sitting around listening to Lucretia and Chalmers sing that God-awful song and trying to make excuses for the fact that, once again, nobody has shown up. If I had a single vertebra left in what used to be my spine, I tell you, I'd not show up at another one of her little gatherings.

AMELIA: I dare say, with Aunt in the picture, I shall never have my own life. What shall we do tonight, Doctor, at the dinner party?

DR. CONSTANCE BOSWELL: Humor her, I suppose. And let her sing her songs ad nauseam.

AMELIA: I suppose. Oh, now look here. Why are we being so glum? It's splendid to see you again, Doctor. Let me play you something on the piano. What would you like to hear?

DR. CONSTANCE BOSWELL: How about "Auld Lang Syne?"
AMELIA: Certainly.

(*They sing the first lines of "Auld Lang Syne." Blackout.*)

(*Enter AMELIA. She goes to her secret hiding place and pulls out her diary.*)

AMELIA: Dear Diary, what a breathtaking day this has been. I've really run the gamut of emotions from laughter to tears. My heart broke all over again telling dear Dr. Boswell about my beloved Violette. But, as Madame always says, "The storm is always heaviest before the silver lining." And, lo and behold, just as the doctor and I were despairing as to how we would get through another one of Aunt's dinner parties, real guests actually arrived! They all seem to be quite lively and one in particular has captured my over-active imagination.

(*Enter MADAME ST. VINCENT MILLAY.*)

AMELIA: Oh, Madame! I'm so glad to see you! I so desperately need your advice. You know when we were in—
MDE. ST. VINCENT MILLAY: Paris.
AMELIA: Yes. I fell in love with a—
MDE. ST. VINCENT MILLAY: Flower girl.
AMELIA: Yes, and now I find myself attracted to—
MDE. ST. VINCENT MILLAY: Miss O'Shaughnessy.
AMELIA: (*Sobbing.*) Yes! Oh Madame, what am I to do?
MDE. ST. VINCENT MILLAY: Remember dear, "Pretty is as pretty does." Don't judge a woman until you have walked a mile in her moccasins.
AMELIA: Oh, thank you Madame. You always know just the right thing to say.
MDE. ST. VINCENT MILLAY: The evening meal approaches, my little cauliflower. We must make our ablutions.
AMELIA: I'll be along in just a moment, Madame.

(*Exit MADAME. AMELIA writes. Enter BOSWELL.*)

DR. CONSTANCE BOSWELL: Still musing over your petite fleur, my dear?
AMELIA: I poured my heart out to Madame, Doctor, and I'm feeling ever so much better.
DR. CONSTANCE BOSWELL: The Madame. Yes . . .
AMELIA: Doctor, I've always wondered . . . and I know this is probably some silly romantic tale I've concocted or perhaps just a frivolous schoolgirl day-

dream. But I've often thought that there was once a spark of something between you and Madame. Is there, perhaps, a little grain of truth in that, Doctor?

DR. CONSTANCE BOSWELL: I'm not going to pussyfoot around with you, Amelia. I'd say you're old enough to know the truth. I'd like to say at the outset that I'm not very proud of what happened.

AMELIA: What happened?

DR. CONSTANCE BOSWELL: Well, you know dear, the Madame is a very attractive woman in a supernatural sort of way. She can make a woman forget who she is and how she should behave. I withstood the Madame's formidable charms for quite a while until, I'm afraid to say, one infamous night when the moon was full and my defenses were down and she got the best of me. Forgive me for telling you all this, Amelia, but I find this little revelation you so deftly pulled out of me has turned into a catharsis of some sort. (*Hungarian tango music up.*) The Madame had her way with me for four days and seven nights. She turned me into some wild animal. My years of study in civilized thought and behavior deserted me as I cared only about glutting myself with every sort of sensual pleasure two women could possibly endure, and then she dropped me like a hot potato and left me for another woman. And so there you have it.

AMELIA: Oh, Doctor . . .

DR. CONSTANCE BOSWELL: So you see, dear, life isn't all romance and flower girls in the street. It's often sad and lonely, brutal and cruel; disappointments and disillusionment in alternating shattering waves crushing the life out of you until you're broken and old and too tired to care.

AMELIA: Poor Doctor.

DR. CONSTANCE BOSWELL: Yes. Poor me. Poor me. Pour me a drink.

AMELIA: The usual?

DR. CONSTANCE BOSWELL: Make it a double.

AMELIA: Double the usual? (AMELIA *brings two tumblers.*) Here you are Doctor.

DR. CONSTANCE BOSWELL: Run along now, dear. Leave the old Doctor to reflect on her wasted youth.

AMELIA: Very well. See you at dinner.

(*Enter* LUCRETIA, *singing her favorite selection from* The Merry Widow. *Dr. Boswell cringes.*)

LUCRETIA OWNER: What a lovely surprise! If it isn't Dr. Constance Boswell, M.D., Ph.D., D.D.S., M.S.W., drunken, ruined, failure! How lovely to see you.

DR. CONSTANCE BOSWELL: Hello, Lucretia.

LUCRETIA OWNER: Was that Amelia's voice I just heard?

DR. CONSTANCE BOSWELL: Yes, it was.

LUCRETIA OWNER: Such a pretty girl, Amelia. Pretty, pretty Amelia. Sometimes I think she's too pretty for her own good. Don't you, Doctor? It goes to her head. She's always all aflutter about one thing or another. Usually that nasty horse of hers. Champ! I'd say Champ is about ready for the glue factory, wouldn't you, Doctor?

DR. CONSTANCE BOSWELL: You can make my life a living hell, if you must, Lucretia. But I won't have you speaking that way about Amelia!

LUCRETIA OWNER: Oh, you won't, will you? And just what do you plan to do about it, Connie? You seem to forget. I own you.

DR. CONSTANCE BOSWELL: You're a sick and twisted woman, Lucretia.

LUCRETIA OWNER: (*With delight.*) Oh Doctor, stop! I think it's ever so amusing that you fancy yourself so morally superior to me. Does the name Daphne Rodriguez ring a bell?

DR. CONSTANCE BOSWELL: For God's sake, Lucretia. Stop.

LUCRETIA OWNER: Let's see, where have I heard that name before? It seems to me I read it in the paper 10 or 15 years ago. Wasn't she a renowned plastic surgeon who died under the knife of another not so renowned plastic surgeon during a relatively simple office procedure?

DR. CONSTANCE BOSWELL: Oh Daphne, Daphne forgive me.

LUCRETIA OWNER: Oh look. The Doctor's turned into a blubbering idiot.

DR. CONSTANCE BOSWELL: If you'll excuse me, Lucretia . . .

LUCRETIA OWNER: Oh, Doctor, please don't go.

DR. CONSTANCE BOSWELL: Is there any reason for me to stay except so that you can humiliate me over and over again?

LUCRETIA OWNER: No. That's the reason.

DR. CONSTANCE BOSWELL: Let me remind you, Lucretia, that I'm not the only one around here with a secret. I seem to remember, about 20 years ago, a certain socialite who dropped out of sight for a while . . . about nine months!

LUCRETIA OWNER: Shut up! You may go now, Doctor.

DR. CONSTANCE BOSWELL: So you see how easily the tables can turn.

[. . .]

DASHIEL O'SHAUGHNESSY: I'm sorry to summon you all so abruptly. But a murder has been committed. And the sooner we get to the bottom of this, the better for everyone involved.

DR. CONSTANCE BOSWELL: Alright then, do what you have to do and let's get on with it. As you can see, the child is quite distraught with grief. How did you sleep, Amelia?

AMELIA: I'm afraid I didn't sleep a wink thinking of the awful way that Aunt died. That heinous picture will be imprinted on my brain forever. Aunt cooked! Like a fish in a bamboo steamer.

CECILY: (*Hung over.*) Emililia. I realize you've had a difficult time, but could you quiet down just a bit? Thank you. Alright, O'Shannahan, blast off.

DASHIEL O'SHAUGHNESSY: Well, I'm afraid I'm going to have to be quite brutal about this.

GWENDOLYN: Yes. Yes. We know. Just get on with it.

DASHIEL O'SHAUGHNESSY: Alright. We'll start with you, then Fifi—oh, excuse me, Gwendolyn. I noticed how your mouth was watering last night over the mistress' necklace. I also noticed that the necklace was missing when we discovered the body. What do you have to say about that?

GWENDOLYN: Yes, it's true. I have pilfered a few trinkets during the course of my career. But pilfering and murder are two entirely different things. You must know that. Oh, blast you, Cecily! We innocently climb through the window with perfectly straightforward intentions, and then a few cocktails here, a bit of charming conversation there . . . the next thing I know, we're invited guests, with perfectly common surnames. Involved in murder, mystery, and madness. Oh, I could just strangle the living daylights out of you. Watch your eyes bulge, your skin turn blue, your body fall limp, as you take the last gasp of your pathetic life. In a manner of speaking. So then who? I wouldn't have imagined any of you capable of such an act. Although the woman would have driven even the meekest of souls to it. Yes, the meekest of souls. The meekest and the sweetest, and ineffectual of souls. Amelia!

AMELIA: Me?

GWENDOLYN: Yes, Amelia! You certainly had a motive, didn't you? A European adventure cut short by a maniacal Aunt who was squelching the youth out of you. Ha! I think I'm on to something. And you, hiding behind that demure facade and a rapscallion at heart. If I were you, Leslie—oh, Dashiel—I'd keep an eye on that girl.

DASHIEL O'SHAUGHNESSY: Yes. Well. What about Dr. Boswell? The very loyal Dr. Boswell. Weren't you the only one with a gun? And weren't you overheard to say that you would kill for a key to the wine cellar?

DR. CONSTANCE BOSWELL: I suppose I may have done it? I thought I'd sunk about as low as I could possibly go, but I've been mistaken before. What am I saying? I may be a drunk but I'm not a murderess. I never could have done such a thing to my life-long friend. I hated Lucretia, true. But not enough to jeopardize my life. Life? Is that what I call this paltry existence? Hardly a life worth living. Pickled. That's what this life is. Preserved in drink. Could I, in a drunken stupor, have lunged and delivered that fatal blow? Am I, the once prominent Constance Boswell, M.D., Ph.D., D.D.S., M.S.W., capable of this heinous act? Quite possibly. Lucretia was the only living soul with knowledge of what really happened the day my colleague Daphne died. Daphne. You came to me for a chin-tuck and got eternal happiness. A bargain, really. Is it mere coincidence that these two dear friends have met their maker? Yes. It's coincidence. I've proved my innocence once, and I will again. Incarceration is out of the question. There's no cocktail hour in the big house.

DASHIEL O'SHAUGHNESSY: Yes, well. We'll take that into consideration. What about the ever joyful, ever happy, ever feeble, Cecily? Yes. Yes. Yes. The mistress didn't take a liking to you, did she? She even went so far as to criticize your dental work. Asking you if you could open things with those front teeth of yours.

CECILY: Well, I really don't think it's very nice of someone to invite you to their house for dinner and a weekend in the country and the moment you arrive they start insulting you and then they die. Well, it would be just like you, O'Shalimar, to think that I did it. I knew you never really liked me. You were only pretending to, weren't you? I can see you going to all the trouble of killing someone and then trying to hang it around my neck to make me look bad in front of Gwendolyn. Although, after that song of Aunty's, any of us could have done it. Even Gwendolyn. My goodness, Gwendolyn. I'm beginning to think that you did do it. Yes! You've been acting suspicious all night. I've seen the looks between you and that Dashboard going back and forth. Then you disappeared there. I knew I never should have let you out of my sight with that Dachshund about. Yes. This certainly sheds new light on things, doesn't it? I've been gadding about the globe with a murderess. Well, O'Shanihan, you see you've gotten me all aflutter, and clearly you can tell that Gwendolyn did it and not me.

DASHIEL O'SHAUGHNESSY: Yes. You might be right. But then, what about the truly sweet, truly sensitive, Amelia?

AMELIA: Yes?

DASHIEL O'SHAUGHNESSY: Yes. Yes. But deep down in that poetic heart and soul of yours, the thought of your Aunt going away on a long, long trip was liberation, wasn't it? Wasn't it ecstasy? Isn't that true?

AMELIA: No! No! Dashiel! How could you be so heartless? And just when I was beginning to think that you were my true love and not Violette as I thought this morning. Oh well. Things change so quickly when you're young and headstrong and romantic and impetuous. But enough about me. What about Aunt? And what about our lovely party? Everything seemed so gay. And for once there were guests, real guests in the house.

A few more live bodies to absorb the shock of that horrid song that Aunt and Chalmers used to sing. Now it appears that one of our most welcome guests is a murderess. Although, you all showed up voluntarily, which, in the case of my Aunt, demonstrates a superhuman level of loyalty. So who? Dr. Boswell is, by her own admission, too spineless to have done it. And that leaves only . . . oh! . . . But it couldn't be. You've been my devoted companion for years. But this is not time for loyalty, is it? A murder has been committed and it's every man for herself . . . as it were. It's time for little Amelia to grow up and smell the coffee, as Madame would say. I'm afraid I shall have to keep a close and skeptical eye on you from now on.

[. . .]

*Group Interview by Holly Hughes and Carmelita Tropicana
with the Five Lesbian Brothers, Maureen (Moe) Angelos, Babs
Davy, Dominique Dibbell, Peg Healey, and Lisa Kron (2000)*

WOW Women in Their Own Words
A Fine Bromance

The [few heterosexual women who worked regularly] at WOW
were beloved because they wore their heterosexuality with humil-
ity. Women who came in not getting the picture that at WOW
lesbos were the rule, not the exception, didn't last very long. We
called ourselves a "women's" collective, but WOW was all about
being dykes.

—Lisa Kron

I do recall when someone would say, "Bye, girls," the response
was, "No bi girls here." Of course, there were some het and bi
girls, but man, that was a lesbian space. It reeked of lesbianism. It
was a den of Sapphism. Really, a hot bed.

—Dominique Dibbell

The Five Lesbian Brothers, as they explain in this interview, began performing together at WOW in the early 1990s. Their first production, *Voyage to
Lesbos* (1990), was a wild, highly sexual romp. After more work at WOW,
they produced *Brave Smiles . . . Another Lesbian Tragedy* (1991) at the New
York Theatre Workshop (NYTW), an Off-Broadway, mainstream theatre
half a block down E. 4th Street from the WOW Café. *Brave Smiles* parodied
the history of lesbian stereotypes in film and television with a wry, smart,
tongue-in-cheek style that won the Brothers audiences beyond the regular
denizens of WOW.

The Secretaries (1994), also produced at NYTW, satirized the caricature of
lesbians as man-hating Furies by taking the archetype to its extreme. A group
of women working at a lumber mill engage in a monthly ritual that coincides
with their menstrual cycles, one in which they offer up a man for a murderous

blood sacrifice. Needless to say, the production raised some eyebrows in the local theatre scene. Although it was wildly successful at NYTW, the production's run wasn't extended, nor was it picked up for a commercial transfer.

As the Brothers detail below, their working methods and the politics of their plays' content seemed to keep them outside more lucrative production venues. Their collaborative lesbian feminist working methods, too, both empowered and finally constrained them. Despite their success, they hit a lavender ceiling.

This interview, conducted in 2000, details the group's genesis and its working process, and lets the women speculate about the arc of their collective careers to date. Since that conversation, the Brothers reunited at NYTW in 2005 to produce and perform in *Oedipus at Palm Springs*, their knowing, queer revision of Sophocles's canonical play. Although it, too, was well-received, the production marked the last Brothers' collaboration. Lisa Kron has gone on to write—and sometimes act—in her own plays (including *2.5 Minute Ride*, *Well*—first produced at New York's Public Theatre and then on Broadway—and *In the Wake*). Moe Angelos has worked for many years with the Builders Association, another theatre group; she recently wrote and starred in *Sontag: Reborn*, a critically acclaimed solo performance directed by Marianne Weems and produced at NYTW. That show, too, has not garnered interest from commercial producers.

The Brothers' conversation demonstrates the ongoing struggle of women and lesbian artists to find their way through a theatre scene that continues to marginalize them and snubs work critical of mainstream cultural norms.
—*Jill Dolan*

DOMINIQUE DIBBELL: When I came to my first WOW meeting, there were like 30 women in the room. I remember feeling this incredible relief because I had been in San Francisco for a year, and the kind of performance that they were doing there was very political and serious and boring to me. This was a room full of 30 lesbians who seemed to have the same sense of humor as I did. I was always so scared when I went to WOW because it seemed like such a socially intense situation and I was so shy. It wasn't until I really started performing that I began to feel comfortable.

BABS DAVY: I was an audience member for a really long time. Then I decided to go to a meeting by myself, which was really scary. You had to call up for the key. There was no buzzer, so you had to shout out, "WOW!" Then somebody would poke their head out the window, and I guess they'd size you up, and they'd throw a key down, wrapped in a sock. That was the litmus test for WOW girls.

PEG HEALEY: Like you had to have the guts.

MOE ANGELOS: If you were brave enough to yell "WOW!" in the middle of a crowded street. Once you did, and once you got up there, you learned that you didn't have to yell "WOW!" You just had to go, "Woohoo . . . !"

DOM: The most amazing thing about WOW was how disposable everything was. You threw it up, and it was brilliant, or it wasn't brilliant, but it was down the next day. There was something so absolutely thrilling about that. Deb Margolin and Joanie Wong had asked me to be in *Hamlet*, and I already had a gig at Dixon Place. But the play was such that I could be on as Laertes at the beginning, go do my gig at Dixon Place, and come back and finish *Hamlet*. There was so much going on at the time, and it was so fertile. It was all happening so quickly that you had to do two shows in one night.

LISA KRON: You really didn't have the chance to think about what you were doing. You didn't have the chance to stop and be scared and be paralyzed by the fear.

MOE: It seemed like such a carefree time. Given the economic environment, we didn't have to worry so much about working at our day jobs. It was a little bit easier to get by.

BABS: You felt like you were safe to fall on your face, because the next day would come, and it would be over, and you didn't have to feel terrible about it. That's the same reason that nobody knows about WOW, because nobody decided what could be on and what couldn't, so there were a lot of real stinkers, too. I was in many of those and lived to talk about it. I would never get on the stage anywhere else. I'm so glad I did.

LISA: One reason I think it was such a rich fertile ground for artists is that you were able to perform yourself. You were able to discover your identity, and at the same time you were discovering your work. If I had worked anywhere else in the theater, I would have just been an actor. I don't think I would have become a writer, and I always was a writer. Nothing teaches you about writing faster than writing something, saying it in front of an audience, and getting their response. To have that kind of knowledge in your body, it changes the way you work. Another big thing for me was working with the designers, Alice Forrester and Susan Young, in particular. I still feel the part of my work that's really underdeveloped, that's my withered limb, is my visual sense. But my early shows were totally lifted into something way more interesting by Susan's work. The audiences at WOW had a certain energy. Audiences got dazzled, and to perform in that environment was so exciting. It felt especially exciting because of the jaded summer stock environment that I had come from. For instance, in *Paradykes Alley* [*the Brothers' first show*], there was a bowling alley in the theater and we really bowled in the show. People had so much fun sitting on both sides of that bowling alley and watching that ball go down. And *Fear of Laughing* was incredible. My most indelible memory of WOW was being in those skirts made of shredded newspaper as the June Taylor dancers. All these dykes were performing in shredded newspaper. There was a moment in the show when we'd turn into the center and see each other performing. Every night, we had that same feeling: we were a bunch of loser dykes, and all of a sudden we were starring in a musical! We're just so fabulous! I remember thinking people walking down the street didn't have any idea what was going on up there. This is the center of the universe, and nobody knows it.

MOE: We assumed a lesbian world in the work and in the sensibility. It was a very messy, haphazard lesbian world that sometimes was really sad and sometimes very, very funny. We were beyond educational, explanatory theater. It was just, "We're lesbians, and you can come along for the ride, but if you miss the boat, you gotta catch up, because we're not gonna turn around to explain." But we made this little lesbian world, this queer little world for ourselves. I was able to play so many different kinds of characters, just in the plays written by the people that are sitting in this room right now. I had gone back to NYU to finish my degree, and all the other kids were rehearsing their scenes, and I said, "I gotta go do a show."

HOLLY HUGHES: How did the Brothers start?

DOM: I recall a very specific moment when I was working with Lisa and Peggy and Moe on the *Seven Year Itch*. I was very excited that you asked me to be in it because you guys were my favorite actors and writers. We were rehearsing and it was near opening and we didn't have the last scene and we were sitting around talking about what the characters might say, and that was the first time that I started collaborating. I made some suggestions and they liked them and that was, to me, the very beginning of the Brotherhood.

HOLLY: Tell us about the name . . .

DOM: I was working at a law firm on the graveyard shift. I would write scenes at work or try to finish the program. I was drawing little pictures of each performer, and I just labeled the drawings the Five Brothers. When we do our writing sessions or our rehearsal sessions, we do all these physical exercises and act like a circus company. We were starting to feel that we had this bond, which was like a brotherhood. Since gender was up for grabs, "brotherhood" made sense somehow.

HOLLY: Can you say what you learned from the Brothers in terms of your writing?

LISA: How not to impose an idea on something, to just let it come from inside of you, instead of having a situation and putting that in the writing.

PEG: We developed the plays through improvisation and writing together.

When the draft was written, which was generally enough to go into re-hearsal, two weeks before, Kate Stafford, the director, said, "You have to give me a script now." At the very last meeting, we sat down and made a list of all of the characters. Everyone would make a list of which characters they wanted to play, from most desired to least desired. The rule was that you should really write what you wanted to play, and then we would read to each other, with no comment. Then there'd be a long silence.

BABS: We would always try to get the closest we could to each person getting the roles that they wanted.

PEG: Right, it's important also that people had an equal amount of things to do.

DOM: We struggled to create five good roles. We were taking a lot of risks. That was a very scary time, because we were trying to find a way to work together.

HOLLY: How do you get from free writing to scene work?

PEG: Some scenes are directly transcribed from improvs. Sometimes, I would transcribe them and get them wrong. Like when Moe said, "I'm cleanin' the house," I wrote, "I'm Queen of the house." Or we would mishear a name. As we develop recurring characters, we might say, "Alright everybody, do it in rehearsal. Everybody write a scene between Susan and Patty" [*in their play* The Secretaries, *for instance*], and everyone would write, then we'd read them all, and say, "Oh, I like this, this, and this element." We would just put them together, or we'd go home and write, bring it in, and put it together. Or we'd write it in rehearsal, and then it would be someone's assignment to go take those five versions and put them together. So, that's like really the step right before you put the whole play together, and then editing. There is also a process of generating material when you're just totally free. Usually, we go on a retreat to do that. We get into a bubble; we're all free writing, we all go to bed, and we all wake up at the same time and do our morning writings and come down and read them before we eat. We try to feel where everyone's at and find common themes.

BABS: For the first *Voyage to Lesbos*, we were all writing for ourselves and it was really loosely thrown together. When we decided to workshop it, we got Lois Weaver in to help us. She was the one who gave us constructive ways to organize the ideas that bubbled up for us and put them on a list of characters, locations, songs, what have you, and then mix them up.

LISA: First, we'd do the free writing before anything else. We tried not to discuss so much, which was very difficult for me, because all I wanted to do was discuss. When we were on retreat every morning, we said, "Okay, we're gonna get up at 7:30, and we're all gonna meet down at the table." You could pee, but you couldn't brush your teeth, you couldn't have a drink of water. You just sit and write for 10 minutes. Then we'd get up and get ready. We'd have an hour and a half to eat, shower, do whatever you want, and then come back down and start the day by reading what we had written. We wanted to write right out of our sleep. Then our days would be a lot of reading, then writing, then reading, then writing. We'd say things like, "Five minutes, write out the plot." "Ten minutes, write the scene between these two characters." "Five minutes, write what happens in this location."

HOLLY: Could you opt not to read your free writing?

LISA: It was always optional. But the most important part of our bonding as collaborators was the vulnerability and intimacy involved in reading and sharing your writing. You would say things in your free writing that you wouldn't say out loud. Then you would read them, and we respected that, and didn't comment on it and say, "Oh My God, I can't believe you did that . . ."

PEG: We borrowed a lot of exercises from other people and things we had learned in school. But we learned from each other how to collaborate with five people, because nobody taught that. That just developed through a lot of blood and tears. "Check-ins" have always been a part of our process. You take however long you need (though we usually limited the time) to go around and speak your peace about what was going on for you, emotionally, with the dynamics of the group without anybody commenting or interrupting. It would often become a dialogue if that's what it had to be, but that's one of the main ways we learned to work together.

LISA: It really stopped the natural paranoia, just to hear everybody be vulnerable. As we went through this process of writing and reading, other people's images would come into your writing, so that Moe's dream would go into Dom's writing, and Dom's story about when she was three years old would go into Peg's writing, and the funny description that Babs wrote of the guy in the car on Second Avenue would go into my writing. The weird, dense fabric of the Brothers' writing came a lot from that.

PEG: Everyone was really generous—

MOE: There wasn't a thought of, "Oh, this is mine." But I don't know why we wanted to do collaborative theater. Split Britches and WOW were the models for everybody, and you didn't even question it.

HOLLY: What were some of the other challenges you had working together?

PEG: It was different at different times. *Brides of the Moon [which premiered at NYTW, directed by Molly Smith, who went on to become artistic director of Arena Stage, a prominent regional theatre in Washington, DC]* was a play where we never clicked. We never got that bubble, where we were all in one head about what the play was about. Ultimately, we got so burnt out and tired that nobody was willing to fight anymore. What made our early work so dynamic and so much fun was that we were willing to fight and argue until we all reached consensus. By *Brides of the Moon*, people had gotten so tired that someone would say something and the other four would respond, "Yeah, okay."

HOLLY: You were tired because you were working so much?

PEG: We were turning out so much work. We did things for HBO that we were very proud of. Then the person from HBO who was going to do them left, and the person who took their place hated them. So they didn't get done, which was disappointing, although we did really love writing them.

BABS: Before that, we had just poured our hearts and souls out doing *The Secretaries* and made what most of us felt was our best play. We were so proud. We were very hopeful that that play would have the longer run or that it would move. It was a big hit at New York Theater Workshop. We got reviewed in every major paper, almost always favorably, and we thought it would move. When it didn't, that really was a big disappointment.

PEG: We had been pushing it and pushing it and going on our own steam and working day jobs and spending our nights at New York Theater Workshop so we could wake up early and finish scenes. We thought, well, now somebody will give us a little money and we'll be able to rest a little bit. It didn't happen.

LISA: I wasn't surprised that it didn't move. But nobody even asked about it. It wasn't even like one producer came sniffing around—

DOM: They all said it was great but they wouldn't touch it with a ten-foot pole because of the content.

LISA: People move commercial things, and it wasn't a particularly commercial play.

BABS: Men moved plays, and a lot of men thought it was anti-male.

PEG: That play was very rare, because it was about things that were so female and so underrepresented. It was about something that hadn't been presented before. These male reviewers, they had never seen it, so they didn't know how to describe it.

LISA: Reviewers never talk about our writing . . . they talk about the performance.

PEG: Probably every lesbian artist thinks something good is going to happen—

MOE: And then you realize you're a lesbian!

[. . .]

MOE: *The Secretaries* was our most well-developed play. We really got somewhere near our potential to harness the power of five lesbians.

DOM: The success that we had, which I think was considerable compared to lesbian artists who were before us or were our contemporaries, I think so much of it had to do with our name, the "Five Lesbian Brothers"—the word "brothers" and the fact that we were not the "Sapphic Sisters." There was some sort of irony in there, some sort of borrowing of that authority of maleness. It totally reassured people that they could come to the theater, because maleness is interesting. We tapped into that. I totally believe that we would not have had the success we did have without that name.

PEG: If we were men, producers would have been interested in us for commercial production, no doubt. But on the other hand, we had two plays produced by the New York Theater Workshop, which is incredible. We had more success than many other struggling artists.

DOM: How do you take a group that makes every decision collaboratively and move that into a corporate situation?

LISA: We always considered ourselves entertainers. We always wanted a TV show. We wanted the Five Lesbian Brothers to be the Monkees. But the world just wasn't ready for the Lesbian Monkees, I guess. But we never sought that work out, either. We did not go after that kind of work.

MOE: TV comes after everyone downtown who has a dick.

PEG: Well, even if we don't write another show, it's really nice to know that we didn't stop working together because of artistic differences, or because we just couldn't agree on something, or because we're fighting over money, or anything like that. We're tired, and poverty is grinding us down, but—

DOM: Another contribution to the exhaustion factor: When you're working with four other people, it really cuts into your life. Our lives started pulling us apart. We had other places we needed to be and go. Getting five people in a room was really difficult. There are personal factors, too. I didn't want to stay in New York anymore. [*Dom moved to Los Angeles to find work in TV and film.*]

LISA: I remember a time when I couldn't imagine there not being a WOW and that being the center of my universe. The Brothers talked about what would happen if we didn't stay together. I felt like I was going to die if I didn't have the Brothers anymore. And then things change and you move on and you do other things. I've had a couple good years. But it's hard to imagine anything that will happen in my creative life that will be as rich as those experiences were.

BABS: When the WOW season would come to an end, I would have such withdrawal for the summer. I just couldn't wait to get back there in the fall. I felt like I didn't have an identity all summer.

DOM: I feel like I was part of an historical moment in time, about which books will be written, and it gives me chills remembering it all. Our work will not be forgotten [*because the Theatre Communications Group published the Brothers' collected plays in 2000*] and now other people will perform it and people will read our plays in college and stuff. Whatever happens from now on is gravy. (October 2000)

Deb Margolin

Hamlet (1989)
Scripted after Shakespeare's *Hamlet*

Joni Wong, who had served as the brilliant lighting designer for Split Britches, Joni Wong, who lit my solo show with four clip-lights and somehow
made it look like a Broadway opening at Franklin Furnace, was the one who
had earned the time for a show at WOW. Having lit almost every show that
went up there, she was allotted a bunch of weeks for a presentation of her
choice at this women's theatre space, where presentation time was given on
the basis of work offered on other shows during the year.

Joni and I had the kind of friendship that's earned on the road. We
roomed together whenever Split Britches toured, and we enjoyed the kind
of mutual respect and love that's earned while swatting mosquitoes out of
one's teeth on the roof of a pension in Italy because it's too hot to sleep in
the hotel room, the kind of enduring tenderness that comes from discussing
one's deepest feelings while trying to sleep on the floor in a squatter's apartment in Europe. It was a love and respect Joni and I shared from these kinds
of experiences together on tour with the Splits that gave Joni the impulse to
use her hard-earned and precious WOW time to honor my obsession with
the play *Hamlet*.

I was totally taken over by the sexiness of *Hamlet*, not for its brawls, its
uncertainties and equivocations, its eloquences, arrogances, postures, and
masculinities; rather it was the somehow erotic way in which Platonic love
was drawn and celebrated that made me want to play, to explore, to exhaust,
to repulse, to parodize, to own and possess Shakespeare's *Hamlet*. I wanted
to play Hamlet really bad, not, as Carl Sandburg said, because "it is sad like
all actors are sad" but rather because it was a *bromance,* a buddy play, a play
that dignified a profound, enduring friendship, not unlike the one I had with

Joni, or the one I had with Nobs. My closest relationship was with my friend Nobs, the stalwart who had grown up across the street from me and with whom I shared what we both felt was a holy alliance. We saw ourselves as Bill Cosby and Robert Culp in the TV show *I Spy,* and eventually, as Hamlet and Horatio in an unjust universe. To my knowledge, there were no artistic representations of such pure, intelligent, muscular, and immortal relationships between women; so, being young, I just regenderized myself, and of all the men to choose from, I was going to be Hamlet. At WOW everyone understood this; it needed no explanation. As a straight woman (a congenital defect to which I had trouble admitting sometimes at WOW), this expansive, unrestricted conception of gender was a wonder, a miracle, and a relief to me. WOW was, as a theatre, the answer to there being no plays celebrating bromances for women.

Joni set me up in her living room, typing up our own version of the script. Hamlet had an offstage voice he used when he needed to complain about the script, express his political opinions concerning the way women were treated, or opine about mortality in more detailed or colloquial ways than those permitted by the Shakespearean text. Some pretty brutal things happened to the text in terms of bad puns and such (see, at the end of act I, scene V, "O cursed Sprite! That ever I was born to set it right!" after Hamlet has not only engaged in a demented discussion with the ghost in which the best way to tell a certain Yiddish joke was added to the ghost's lament of the crime of regicide, but has also thrown away a can of soda given to him by Horatio following this sepulchral visit and the offstage voice commands him to pick it up). Somehow, despite and because of these hideous bowdlerizations, the entire story of *Hamlet* was in that script, including all the major monologues and key plot points. We finished a version of the script within a few weeks of production.

Susan Young, a resident costume and set visionary at WOW, found all kinds of magnificent street items for our set, including some kind of huge, gaudy roulette wheel, which had a prominent place on the stage and somehow came to signify both the vaudevillian roots of WOW tradition and the tragic vagaries of chance. Lisa Kron, playing both the ghost of Hamlet's father and the offstage voice that yells at Hamlet and tries to keep him on track with the text, sat on a stool behind the arras stage right and knitted an entire afghan while speaking into a microphone night after night when Hamlet needed help negotiating the responsibilities of his character. Puppets were sometimes used by Heidi Griffiths and Betsy Crenshaw as Rosencrantz and Guildenstern, who took over some of the dialogue between Ophelia and her brother Laertes and served to mock and tragedize Ophelia's docility and lack of agency. Dom Dibbell made a magnificent, dignified Laertes. The same redoubtable actor, the very brilliant Mary Neufeld, played both Horatio and Ophelia, since it was the firm belief of all in our production that if Hamlet could have forgotten about murdering someone and instead had sex with his boyfriend and/or discussed philosophy with his girlfriend, or had sex with his girlfriend and/or discussed philosophy with his boyfriend, or something, either way, his more integrated life would have obviated the entire tragedy. There was a guest star invited onstage during each performance, and I remember in particular the éclat that Carmelita Tropicana brought to that role, declaiming in Espanol in the middle of the proceedings. There was no curtain call at the end of the play; we stood together and bowed right before intermission, telling the audience that, if they wished to applaud, now was the time to do it, since in just over an hour and a quarter, most everyone on the stage would be deceased. People leaving the theater had to step over the dead bodies to get down the stairs and out onto East 4th Street.

It is important, I think, to note that, although this was a cast comprised entirely of women, it was never conceived as a play done in drag; neither was it conceived as a play that in any way altered the genders of Shakespeare's characters. The enactments of these characters fell into a sacred and liminal space, a WOW space, a space in which gender was a matter of choice in the moment and needed no explanation or defense. This followed the precept that hallowed the WOW theatre: follow your desire, do what you want.

I always wanted to play Hamlet, and I did. —*Deb Margolin*

HAMLET
Scripted by Deb Margolin after Shakespeare's *Hamlet*
Directed by Joni Wong

HAMLET:
O, that this too too solid flesh would melt
Thaw, and resolve itself into a dew,
Or that the Everlasting had not fix'd
His canon 'gainst self-slaughter. O God, God,
How weary, stale, flat and unprofitable,
Seem to me all the uses of this world!
Fie on't! ah fie! 'tis an unweeded garden,
That grows to seed. Things rank and gross in nature
Possess it merely.

(*Sigh.*)

VOICE: Keep going!

HAMLET: No. Keep going. Cosi fan tutti!

VOICE: In English!

HAMLET:

That it should come to this!

But two months dead, nay, not so much, not two,

So excellent a king that was to this

Hyperion to a satyr . . .

(*Sigh.*)

VOICE: Keep going!

HAMLET: No! I hate this part!

VOICE: Which part would you rather play? Voltimand? Fortinbras?

HAMLET: No! I meant this part of the speech.

VOICE: The noun you don't like? The verb?

HAMLET: No! No! The sonologue! The sonologue! I don't like talking about how Frailty Thy Name Is Woman! Or those analogies to Niobe All Tears! It sounds like a rock band at the World or something!

VOICE: Ars gratia artis.

HAMLET: And don't talk that foreign language to me! This fancy chit-chat here is bad enough!

VOICE: Ars gratia artis means art for art's sake. It means we're not interested in your politics, we're interested in your feelings.

HAMLET: Everything is political . . .

VOICE: Oh, come on. This monologue is not political! Both Republicans and Democrats prefer it! It is not political! It's emotional! This monologue is a gem! It's FAMOUS! It's a lapis lazuli of limpid language! It's a ruby, a diamond, a beautiful thing that just exists beyond politics.

HAMLET: Those fucking gems cost a lot of money! THAT'S POLITICAL!

VOICE: I can see what's with you. You turn to politics to avoid emotion. In fact, the King just told you you're next in line to hold a powerful political office!

HAMLET: That's the kind of politics that makes me prefer emotions!

VOICE: What's the problem? Why is it so difficult to talk about your Mother? That's what's coming up next, isn't it? Is it painful for you?

HAMLET: And don't give me that SHRINK rap either. I'm not crazy you know.

VOICE: The point has been argued both ways in prestigious universities.

HAMLET: Right, big deal . . .

VOICE: But talking about women . . .

HAMLET: I'm sexually mixed up, all right? That's what you wanted to hear, isn't it? Unmanly grief! Common theme is death of Fathers!

VOICE: Don't get so emotional!

HAMLET: Jesus! You just said . . .

VOICE: Don't take everything so personally. Try a British accent. It's like a costume for the voice!

HAMLET: Okay. (*With an accent.*) I feel sort of sexually mixed up . . .

VOICE: Not that cockney . . .

HAMLET: (*Laughs.*) No punning . . .

VOICE: The accent.

HAMLET: I feel sort of awkward . . .

VOICE: Back to the monologue . . .

HAMLET:
So loving to my mother
That he might not beteem the winds of heaven
Visit her face too roughly. Heaven and earth,
Must I remember? Why she would hang on him
As if increase of appetite had grown
By what it fed on, and yet within a month—
Let me not think on't. Frailty, thy name is HUNH hunh—

VOICE: Woman!

HAMLET: HUNH Hunh—

VOICE: Woman!

HAMLET:
A little month . . . or 'ere those shoes were old
With which she followed my poor father's body . . .

(*Sigh.*)

VOICE: Shh! Now come on sweetheart. Let's just get through the speech here.

HAMLET: It's just PI, the whole thing . . . [*meaning "politically incorrect"*]

VOICE: This is an immortal speech!

HAMLET: Well, whose fault is that? Mine? And what is an immortal speech doing in a play about mortality?

VOICE: Just stay present! Let's follow the action and see where it takes us!

HAMLET: Oh come on. You know where it takes us! It takes us to where I only have one friend. One friend! One friend! What if he gets sick or has to travel on business? What about that? Have you thought about that? It takes us to where my girlfriend is not allowed to speak to me or open her chaste duh-da-da to my—to my unmastered importunity! Have you thought about that? And then I have to insult her while her father and Mayor Koch lurk behind a curtain! Doesn't it! Doesn't it! It takes me on a boat! I throw up on boats! And it takes me into my Mother's bedroom . . .

VOICE: And . . .

HAMLET: And it . . . it takes me to the grave . . . first I have to talk to a skull. Have you ever done that, have you ever tried to chew the fat with a skull? Then I bury Ophelia and then I die myself.

VOICE: But that's—

HAMLET: And it's all written out! And there's nothing I can do to stop it!

VOICE: There are ways of handling this—

HAMLET: Don't patronize me!

VOICE: Just keep to the script and call me if you get too anxious.

HAMLET: Couldn't I play one of the comedies?

VOICE: Another way of hiding from emotion.

HAMLET: Comedy is all emotion! Emotion and timing! Oh please! Or I could do modern dance! I love modern dance!

VOICE: Sure, go ahead! Do modern dance!

HAMLET:

(*Dances.*)

Break my heart for I must hold my tongue. Horatio, or I do forget myself.

(*Enter* HORATIO/OPHELIA.)

HORATIO/OPHELIA:
The same, my lord, and your poor servant ever.

HAMLET:
My good friend, I'll change that name with you.
And what make you from Wittenberg, Horatio?

HORATIO/OPHELIA:
A truant disposition, good my lord.

HAMLET:
I would not hear your enemy say so,
Nor shall you do mine ear that violence
To make it truster of your own report
Against yourself. You're not that bad.

VOICE: I KNOW YOU ARE NO TRUANT is the line!

HAMLET:
I know you are no truant.
But what is your affair in Elsinore?
We'll teach you to drink deep 'ere you depart.

HORATIO/OPHELIA:
My lord, I came to see your father's funeral.

HAMLET:

How'd you like it?

VOICE: You want to collect unemployment? What's the matter with you?

HAMLET: I told you I prefer comedy.

VOICE: Why?

HAMLET: There's room! There's more room! In comedy there's room for ugly people or weird people! You don't have to sing or get your hair done.

VOICE: Look, we don't have a whole lot of time for this discussion.

HAMLET: Time, time, time! I think time is just a bacterial infection! And lines and wrinkles are just symptoms!

VOICE: Listen. If you don't want this part there are plenty of actors who would kill for it, and most of them are Jewish. Now this is the scene in which your dearest friend makes an appearance.

HAMLET: The beautiful friendship . . . I always loved this friendship . . . It's the best thing in the play . . .

VOICE: So get back there.

HAMLET: Where were we?

HORATIO/OPHELIA: I was just saying that I came to see your Father's funeral. By the way, I'm terribly sorry about all this, really.

(HAMLET *and* HORATIO/OPHELIA *hug. They see each other for the first time, really.*)

HAMLET:

I prithee do not mock me, fellow student.

I think it was to see my mother's wedding.

HORATIO/OPHELIA:

Indeed, my lord, it followed hard upon.

HAMLET:

We're alone, why don't you just say: Jesus, your old lady wasted no time?

HORATIO/OPHELIA:

My, lord, I—

HAMLET:

Christ, you look gorgeous. I miss you so much.

HORATIO/OPHELIA:

And me too you, my lord, and yet I—

HAMLET:

We're alone, Horatio! Tell me everything! How's Chlamydia? Do you love her yet? Is there anything to smoke in Wittenberg?

HORATIO/OPHELIA:

You are ruthless!

HAMLET:
Only if you are Naomi, and depart this State without me!

(*They hug.*)

HORATIO/OPHELIA:
I flunked my Chemistry exam!
HAMLET:
Shit! And Marcellus? He passed?
HORATIO/OPHELIA:
Like time on a rainy Sunday.
HAMLET:
You speak so beautifully! I love the way you speak!
HORATIO/OPHELIA:
My speech is well-weighed in your love, my lord.
HAMLET:
See what I mean? That way you have of turning everything around! Like I
    said: "I love the way you speak," and you said, "I speak the way you love . . ."
    or something . . . What was it you said, where you both answered me and
    mirrored my comment back to me . . . I love you, Horatio . . . ! I don't care
    if the structure of ferrous electrons eludes you—
HORATIO/OPHELIA:
I can only study in the morning, my lord. Morning becomes
Electrons!
HAMLET:
Touché!
HORATIO/OPHELIA:
But thrift, thrift, my lord, the script police!
HAMLET:
Thrift, thrift, Horatio! The funeral baked meats
Did coldly furnish forth the marriage tables.
Would I had met my dearest foe in heaven
Or ever I had seen that day, Horatio!
My father!—Methinks I see my father.
HORATIO/OPHELIA:
Where, my lord?
HAMLET:
In my mind's eye, Horatio.

END OF EXCERPT

Madeleine Olnek

Codependent Lesbian Space Alien
Seeks Same (1992)

Several women who arrived at WOW with acting training (or at least aspirations) later evolved into writers as well, among them Lisa Kron, Moe Angelos, and Claire Moed. But Madeleine Olnek had set her sights on writing before she started working at WOW. She had studied at New York University's Experimental Theatre Wing, an acting program that also teaches a variety of self-scripting methods. Later Olnek worked with David Mamet at the Atlantic Theatre, and with Bad Neighbors, a downtown theatre company that produced a weekly soap opera. Her skills were recognized in these venues, but Olnek came to WOW very discouraged. Collaborators tried to talk her out of bringing lesbian material into her writing. Even when she managed to get past the gatekeepers and get lesbian-themed scripts staged, she found a lukewarm reception at best.

But as this 1992 script makes clear, Olnek had nonetheless developed a clear and original voice as a writer. *Codependent* is a romance, and a girl-meets-girl, girl-loses-girl, and finally, following the rules of comedy, girl-reunites-with-girl comedy. Jane is in therapy. She seems completely stuck. She works in a dead-end job at a West Village card shop. She doesn't have friends let alone dates. And lately she dreams about love notes falling from spaceships. Are these only dreams?

Turns out the aliens are real. The distant planet Zots is in crisis. The ozone layer is being destroyed by toxic substances that turn out to be big feelings rather than carbon dioxide. Denizens of Zots who can't control their feelings receive counseling, and if that doesn't work they're deported to Earth, where their hearts will be so severely broken they'll be unable to love again. Only then will the emotionally transformed aliens be allowed to return to Zots.

Perhaps no piece in this book redresses as many canons as *Codependent*. Olnek frames the play within the sci-fi genre, but she also sends up game shows, pop psychology, and network news anchors. If we buy Susan Sontag's formulation of camp as "failed seriousness," then Olnek reveals the performance of normative femininity to be one failure after another. She creates an extremely funny play highly charged with political satire.

In the mid-1990s, Olnek received an MFA in Playwriting from Brown University, under the guidance of Paula Vogel. In 2011 she premiered a film adaptation of *Codependent Lesbian Space Alien* at the Sundance Film Festival. The film is available for download at www.codependentlesbianspaceali-enseekssame.com. —*Holly Hughes*

CODEPENDENT LESBIAN SPACE ALIEN SEEKS SAME

News Reporter/Aliens News Reporter/Bouncer . . . . David Chelsea
News Anchor/Alien News Anchor/Jachimo . . . . Kevin Seal
Earth Scientist/Alien Scientist/Suzanne Sommers/Roz . . . . Carolin
   Walton-Brown
Jane . . . . Donna Evans
Zoinx . . . . Susan Ziegler
Zylar . . . . Betsy Crenshaw
Bar . . . . Carolyn Patierno
Jane's Therapist/Cyndi . . . . Lynn Shelton
Tina/"Bill" The Studs Host/Bartender . . . . Kathleen Dennehy
(All cast members present in the club scene.)
Costumes by Linda Gui
Music and sound effects by John Morace
Dramaturged by Deb Margolin
Dance in nightclub choreographed by Stormy Brandenberger
Lights by Joni Wong
Tiny spaceship designed by David Zinn
Stage-managed by Nora Mynchaca
Poster designed by David Chelsea

The play was dedicated to Wylie Goodman.

The production was directed by the author and was presented in a double bill with another one of her plays, a one-act entitled *The Jewish Nun,* with Kathleen Dennehy and Kevin Seal. In advance of the WOW production, both plays had their first reading at Dixon Place, with the assistance of four of the Five Lesbian Brothers.

ANNOUNCER: We interrupt this broadcast to bring you an ABC News bulletin. Geologists operating in an official government science lab have detected asteroid movements that defy standard patterns of meteor showers. We now go live to outside the National Geological Institute.

REPORTER: Thank you, George. I am standing here with Joanna Johncon, chief of rock study at Nupar.

JOANNA: That's asteroid study, Steve. I don't want your viewers to think I'm a musician.

REPORTER: Alright, point taken. What is the significance of these findings, Joanna?

JOANNA: Well, primarily asteroids orbit the Earth at a certain velocity because of their molecular structure, which causes their aerodynamic capacities to be within a certain range, but the recent readings on the seismograph have shown us that—

REPORTER: Give it to us in simple language for the folks at home.

JOANNA: If you throw shit at a fan it splatters.

REPORTER: Thank you very much! Back to you, George.

ANNOUNCER: Steve, if I may ask you one question, does this mean that we should expect falling rock debris on our person?

REPORTER: No, no not at all, George, so far all this finding has signified is that there are asteroids, or unidentified matter, that have descended into the stratosphere. Whether or not they descend further down remains to be seen.

ANNOUNCER: So, in other words we should *not* expect falling rocks.

REPORTER: No, at least not at the moment. The computer print-outs have shown the asteroids or unidentified matter to be remaining within a certain orbit close to, but not yet at, the Earth. That's not to say that the unidentified matter might not eventually land.

ANNOUNCER: I notice you use the term: unidentified matter. Then could it be other than a rock formation?

REPORTER: Well technically it could be anything, George, it could be anything.

(*Lights fade.*)

(*Lights up on* JANE *and her* THERAPIST.)

THERAPIST: Tell me the entire dream from the beginning.

JANE: I saw—

THERAPIST: You saw a spaceship.

JANE: Yes, and—

THERAPIST: And a bright, bright light.

JANE: And a note dropped out of the spaceship.

THERAPIST: And what did the note say?

JANE: It said, "What are you doing later?"

THERAPIST: Interesting, interesting. Did anything else happen in the dream?

JANE: No.

THERAPIST: So after you got the note that said, "What are you doing later?" you woke up?

JANE: Yes. Yes I did. Except—

THERAPIST: Except what?

JANE: Except I don't remember waking up.

THERAPIST: You don't remember the exact moment of it? Or—

JANE: I don't remember waking up at all. I mean, like what I'm saying is that either, either I never went to sleep or—

THERAPIST: Or you never woke up!

JANE: Well, I guess—yeah. I mean, I don't know.

THERAPIST: Do you think you're dreaming now?

JANE: No.

THERAPIST: Alright. You know when you're awake and you're asleep. That's not the issue here. The issue here is that your fantasy life revolves around images of special beings just plopping down into your life, instead of you going out and doing those things that will put you in positions where real people will be able to approach you. Do you know what I'm saying?

JANE: Yes.

THERAPIST: You do?

JANE: Yes, my fantasy life revolves around special beings just plopping down into my life instead of going out and doing those things and having real people approach me.

THERAPIST: And a fantasy life is nothing to be ashamed of. However . . . however, it can be . . . problematic when that fantasy life is our entire focus. When it prevents real things from happening. Okay?

JANE: Yes.

THERAPIST: I'll see you next week. And keep away from the flying saucers until then.

JANE: (*Sheepishly.*) Alright.

(*Lights fade. We see a tiny spaceship cross the stage, and the flash of a bright light.*)

(*Lights up on the Planet Zots. There is a news bulletin.*)

ALIEN ANNOUNCER: Welcome to *PDQ Zots News Tonight*. You give us 22 minutes, we'll give you Zots. Sponsored by Ozaltine. Ozaltine. When the ozone is disappearing you need a delicious drink. Now—we will give you the newest information possible on the state of our planet's ozone.

ALIEN REPORTER: I am very grateful. I am parabollically situated with Zots' premiere ozone monitorician Quarina Quarzitz. (*To Quarina.*) Please inform our fellow inhabitants as to the present state of our planet's ozone.

QUARINA: As all inhabitants are aware, the ozone is disappearing. The planet is in great danger. The planet is in great danger.

ALIEN REPORTER: Is it possible for you to modify your comments for the inhabitants who are listening to this broadcast in their living units?

QUARINA: The ozone layer, which shields our planet from excessive ultraviolet radiation, is currently experiencing self-substance decomposition from toxic sources.

ALIEN REPORTER: And what is the composition of these toxic sources?

QUARINA: Big feelings.

ALIEN REPORTER: Explain.

QUARINA: As our computer monitors have recently ascertained, when an inhabitant loves too much, their feelings become so big that the body is no longer able to contain them. The feelings then rise up into the sky and widen the hole in the ozone.

ALIEN REPORTER: And is love the only big feeling which causes this problem?

QUARINA: Yes. Hate and jealousy stay within the person and destroy them. Love transcends the person and destroys the ozone.

ALIEN REPORTER: Frightening. What is being done to arrest this life-endangering emotion?

QUARINA: We have set up 27-hour emergency services. Any inhabitant experiencing big feelings, or aware of any other inhabitant experiencing big feelings, should report to the state services.

ALIEN REPORTER: And how will they be dealt with?

QUARINA: In a manner befitting the dimensions of their emotions.

ALIEN REPORTER: The dimensions of their emotions. That sounds like it could be a popular song lyric. (*Sings.*) The dimensions of their emotions...

QUARINA: Perhaps you yourself should be reported.

(*Lights fade.*)

(*Lights up on* ZOINX *and her* COUNSELOR.)

COUNSELOR: You were reported.

ZOINX: Yes.

COUNSELOR: And you yourself did not notice?

ZOINX: What?

COUNSELOR: That each time you cried, it got warmer?

ZOINX: No.

COUNSELOR: (*Pause.*) We have a special program. Inhabitants such as your-self who have feelings that are discovered to be a threat to the ozone are sent to the planet Earth. There you can get your heart broken so that you cannot love anymore. Then you may return to our planet, numbed and apathetic, once more a valuable addition to the work force.

ZOINX: Why would my heart become so broken on this planet Earth that I would no longer be able to love?

COUNSELOR: It has something to do with the behavior of earthlings. (*Pause.*) Wouldn't you like to be relieved of your feelings?

ZOINX: How do they know it will work?

COUNSELOR: We have persons such as you there already. Including two in-habitants from your own municipal sector. Our intelligence on their activi-ties informs us that they are currently engaging in behavior that may lead to romantic liaisons even at this very moment.

(*Lights fade.*)

(*Lights up on an NYC cafe. BAR, an alien, is seated at a small table. A WAIT-ER is describing the specials. TINA enters.*)

TINA: Hi—Are You—?

BAR: Codependent lesbian space alien.

TINA: Yes. Ha, ha! You know—that was really an original ad!

BAR: Which planet do you hail from?

TINA: Oh. I—

BAR: Let me guess. You are blonde with a strange sensibility towards gar-ments. You must have arrived from Eucladia.

TINA: Uh—yeah . . .

BAR: I myself am from Zots. A tiny planet oxyparallel to the rings of Saturn. A planet faced with extinction if my mission is not successfully completed.

TINA: Tell me something—uh . . .

BAR: Bar.

TINA: Bar. Do you hold a paying job?

BAR: A paying job. Yes. My job is to have my heart broken on the planet Earth. My payment is that I will be allowed to return. Yet I have not been successful in interesting Earth inhabitants. I have written over 2,000 one-lined love letters and have scattered them about but to no avail. I decided to seek out a fellow alien in the hopes that she could advise me.

TINA: Advise you?

BAR: On how to score.

TINA: Look, I think—I think I was expecting someone else. Or maybe . . . I thought I was someone else. I have to go.

(TINA *gets up to exit*.)

BAR: Someone . . . Excuse me—are you—Stop! I feel you are not truly an alien.

TINA: Yeah. I wish it was mutual.

(*Lights fade* as TINA *exits*.)

(*Lights up on* ZYLAR, *another alien who is seated on a couch*. CLAIRE *is also on the couch with her head in* ZYLAR'*s lap*.)

CLAIRE: (*Dreamily*.) Tell me what you think about love.

ZYLAR: I think it comes along once in a lifetime. I think that for every person there is a perfect match in the world and the feeling of being in love is finding that perfect match. I think that love is the only real thing, the only time people act honestly towards each other. I think it is the only time we truly enjoy being alive. I think it is the only experience that can really change us. I think it is the only emotion people live and die for. I think every effort in life is ultimately an attempt to get or receive love. I think it is the be-all and end-all of existence.

CLAIRE: Is that what you really think?

ZYLAR: No. I think that the state of being in love is an illusion. It is people wallowing in a mirror reflection of themselves. It is people wanting to collapse into each other rather than stand on their own two feet. It is the idea that we do not have to contribute anything to the world as long as we are feeling a lot. It is a regression to when we were being breast fed. Or, if we were not breast fed, it is an attempt to rectify that inequity. It is as inexplicable and random as a traffic light, yet we attach great meaning to it. The number of times we are fallen in love with is directly proportional to how good-looking we are. The number of times we fall in love is dependent on whether we live in a big city or a small town. Falling in love is the emotional equivalent of emptying your bladder—things well up in you and you just let them out on whoever comes along. Whoever is convenient. (*Pause*.)

CLAIRE: Do you think that you're a "convenient" person to fall in love with?

ZYLAR: No.

(*Lights fade*.)

(*The following exchange takes place between* ZOINX *and her* COUNSELOR *while the stage is in blackout and as we see the tiny spaceship crossing.*)

ZOINX: But I have an additional question. How will I find my way through Earth customs and manners?

COUNSELOR: Upon your arrival you will turn on a box. In this box you will find the emblems and signals of American culture. Remember, do not forget to turn on the box.

(*We hear the sound of a "click." Lights up on a Game Show set.*)

HOST: Hello and welcome to "Torture Yourself with Details"! The game show that asks the why, why, and why of what happened! Today's guest artist is the inimitable Suzanne Sommers!

SUZANNE: Hello, Jack.

HOST: Hello, Suzanne! You know I loved your work as Macduff in the cross-gender Toronto version of *MacBeth*!

SUZANNE: I wasn't in that show, Jack! Rather, I appeared on television's *Three's Company*!

HOST: Right! Now meet today's contestant! She's a self-flagellating ex-dental student from Des Moines! Meet Jane Chernoff! Hello, Jane!

JANE: Hi, Jack. I'm sorry.

HOST: Why are you sorry, Jane!

JANE: I just am.

HOST: Well you know the rules. The guest artist and today's contestant sit opposite each other in comfy chairs! And questions are asked! And there's dinging! And buzzing! Are you ready?

SUZANNE & JANE: Yes, Jack.

HOST: Okay, start the clock!

(*Melodic ticking starts.*)

SUZANNE: She was wearing a blue dress and smiling. She was running her fingers through his hair. She kissed him. She smiled at you.

JANE: Okay.

(*Sound: DING!*)

SUZANNE: You didn't call her on the 25th. You talked for too short a time on the 26th. You were distracted by your taxes on the 27th. When she said,

"We should come back and eat there sometime," you didn't respond because you were too stunned, but it read as indifference.

JANE: Okay.

(*Sound: DING!*)

SUZANNE: You have never been alone. You have always been alone. You are too picky. You are not picky enough. Those are men's shoes.

JANE: Yes.

(*Sound: DING DING DING!*)

HOST: Okay, that's the end of Round One! How are you feeling, Jane? Sufficiently tortured?

JANE: Actually, Jack, I feel about the same as I did when I got up this morning. (*Pause.*) I forgot to buy shampoo.

HOST: Well, you'll have plenty of time to buy shampoo where you're going! After winning no money and no prizes in a no-win situation, Jane Chernoff, we're sending you back to your lonely dead-end job as a cashier in a greeting card store on 12th Street and University Place! How does that make you feel?

JANE: Um—

SUZANNE: It sounds absolutely repulsive to me, Jack!

HOST: Yes, it is! It's pathetic! Thank you, Suzanne! And thank you to our lovely studio audience! Please tune in tomorrow for another round of "Torture Yourself with Details!"

(*Applause. Lights fade.*)

(*Lights up on a greeting card store. JANE is behind the counter. ZOINX enters.*)

JANE: Can I help you?

ZOINX: Yes. (*Long pause.*)

JANE: Are you looking for anything in particular? A special kind of gift or whatever?

ZOINX: Do you have a radio transmitter?

JANE: Where are you trying to transmit to?

ZOINX: Outer space.

JANE: I'm sorry. Did you try Radio Shack?

ZOINX: Is this not Radio Shack? Is this not?

JANE: No—it's not. But we do have plenty of other things here.

ZOINX: I have seen you on TV.

JANE: Oh.

ZOINX: You sell greeting cards?

JANE: Certainly. We have all sorts. Birthday, Thanksgiving, Halloween, Valentine's Day.

ZOINX: May I have a Valentine's Day card?

JANE: Certainly. For your sweetheart?

ZOINX: Yes.

JANE: That'll be two dollars.

(JANE *hands* ZOINX *the card.* ZOINX *hands* JANE *two dollars.*)

JANE: Thank you.

(*Then* ZOINX *hands* JANE *the card, and exits.* JANE *looks around confused.*)

(*Lights fade.*)

(*Lights up on* ZOINX *and* JANE *sitting next to each other at the movies. We hear the soundtrack of voices speaking seriously.*)

ZOINX: (*Very loudly.*) Ha. Ha. Ha. (*Pause.*) Ha. Ha. Ha.

VOICE #1: Could you keep it down in front?

VOICE#2: YEAH, KEEP IT DOWN!

ZOINX: Ha. Ha. Ha. (*Pause.*) Ha. Ha. Ha.

(*KLONK!*)

(*A popcorn bucket hits* ZOINX *in the back of the head.*)

ZOINX: Ha. Ha. Ha.

(*Lights fade.*)

(*Lights up on* JANE *and* ZOINX *at* JANE'S *apartment.* JANE *hands* ZOINX *a mug and they sit down.*)

ZOINX: What is this beverage?

JANE: It's coffee.

ZOINX: Is it a relaxant?

JANE: No. Haven't you ever had coffee before?

ZOINX: No.

JANE: Really? Huh. Well, be careful! Don't drink too much of it. It can make your heart beat all fast and your hands shake.

ZOINX: Your hands are shaking already.

JANE: Huh! Well they are! Look at that—ha ha! (*Long pause.*)

ZOINX: Is it permissible for me to touch you?

JANE: (*Nervously.*) Yes.

(ZOINX *puts her hand on* JANE's *nose. There is a long pause. Then* JANE *speaks.*)

JANE: Your hand is on my nose.

ZOINX: Yes.

JANE: How come?

ZOINX: I am expressing my affection for you. Do you find that unpleasant?

JANE: No—I just—I'm not exactly sure what to do.

ZOINX: This.

(ZOINX *takes* JANE's *hand and puts it on her* (ZOINX's) *nose. They each sit there with each other's hands on each other's noses for a moment. Then* ZOINX *takes her hand off* JANE's *nose and* JANE *takes her hand off* ZOINX's *nose.*)

ZOINX: I have never done that with someone so quickly.

JANE: I've never done that with someone at all!

ZOINX: Never? Astonishing. Why not?

JANE: Why not? Well, I don't think anyone has wanted to.

ZOINX: We have had similar lives.

JANE: Gosh. That's funny you should say that.

ZOINX: Funny. (*Pause.*) Like the movie?

JANE: No—I mean it's funny because I barely know anything about you. Whenever we spend time together you never really tell me about yourself. Like I don't even know where you're from.

ZOINX: Where I am from.

JANE: Yeah. Where did you grow up?

ZOINX: (*Takes a long pause.*) Not here.

JANE: Well, I hope not. I'd be really upset to think that you've been here my whole life and it's taken this long to meet you.

(ZOINX *puts her hand back on* JANE's *nose.* JANE *turns off the light.*)

ZOINX: Ow!

JANE: I'm sorry. Did I poke you in the eye?

ZOINX: It is okay.

END OF EXCERPT

WOW Women in Their Own Words

HOLLY HUGHES: How did you get involved in WOW?

MADELEINE OLNEK: This was '86, '87, and I was in this avant-garde production that was in the East Village that was called *Lives of the Saints*. That was the end of me as a performer, that production. It was four months of rehearsal and it was so avant-garde, it was beyond language. And everyone played a saint. I wrote my own material. Every night we'd go out drinking. Nancy Swartz, who was a WOW person, was in it. She had a show at WOW, and she asked me if I would write it with her. I've never done something so breezily with such a big pay-off. The show was called *Fan Mail*; it was about celebrity, and we loosely based it on a rumor about Jodie Foster. [*At that time, Foster was rumored to be a lesbian, but her sexuality wasn't publicly confirmed until 2013.*] Some people from Yale came who were very upset that we intruded on Foster's privacy. One of those people ended up being an editor of *Out* magazine.

I was coming from New York University, where you would do a show and the whole audience would be other student actors or theater people. They were very judgmental. I know that WOW is always sometimes accused of "preaching to the converted," but I was putting on a show in front of an audience of people I didn't know. They weren't necessarily people from theater. It felt like a broader theater experience than what I had been used to at NYU. I was really interested in things that were happening in the East Village. After I did the show at WOW, I met Deb Margolin, who was the writer for Split Britches. I was amazed by her use of language and comedy. It struck me as so original, unlike anything I have ever seen.

I wanted to find a way to combine the structure of a play with the edge of performance art. People go to a play and they just sink into their seats and it's a dead evening. I don't believe in theater that tries to be interesting for interesting's sake. I believe in trying to key into something very vital and essential. So much of institutionalized theater I see is cut off by that impulse, or getting these sort of pre-packaged playwrights where it's as much about their personality and their social skills in the theater world as it is about their writing and their work. What's really essential here? Is this writing alive? Is it important?

Really good comedy can turn your perspective on its head. If you go see a comedy, you walk out and you're a changed person, even if you don't change your life. It really affects your body chemistry for an hour. So much in life is already drama or already a tragedy. If you write a tragedy, you're actually not being very creative, because you're just reiterating the circumstances of our lives. Anyone who's seriously interested in comedy is interested in the universal impulse of laughing. I don't know of anyone in comedy who only wants to make certain groups of people laugh. But the perception is that lesbians aren't funny. WOW became a cooking pot for these really fine comic sensibilities. When the Five Lesbian Brothers first formed, having social nights out with them, they were so funny, I almost didn't want to talk because people were just topping each other. It was this incredible verbal and mental comedy battle and the comedy there was so good that it just inspired you to get to the next level.

WOW was vital because they were saying things that you couldn't hear anywhere. The production values were so inexpensive that the writing and the performances really had to be really good; you had to really kill, since people weren't coming in and having a cushy time in a lush theater. There were also so many obstacles to putting up lesbian material, which was always much more difficult outside of WOW. At WOW, lesbians were the majority, so the lesbian stuff was never an issue. You could actually focus on making the work better, because the lesbian content wasn't an obstacle. You didn't have to spend energy being the "lesbian weirdo" or assuring people putting on the production it was okay. I just wanted to be a better writer, and a better director, and I wanted to put my energy into making the pieces work.

At WOW, the work was better, but it didn't exist in the world. We got zero press coverage. I was really stunned; when I had previously worked with the Bad Neighbors Theater Company, everything I did got a couple of reviews, and that would be a way of marking it, not just getting feedback as an artist but also giving you professional credentials, and building an audience, giving you a future as an artist. I was shocked that WOW got no press coverage. So I became the WOW publicity person.

I remember one week, *Outweek* magazine had done their fall theater picks, which included three gay men and a straight person. And it's a gay New York weekly! I wrote a letter, complaining, "Don't you think there should be some lesbian theater events highlighted?" They answered, "Well, we're inundated for requests to review stuff by gay male artists whereas lesbians don't call." In the magazine, several times, in bold, in the Arts Section it said, "DO NOT CALL, DO NOT CALL, WE DO NOT ACCEPT PERSONAL SOLICITATIONS." Women would see that and say, "Do not call, I'm not going to call." But men would think, "That doesn't apply to me; I'm going to call." The magazine would break its own policy and honor the people who were pushy.

So many gay men are involved in theater; it's really bizarre that it's such a hostile place for lesbians. The *New York Times* has never been to review anything at WOW, whereas the Ridiculous Theatre [*New York's preeminent gay male theater, which at the time was the male equivalent of WOW*] has been honored frequently by the *Times* as an "important place." What they were doing there was very quirky, bizarre, and very much for an in-house audience but the *Times* saw its value. The *Village Voice* honored WOW with an Obie, but even the *Voice* wouldn't list WOW shows sometimes. Michael Feingold, the head critic of the *Voice*, he can make or break your reputation downtown. He's a very powerful man, very well respected, very smart, very articulate. But he's never been to WOW, never walked inside to see a show there. WOW is two blocks from the *Voice;* I mean, what's that?

What happens to a lesbian playwright versus what happens to a gay male playwright is the same as what happens to men and women more generally in our society. When I did my play *Wild Nights with Emily* at WOW, Sharon Jane Smith very generously produced me, and Deb Margolin played the lead part. It got a good review in the *Voice*. Because of that review it went to Boston. Because it went to Boston, a regional theater in Alaska thought, "Oh, this play is going places, we better produce it." That play would have died at WOW had there not been a review; instead, it had a future.

The idea of a woman writer is very dangerous; even more so for a playwright, because she puts words into the mouths of other people. There's something incredibly subversive about being a woman playwright.

HH: If you saw there was this indifference to WOW from the larger theater world, why did you stay for so long?

MO: My career has been a downward trajectory to the more obscure. When I was in college, I did comedy shows and worked with Molly Shannon [*the comic who went on to star on Saturday Night Live from 1995 to 2001*]. I was part of the Atlantic Theater Company, and that was definitely going places. But I knew I had to leave because I knew I would never be the writer I wanted to be if I stayed in that group. It's a very complicated answer for me . . . the first time I came to WOW, I was sure I was not a lesbian, although I did notice that everyone dressed like me. Nancy Swartz said to me, "When we go to WOW, if anyone assumes that you're gay, don't correct them," because that would be seen as very rude. And I was like, "Oh, okay."

HH: I don't think that people at WOW really thought that heterosexuality existed.

MO: People would often play a lesbian in a play, and realize, "Oh my god, I'm a lesbian." It was only by entering an imaginary world that you could really see the possibility for yourself. At the same time, many straight people, including straight men, were involved in my shows. They were very successful and no one was talking about whether the people were gay.

HH: Can you talk about how your writing developed at WOW?

MO: WOW was a great place for writers, even though the idea was that everyone was there to perform. I was one of the few people there who was absolutely not interested in performing and I got tapped on as a writer for a lot of projects. WOW operated the way Café Cino served as a laboratory for artists like Sam Shepard. You just booked a date and then whatever you wrote was going to be put on. When Shepard talks about the East Village as a writer's paradise, WOW was one of the few places that retained that environment. You had to put in sweat equity on someone else's show to get your own show, rather than a group of people deciding whether or not your group or your script was "worthy" to put on.

I've often been told that my plays don't read like much. They really have an impact when you see them, because I write things to be performed. WOW really benefited from the immediate sense of, "Oh, my God, in a couple of weeks, this has to be up!" That helped remove writer's block. Many things that happened at WOW were things that Paula Vogel had structured into her playwriting program at Brown University. For instance, you were given an assignment at the beginning of the week and you had to write something that would be put on that weekend; and it had to have certain pre-assigned elements in it. The difference at WOW being perhaps you had to have certain people in it, if it was their time in the space.

We were also lucky because people would get to know your work and maybe, hopefully, want to work with you. They would have faith in you that contributed to the success of the project. The most important thing WOW contributed was the opportunity for writers to really work on the play until it works. Maybe WOW was spared from the corruption of the writer's process in the commercial theater world because it was such a status-free environment.

Flyer for the WOW Festival, October 1981, designed by Peggy Shaw. Even alternative publications such as the *Village Voice* were unlikely to list WOW events, so artists turned to advertising their own productions, often by illegally attaching flyers to buildings (a practice known as "sniping"). Established institutions could hire others, but WOW artists did their own sniping.

Below: Membership card for the WOW Festival, 1981, designed by Peggy Shaw (Collection of Debra Miller)

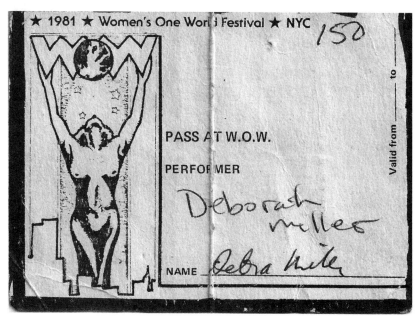

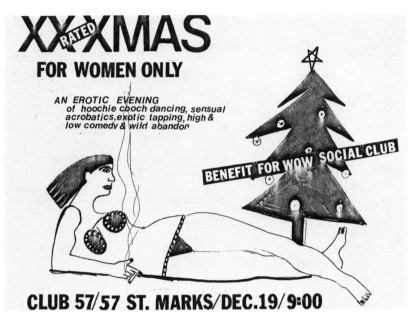

XX~~RATED~~ XMAS

FOR WOMEN ONLY

AN EROTIC EVENING
of hoochie cooch dancing, sensual
acrobatics, exotic tapping, high &
low comedy & wild abandon

BENEFIT FOR WOW SOCIAL CLUB

CLUB 57/57 ST. MARKS/DEC.19/9:00

Flyer for a WOW benefit, December 1982 (design by Cathy Quinlan, collection of Diane Torr). The benefit was to raise funds to acquire a permanent space at Club 57, one of the earliest and most iconic East Village performance clubs, located in the basement of a Catholic church at 57 St. Mark's Place. Torr notes, "Cathy Quinlan, Peggy Reynolds and I hosted this event at Club 57 to raise the money for the first month's rent on a WOW Café. . . . I had performed a lot at Club 57 via Ann Magnuson, Steve Brown and other Club 57 event organizers, so I had an 'in' and asked for the use of the space. I invited some of my go-go dancer friends to participate. A little-known event is the 'anti-feminist demonstration' . . . that consisted of anarchists holding placards saying 'Women get back in the kitchen.' It was an anarchist friend of mine, Lee . . . just to raise hackles."

Right: Diane Torr, Erotic Night at the WOW Café, 1983. (Photo by Saskia Scheffer)

© Saskia Scheff

Interior of the first WOW Café at 330 East 11th Street, circa 1983. Moe Angelos is in the foreground with Peggy Shaw in back. A photo by Eva Weiss hangs on the back wall. (Photo by Debra Miller)

MS GAY PRIDE
1983

"Ms. Gay Pride 1983," Alice Forrester. (Photo and design by Eva Weiss, collection of Claire Moed)

In the 1980s, the New York City Gay Pride March began in the Village and ended in Central Park. WOW marched as a group, dragging a cooler of beer, which we sold until we covered our expenses and then drank. Lori Leckman (*standing*) has Jackie Rudin on her shoulders. (Photo by Saskia Scheffer)

Interior of the first WOW Café at 330 East 11th Street, circa 1984. Sunday brunches provided income and confirmed the Café as a social space as well as a performance venue. (Photo by Saskia Scheffer)

The Well of Horniness, 1984, written by Holly Hughes and directed by Lois Weaver. *From the left*, Sharon Jane Smith and Helen Frankenthal. (Photo by Eva Weiss)

Ciao to WOW. Exterior of the original Café on East 11th Street, circa 1985, with Claire Moed (*left*) and Alice Forrester sitting in the doorway. Claire would frequently stand in front of the Café handing out flyers for WOW events. On this occasion, we were preparing to move to the location on East 4th Street. (Photo by Joni Wong)

The Lady Dick at WOW on East 4th Street, fall of 1985. *Back row:* Susan Young (*left*) and Eva Weiss. *Front row:* Carmelita Tropicana (*left*) and Sharon Jane Smith. Set design by Alice Forrester. (For full production information, see page 101–2.) Photo by Dona Ann McAdams.

Mundane Devastation, 1985, created by Alice Forrester, costumes by Susan Young. *From the left, back row:* Claudia Giordano Lasky, Debra Miller, Debby Wapshott, Ginny Bowen Miller, Sabrina Artel, and Adrienne Collins. *From the left, front row:* Moe Angelos and Nancy Swartz. (Photo by Amy Meadow)

Photographs from *Cinderella: The Real True Story*, 1985, conceived by Cheryl Moch and Holly Gewandter, directed by Lois Weaver, music by Holly Gewandter, set design by Peggy Shaw, costumes by Susan Young. (*A*) Alice Forrester, (*B*) Lisa Kron, (*C*) Debra Miller, (*D*) Claire Moed, (*E*) Julia Scott, (*F*) Julia Dares. (Photos by Amy Meadow)

Upwardly Mobile Home, 1985. *From the left:* Lois Weaver, Peggy Shaw, and Deb Margolin. (Photo by Eva Weiss)

Snow White, Unadorned, 1986, conceived by Cheryl Moch and Holly Gewandter, directed by Lois Weaver, original music by Holly Gewandter, set design by Peggy Shaw, Susan Young, and Joni Wong. Heidi Griffith plays "The Queen" in a costume by Susan Young. (Photo by Amy Meadow)

Snow White, Unadorned, 1986. Lynn Hayes plays the "Mirror" in a costume by Susan Young. (Photo by Amy Meadow)

Rabbit Plantation, 1987, written by Alison Rooney, set design by Susan Young and Claudia Giordano Lasky. *From the left:* Kate Stafford and Karen Crumley Keats. (Photo by Dona Ann McAdams)

Candela, 1987, created by Uzi Parnes, Carmelita Tropicana, and Ela Troyano. *From the left:* Uzi Parnes, Carmelita Tropicana, and Moe Angelos. Ishmael Houston Jones is on the film. (Photo by Dona Ann McAdams)

Publicity photo of the full cast of *Starstruck*, 1987–88, created by Alice Forrester and Heidi Griffiths, set design by Alice Forrester, Lynn Hayes, Quinn, Serena Heslop, and Diane Jeep Reis. *Back row, from left:* Helen Frankenthal, Dorothy Fradera, Donna Evans, and Claudia Giordano Lasky. *Second row, from left:* Lynn Hayes, Sharon Jane Smith, and Beth Nathanson. *Front row, from left:* Diane Jeep Reis, Betsy Crenshaw, Babs Davy, and Quinn. (Photo by Dona Ann McAdams)

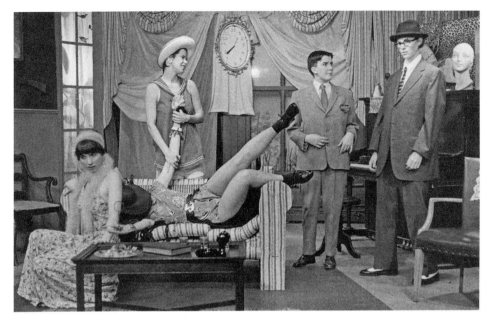

Paradykes Lost, 1987–88, written by Lisa Kron in collaboration with the cast (Moe Angelos, Betsy Crenshaw, Babs Davy, Peggy Healey, Carolyn Patierno, Imogene Pip, Kate Stafford and Susan Young), set design by Susan Young *From the left*: Carolyn Patierno, Imogene Pip on couch, Peg Healey standing, Moe Angelos, and Kate Stafford. (For the full list of production credits, please see the excerpt on page 55.) Photo by Dona Ann McAdams.

Little Women, 1987–88. *From the left*: Peggy Shaw, Lois Weaver, and Peg Healey. (Photo by Amy Meadow)

Publicity photo of the full cast of *How to Say Kaddish with Your Mouth Shut*, 1987, by Claire Moed. *Back:* Claire Moed. *Front, from the left:* Imogene Pip and Lisa Kron. (Photo by Eva Weiss)

Tart City, 1988, Created by Kate Stafford and Karen Crumley Keats. *Left foreground:* Susan Young. *Right background:* Gail Freund. (Photo by Dona Ann McAdams)

Clamcracker Suite, 1988, created by Carmelita Tropicana, Uzi Parnes, and Ela Troyano. *Seated:* Babs Davy. *On lap:* Carmelita Tropicana. (Photo by Dona Ann McAdams)

Voyage to Lesbos I & II, from the 1989–90 season, created by the Five Lesbian Brothers. *From the left:* Lisa Kron, Peg Healey, Moe Angelos, and Dom Dibbell. (Photo by Dona Ann McAdams)

Publicity photo of author Deb Margolin in the title role in *Hamlet*, 1989. (Photo by Amy Meadow)

Of Men and Steamboat Men, from the 1989–90 season, written by Sharon Jane Smith. *From the left:* Sharon Jane Smith, Moe Angelos, Betsy Crenshaw, Harriet Hirschorn, and Gabrielle Hamilton. (Photo by Dona Ann McAdams)

Women and Children First: Outstanding Perk or Tool of Oppression?, from the 1991–92 season, written and performed by Babs Davy. (Photo by Dona Ann McAdams)

The WOW tenth anniversary benefit, 1993. (Collection of
Debra Miller)

Dyke Noir

The overall feeling I get when I think back to my tour at WOW was stomach upset . . . from fear, from adrenaline, from anger, from the excitement of sexual intrigue.

—Dominique Dibbell

In May 1988, *Village Voice* columnist C. Carr changed my life. I was on the cover of the downtown weekly that everyone read, sometimes searching out newsstands that stocked the paper at midnight every Tuesday, so they could be ahead of the curve on what to see, who to see, and, possibly, where to live. Carr's "On Edge" column in the *Voice* mapped the complicated terrain of East Village art making of all kinds. Her story that May not only featured my collaboration with Lois Weaver and Peggy Shaw, *Dress Suits to Hire*, but credited me with creating a new genre of performance she termed "dyke noir." Carr took what might have been seen as failure in the eyes of other critics and turned it into proof of innovation. For instance, she was untroubled by a crime story without a crime, because, she said, "The characters are the crime." She didn't care that these plays lacked a plot; we didn't need it and we were better off without it, Carr said. And because she said so in the paper we venerated more than perhaps even the *Times*, it felt true.

Carr's ideas about "dyke noir" didn't just explain my work. Although WOW was known for its humor, darkness loomed over much of the work, an anger unmasked and given voice on the tiny stage. Ana Maria Simo's *Pickaxe* is one example of a queer lesbian play that owes more to expressionism than it does to a concern with positive imagery of any sort. Moe Angelos and Dom Dibbell's collaborations, such as *I Wish I Had a Real Gun*, and *O Darn! The World Is Not a Safe Place for Little Buttercups*, also advocated a lesbian desire that was as much about vengeance and rage as it was about sex. The lesbian erotic was full of anger. As Eileen Myles points out in *Feeling Blue*, it's very hot to kiss a woman with a gun. Even Lois and Peggy, who were known for a gentler style and tone, served up *Lesbians Who Kill*, working once more with Deb Margolin to produce their take on the renowned lesbian serial killer Aileen Warnos's case.

Carr's dyke noir, in other words, didn't apply to just one show or any one artist but described what many of us knew ourselves to be, at least in terms of our artistic aspirations. We looked at the movie stereotypes of dykes as ruthless, unruly women with murder in their hearts and we refused to get onboard with any movement that would offer up sanitized versions of ourselves. We were done with being nice girls. We were armed and dangerous and didn't care who knew it. —*Holly Hughes*

Holly Hughes

The Lady Dick (1985)

The new space on E. 4th Street felt luxurious compared to the storefront. There was a backstage with a dressing room, and you could fit more than three people onstage. I remember feeling I had to live up to the place. I wanted to stop messing around and do some theatre, whatever that meant. I still didn't know very much about theatre; I'd hardly seen anything that wasn't performed in a bar. Maybe that's why my second play, *The Lady Dick*, was set in a bar. It was as if some of the characters from my first play, *The Well of Horniness*, demanded their own show. And they weren't keen on sharing the stage. The play was a series of monologues strung together by parodies of songs. If the plot was silly in the *Well*, it was entirely absent in this piece, a crime story without a crime. Or, as C. Carr wrote in the *Village Voice*, "The characters are the crime." In the first play, the characters tried to escape from the only plot I knew, the one that is burned into the mind of every girl-child, the marriage plot. But I couldn't imagine what life outside would look like. So the play ended with the protagonist, Vicki, waking up back in heteroville life.

Lady Dick takes place in the world I couldn't imagine but was starting to inhabit. As in the bar the play is set in, WOW was a world apart. No sign, no buzzer; the door closed behind you, and it was easy to forget there was any other world. But the bar in this play is darker, meaner than WOW. It's hazy with sexual tension and all species of pain. Characters flaunt their psychic scars like elaborate tattoos. It's like the Dystopia Bar 'n' Grill. The protagonist, Garnet McClit, moves through the bar like she's traveling the stations of a lesbian cross. At each station, there's another pissed-off and sexed-up woman waiting to snare McClit with her story.

The first excerpt is from the top of the show and introduces Garnet, who was played by Sharon Jane Smith in the first production. In the second excerpt, we hear from a character named Lethal Weapon, who bursts through a side door and holds the denizens of the bar hostage. Rereading this script twenty-six years later, I see Lethal as a later version of Vicki, the runaway housewife in *Well*. She's rejected the marriage plot and has no map. But she does have something to say, and she's going to make sure you hear it.

The original cast of *The Lady Dick* included Sharon Jane Smith, Susan Young, Ana Maria Simo, Carmelita Tropicana, Alison Rooney, Kathy Thomas, and Eva Weiss. Sets were designed and built by Alice Forrester, lights were by Joni Wong, and Sarah Schulman was the stage manager.

THE LADY DICK

GARNET MCCLIT:

It was the usual kind of town. The perfect place to grow up. That's what they said. They also said it was a good place to grow old.

I told myself I'd never find out. I was just passing through.

Where I come from, nothing ever changes. Not the way things are said, not the way things are done. For sure not the style of the clothes because the clothes they wore there had no style. Nobody ever changed their mind. That's why they liked it.

That's right, them and me. Right from the beginning.

The only good thing about growing up there, the only thing I liked, was the weather. We used to have pretty bad weather. Blizzards and tornadoes. On the same day.

You know how it is with girls. One day you're one of them. You're playing with them and you're all the same. And this makes you happy. Then one day it's different. Because you're different. You know how girls get funny at a certain age. They don't want to do nothing. They want someone to do something to them. Ask their parents for money, so they can dress up like they ain't got no parents. Go around looking like they just got beat up.

I never went through that phase.

When all the other girls started looking for shelter from the storm, I started looking for the storm.

When you grow up fast in a town that never changes, it is best to grow up fast and get out of town. No sense being a camel in with the mares.

And I couldn't change. Any more than the town could. Any more than you can change bad weather.

Whatever folks were thinking they stopped thinking and started saying.

Started telling my folks I might be headed down a bad road. But maybe they could head me off at the pass. If I went to a therapist.

So I went to a therapist. And I took one look at that therapist and said, "Okay, Bud. Drop that legal pad and stop trying to comb your hair over that bald spot. I know who you are. You're no therapist. You're a shrink. That's what you do, shrink people like me down to size. Your size. You're like a lumberjack turning a cow into a pile of jiffy steaks. Well, I got news for you. I'm not your TV dinner. You think you know me, you don't know me. I got better things to do than to play word games with someone who wants me to snitch on my own mother. But I'm going to do you a favor, head-shrinker. I'm going to let you live. I'm going to let you crawl on out of here, so you can keep charging people a hundred bucks for an hour that don't even have an hour in it. But you, and your theories, stay outta my way." So you might say I flunked outta therapy.

I know people say that therapy isn't the kind of thing you can flunk outta, but that's just something people say.

I did what dropouts do. I left town with someone else's money. I went to Europe. My parents said they hoped I'd find myself there. That was a nice thing for them to say. 'Course they didn't really mean it. They hoped that I'd find somebody else and become them. Somebody who wore high heels and whistled while she worked.

They didn't have to worry. I didn't find myself. I found her. And I lost what little bit of self I did have.

It was somewhere in the low country. She was seated at a café writing dirty poetry that didn't rhyme. She was a dark and stormy night and for a while, I was her smoking gun.

Then I lost her, too.

By the time I got back to the town that never changes, I had changed. So much, folks didn't recognize me. Cops called me "Boy," boys called me "Sir," and the ladies, well, the ladies called me.

(FEMALE JONES *enters with a bouquet of flowers.*)

FEMALE JONES: Ding dong! (*Looking at card with flowers.*) Garnet McClit, Lady Dick?

[. . .]

LETHAL WEAPON: I know what they call you. They call you sucker. And I know what they call this place. They call it a rathole. Oh, it's not my name for it. I like to think of it as a rattrap, because the rats that are here can't get out, isn't that right? I think there's a couple of rats backstage—why don't you come on out? I feel like buying you a drink.

(*Enter two women,* VICTIM ONE *and* VICTIM TWO. *They cross to bar area, behaving as hostages. Whether or not they are innocent bystanders is open; they believe they are.*)

LETHAL WEAPON: Now you know I know what they call you. But you don't know what they call me. They call me Lethal Weapon. There's been so many, I only remember the first ones, that look on their face the second before they . . . (*Hands* VICTIM ONE *a cocktail glass.*) Drink up, honey. It's not my fault. It's yours.

Before I met you, I could do two things at the same time. Now I can only do one thing to one person. You. You made me a real Johnny One Note.

Lucky for you it happens to be a helluva note.

Before I met you, you were already sleeping inside me like a little germ waiting to turn into a big disease. I was a real nice person. Hard to believe? It was loving you that brought out the killer in me.

I was going to get married. I had a real nice guy, money in the bank, didn't want a thing, and if I did, it wasn't you. My fiancé was a sensitive man. He was going to give up meat after we got married. I'd look into his eyes and see baby booties. He loved me so much it made me sick. He used to grill me steaks on the patio. His baby blues'd get all watery and I'd wonder: Is it love . . . or steak sauce?

After all this time, I still don't know. But I guess you know what I did. I ran out onto the patio and grabbed his flaming sirloins and hurled them as hard as I could and I set his lilies on fire. Then I turned on him. He was a good man but loving me had made him worthless. He was the first.

Then I went to see my mistress. She wears a beret and talks with this cute little English accent she picked up at a yard sale. We talk about ART. She goes for that funny music. You know the kind I mean. The singers sound like two epileptics screaming at each other in a foreign language. Then there's the instruments. And I'm not talking about your piano or your guitar. I'm talking about your steamroller and a dump truck running into each other.

I like it. You just can't tap your toe to it.

But she finds the music inspirational. Says it makes her want to do funny things, like make art. She makes art to the music. She takes Fiesta Ware . . . my Fiesta Ware, and smashes it, to the beat. Then she takes photographs of the damage. The photograph is the art part, the rest is just process, isn't that right?

Myself, I hate art. I miss my Fiesta Ware. I tell her, "I really loved that lavender turkey platter you demolished for your Guggenheim grant."

And she says, "If you love something, SMASH IT. That's the meaning of modern art. And I'm going to make an artist out of you if it kills me."

Well, that was a funny thing to say to somebody who had a killer sleeping inside them. Though I can't say she lived to regret it.

Then I met you. I didn't know, but you might be some kind of cat fancier. So I walked right up to you and said, "Did you see my pussy? It'll come if you call it."

Well, you looked at me as if you were a little bitty frightened Peter Cottontail and I was a great big runaway Chevrolet. Then I got it. You liked being hunted. I could tell by the way you let me get close enough to you to catch your scent. Then you went bye-bye.

You said, "I love Georgia O'Keefe, she's my favorite painter." And I said, "I am Georgia O'Keefe."

'Course you already knew this. That's why you loved me so much. Over the discount cookbooks, we kissed. You left town.

You left me in a bad way, baby. I wanted you so much I could barely walk. Every time I sat down, I ruined the chair. I didn't dare cross my legs.

Then the phone rang. I hoped it was you. I knew it was you—I had killed off everyone else by then.

It was you. You said, "A storm's coming, and I got to see you." I don't say nothing.

And you say, "Forget about art, give up marriage, I want you."

Still, I don't say nothing.

And you say, "What's the matter, baby, can't you come?"

And I say, "When I come, you're going to know about it. But you watch out. I got no brakes."

And you said, "Don't stop for nothing."

So I didn't. I got into my car, and I'm driving. And it's raining, then it's hailing, then it's thundering, and then it's lightning and then . . . all of a sudden, the STORM STARTS.

There is a wall of water on one side and a wall of fire on the other, and the road behind me is history. There is a trailer park over my head. An entire department store with blue-haired salesladies still trying to hang on to the sales tables, spinning around like in spin the bottle, where it will stop nobody knows.

It occurs to me this could be the end of life as we know it. I think you and me are going to have a good time.

I get to your house. You take me in. You say something so sweet. I still remember it. Why don't you say it again? SAY IT.

VICTIM ONE: Isn't there something you want to say, like I love you?

LETHAL WEAPON: Shit no. I don't love you. I LOVE YOU. You get it? You got it. Still you insisted on telling me these stories that weren't exactly funny, but I laughed anyway, so hard I slapped your thigh and you nailed my hand down.

We kissed, and the rain let up. We kissed a little more, and the fog started coming in. I thought if I'm going to get out, now's the time. Looks like a three-day blow is heading our way. In a few days, I'll be socked in.

I should have gotten suspicious when you asked me to wear your dead mother's negligee while you got dressed up in your dead brother's Eagle Scout uniform. The moment of truth came in your parents' bed. Before I could ask for more, you were bye-bye.

(VICTIM ONE *exits*. LETHAL WEAPON *turns her attention to* VICTIM TWO.)

LETHAL WEAPON: Of course I went after you. I had no gas, I had no brakes and the storm was having a relapse; but I was doing 85 in no time.

I didn't even feel the little old lady. The first little old lady. Besides she had eight incurable diseases and no pets, so I figured her time was up. I felt a little bit bad about the family of five.

The first family of five.

Then I remembered my constitutional right to the pursuit of happiness, which says, even if there is no such thing as happiness, I got a right to pursue it.

That's the way it is with me now. Hit and run. I'm gonna run down everything that gets between me and you. Sometimes I feel bad for the people I kill, there's nothing wrong with them, except that they're not you, and that's reason enough for them to die. I know it's just a matter of time before you and me get back together and cause another little earthquake or something even worse. Until then, I send roses to the kin of my victims. We are talking massacre, and I can't stop till I get to you.

(*Blackout.*)

END OF EXCERPT

Ana Maria Simo

Pickaxe (1986)

Cuban-born, French-educated Ana Maria Simo is a New York–based writer of plays, novels, and essays who published her first book, *Las Fábulas*, a short story collection, at eighteen. Three of her plays—*Exiles* (1982), *Alma* (1988), and *Going to New England* (1990)—were staged Off-Broadway by IN-TAR, one of the longest-running Latino theatres in the United States, where she was part of the playwriting lab led by pioneering dramatist Maria Irene Fornes. Ana's *The Bad Play* was presented at Performance Space 122 in 1991, and *Opium Wars* was staged at the New York Theatre Workshop in 1996.

Ana was one of the women who came to WOW with a background in theatre and experience running a lesbian theatre collective. With Magaly Abalau, she founded Medusa's Revenge, the first lesbian theatre in New York City, in 1976. After Medusa's Revenge closed and Peggy Shaw asked her repeatedly to work at WOW, Ana relented, although she never became a "core" member. She was cast in *St. Joan of Avenue C* (1985), and played piano for one of Holly's shows and for *Carmelita Tropicana's Xmas Special* (1985). At WOW Ana saw the possibility for total creative control of her work and for working with an all-dyke cast. She asked for a slot in the WOW season, grabbed an unusual six-week run, wrote *Pickaxe*, cast it with three WOW regulars—Sharon Jane Smith, Kate Stafford, and myself—and embarked on her first directorial venture.

Ana's trajectory was different from that of many Cubans who immigrated to the United States. She was educated in a Cuban culture that was overwhelmingly European, where theatres performed everything from Brecht to Ionesco. When she immigrated to Paris in 1968, she found cultural continuity and learned intellectual discipline. She studied sociology and linguistics at the University of Paris VIII Vincennes and semiology with Roland Barthes.

Ana's European sensibility comes through in *Pickaxe* and separates the play from most WOW productions. Like most of Ana's work, the play's tone shifts between farce and tragedy. It is operatic, presents a rarefied reality, and exhibits her preoccupation with political violence. *Pickaxe* is dark and brutal. The characters are historical figures—Leon Trotsky, Frida Kahlo, and Ramon Mercader—but they are fictionalized, as are the events surrounding them. The drama is set in Frida's house near the volcano Popocatepetl, and like the volcano, emotions seethe. The play opens with Trotsky describing his nightmare and fear of sharks. When he tells Frida that maybe he should die, she grabs his hand, pushes it up her skirt and deep inside her, and commands him to live, live. This is a drama played with heightened speech, visceral monologues, and a stark stage cast with shadows. The characters constantly talk about cleanliness; they speak of a clean conscience, as well as physical cleanliness. Rhonda imagines a man in Pompeii bathing as the lava buries him; Frida tells Trotsky to bathe; and the last image of the play is Frida and her maid Aurora on their knees, rags in hand, cleaning up blood.

Pickaxe was unlike any other show at WOW. It presented many challenges for the Café's members; for audiences who grew to expect camp comedies as their usual theatre fare; and for us actors who had never played such difficult, complex roles. Ultimately, *Pickaxe* opened WOW to a different aesthetic and deeply influenced its writers. —*Carmelita Tropicana*

PICKAXE
Written and directed by Ana Maria Simo
Set design: Peggy Shaw
Lighting design: Lynn Hayes
Costumes: Susan Young
Stage Manager: Sarah Schulman
Sound design: Mary Maier/Ana Maria Simo

CHARACTERS
Frida, Mexican painter, thirties
Leon, Russian revolutionary, early sixties, but appearing to be ten years younger
Ramon, political adventurer, Leon's secretary, late twenties
Rhonda, his almost identical twin sister
Aurora, Frida's maid, a former cabaret singer, early forties

CAST
Frida: Kate Stafford

Leon/Aurora: Alina Troyano
Ramon/Rhonda: Sharon Jane Smith

Time and place: Mexico 1940.

Frida's house, in the shadow of the Popocatepetl volcano.

Scene 1

(*Before the lights go up, the sound of a shortwave radio is heard: Radio Moscow's identification with the Internationale, followed by Stalin's voice, gradually jammed with the sound of a Mexican station playing "Mujer Divina." LEON has fallen asleep in his studio, by the radio. FRIDA enters and stands near him. She turns off the radio.*)

FRIDA: Leon! Leon!
LEON: I don't want to go back. The sea was filthy and it's probably even filthier now.
FRIDA: Are you dreaming, Leon?
LEON: Yes.
FRIDA: Am I in your dream?
LEON: No. You're not.
FRIDA: Why not?
LEON: Because I don't want you there. Go away. Leave me in peace.
FRIDA: (*Hums a nursery song.*) Tell your mother what you see, little boy.
LEON: I see a wooden rowboat. The paddles are attached to the sides with pieces of rope. The boat creaks every time I move. The sun is not out yet, but it is very bright, like the nights in the Arctic. The sea is thick as a green oilcloth. It stinks. I put my hand in the water. I'm afraid a shark will come and eat it.
FRIDA: There are no sharks in the Arctic Ocean, Leon.
LEON: But I see them! They're coming after my hand.
FRIDA: Perhaps you see the shadow of your own hand in the water.
LEON: Go away. I don't know who you are.
FRIDA: I'll go away if you want me to, but I'll still watch you sleep through the crack in the door.
LEON: Not through the crack in the door.
FRIDA: Yes. I'll stick my big right eye to the crack and I'll watch you.
LEON: No, please don't do that.
FRIDA: Then talk to me, Leon. I won't say a word to anybody. I promise.

LEON: Half the men in town have lost a hand or a foot to the sharks. They're proud of it. But I'm afraid of the sharks. I want to go back. I want to go back.

FRIDA: If you go back, they'll pull your nails and your tongue out. You know that.

LEON: Yes, I know, but I want to sleep in my boat. Is that the lagoon in front of us? What is that shadow?

FRIDA: That is a monster. He's harmless. He has no teeth.

LEON: The lagoon was always in shadows, even at noon. (*He dips his hand in the sea, smells it, licks it until the hand is dry and the smell is gone.*) I've lost the smell of the sea. It doesn't smell anymore. I've lost it.

FRIDA: Don't, Leon.

LEON: I don't want to be here. I don't want to be an old man. I want to go back to the lagoon. I don't want to die.

FRIDA: There's a war over there, remember? The lagoon has been drained, so that the tanks can roll by. The mud at the bottom is dry and cracked and it stinks. You don't want to go back there.

LEON: Perhaps I should kill myself.

FRIDA: No. You have to live. (*She grabs his hand and pushes it inside her vagina, sitting on his knees. He tries to pull his hand out, but she is stronger.*)

LEON: Let me go.

FRIDA: You will live because I want you to live.

LEON: No.

FRIDA: (*Overlapping.*) Yes.

LEON: No. No. No. No.

FRIDA: Live. Live. Live. Live. (*He pushes her violently to the floor, disengaging his hand. Pause.*)

LEON: What do you want from me?

FRIDA: I want you to be comfortable and happy. I want you to eat well and sleep well. I want you to take a bath every day. Did you take a bath today?

LEON: You're torturing me.

FRIDA: I'm just your housekeeper.

LEON: You own this house and you think you own me.

FRIDA: I know I do not own you. I just have to keep you alive so you can finish your book.

LEON: Sometimes I wonder if you're trying to kill me.

FRIDA: Let me tell you a secret, Leon. I don't want you dead. I don't care enough about you.

(*Blackout.*)

Scene 2

(*LEON's studio. Morning.* LEON *is dictating to* RAMON *the last chapters of his biography of Stalin.*)

LEON: "Having betrayed the ideals of Leninism, he became a bloodthirsty tyrant." Did you get that?

RAMON: Yes.

LEON: You're very fast. Too bad I didn't find you before. I would have finished this book a year ago. Where was I?

RAMON: ". . . he became a bloodthirsty tyrant."

LEON: Period.

RAMON: A new paragraph would be more elegant.

LEON: Elegance is very important to you, isn't it?

RAMON: Yes, I'm afraid.

LEON: What are you afraid of?

RAMON: I'm afraid that you'll think I'm frivolous.

LEON: I have nothing against elegance. In fact, I am very attracted to elegant women. Unfortunately, they are often the wives or mistresses of the enemy.

RAMON: It's not their fault.

LEON: Oh, yes, it is. They could give all that up, but they rarely do.

RAMON: I'd rather keep them where they are, let them be as rich and as elegant as they can get. That's what I like.

LEON: What is it that you like?

RAMON: Legs. Especially when they're putting on their silk stockings. I like to watch when a woman puts her naked foot on a chair like this. (*He does it.*) And slowly pulls her skirt up to the knee and starts putting on her stocking, little by little, until she reaches the thigh and then she makes it smooth with the palm of her hand.

(*Blackout.*)

Scene 3

(*LEON's studio.* FRIDA *and* RAMON *watch* LEON *write.*)

RAMON: How can he write so fast?

FRIDA: That's all he knows how to do, so he does it quick and well.

RAMON: Look how his hand moves on the paper. It looks like a bee . . . it looks like an ant in an anthill. Does he get paid by the line?

FRIDA: He doesn't make any money from it. He believes every single word he writes.

RAMON: Do you believe everything he writes?

FRIDA: Not everything, but most of it. I haven't read everything he's ever written.

RAMON: Do you believe in world revolution?

FRIDA: Of course I do. What about you?

RAMON: It is a very exciting idea.

FRIDA: It is the most exciting idea I've ever heard.

RAMON: The question is, will it happen in real life?

FRIDA: I have faith in Leon. You should hear him talk about it.

RAMON: I hear him talk about it every hour of the day.

FRIDA: I mean hear him talk as a friend. Forget that you're his secretary.

RAMON: That's precisely what I've done, and it was a big mistake.

FRIDA: Why?

RAMON: Because I'm starting to feel sorry for him.

FRIDA: Oh, I feel sorry for him sometimes. He's old. He doesn't know how to wash himself well. But that doesn't mean that I lose my faith. He's a great man.

RAMON: I wonder sometimes if he's crazy.

FRIDA: He's not crazy. He just doesn't know how to enjoy life.

(LEON *continues writing as* FRIDA *and* RAMON *watch him and lights dim to black.*)

Scene 4

(FRIDA's *studio.* FRIDA *holds a mirror in her left hand and paints with her right hand. She sits before her easel on a regular chair; a crutch rests against it. After a while, she starts using the brush and paint on her own face.* LEON *enters, surprising her during this operation.*)

FRIDA: I was trying to make myself a little more attractive.

LEON: You are already very attractive, you are beautiful. What more do you want?

FRIDA: You don't understand certain things, Leon.

LEON: Such as?

FRIDA: Look at yourself, for example. Did you take a bath today?

LEON: Not yet.

FRIDA: What are you waiting for? It's almost midnight.

LEON: I'll do it first thing in the morning.

FRIDA: You stink, Leon. You're a slob. You're a bad influence on me. I've let myself go downhill since you arrived because no matter how ugly I look, you will always look worse.

LEON: I'm a man. There's no comparison.

FRIDA: Do men have to smell like pigs?

LEON: I mean women smell better and look better than men.

FRIDA: You're wrong. How can you write books if you're always wrong, if you can't think the simplest thought?

LEON: Go ahead. Kick me, beat me. If it makes you happy, it makes me happy.

FRIDA: You'd be happier if you took care of yourself.

(*A scratching noise is heard.*)

LEON: What's that?

FRIDA: What?

LEON: Ssssh! That noise.

FRIDA: It's nothing. A groundhog in the garden, a cat. See what I mean? If you washed more often, your mind would feel clearer, safer, you wouldn't fear so much for your life every minute of the day.

LEON: I have good reasons to fear for my life.

FRIDA: I know, I know. This house is a fortress. We're so safe that we can hardly breathe. You should try to forget the fear, imagine that fear is just dirt stuck behind your ears and wash it away with soap. Try, Leon, please. I'll help you. Let's have a normal life, starting with the bath. I'll show you how to wash properly. I can do it for you the first time.

LEON: I can do it myself. I'm not a child.

FRIDA: You're a stubborn, unpractical, filthy child.

LEON: My mind is clean and that's all that matters. I may have fear, but I have no lust. All I want is to watch and hear your lust. When I was younger, I was very practical. I organized a whole army. You wouldn't have liked me at all. Now I feel more altruistic. The people should have their world revolution and you, Frida, should have sex, since that is what makes you paint.

FRIDA: Come here, give me a kiss. (*He kisses her on the cheek.*) My head is too small, my body is too big. My hands and my feet are the wrong shape. I'm a monster. I'm the daughter of the hunchback who goes up the church tower and jumps out and crashes on the pavement below. Did you ever see that film?

(*Blackout.*)

Scene 5

(*Morning, two weeks later.* LEON's *studio.* RAMON *is shaving* LEON.)

RAMON: My left leg is longer than my right leg. I wasn't born like this. It happened one day. I was in the tub and suddenly the leg stretched a fraction of an inch under the soapy water. I know it sounds incredible, but it's the truth. I don't even limp—the difference between the two legs is tiny. But it's there, and it bothers me. I would have preferred a visible change, something others could see. Instead, you have to take my word for it, or not. But why should you believe me?

Sometimes before I fall asleep, I feel my left leg twitching. I turn the light on quickly, the way you do when you want to catch the fleas in your bed, and I look at it. But the leg isn't moving. It knows better. Is it dead? It has no pulse. I try moving my toes. That always works. And I can go back to sleep. All of these little things take a lot of time and energy. But I have plenty of both to waste. Besides, they're harmless; no one notices. No one knows about them, except me, and now, you.

LEON: (*Trying to touch* RAMON's *face.*) How can your face be so smooth? Do you shave more than once a day?

RAMON: Once a day, before I go to bed.

LEON: That's a strange time to shave.

RAMON: I like sleeping with a smooth face.

LEON: Women like that, don't they? They like boys, not men.

RAMON: I'm not a boy, I'm a man.

LEON: How old are you?

RAMON: I said I was a man.

LEON: I've aged 20 years in this country. The altitude dries out the skin. Look at my hands.

RAMON: The fine hands of a writer.

LEON: Touch my hands. Don't be afraid. The skin feels like parchment, like the skin of a crocodile, the skin of a mummy.

RAMON: Mine are rough, too. That's because we're men.

LEON: No. It's the air. It destroys everything. Have you ever left a fruit out in the garden overnight? Try leaving a fat, juicy plum on a stone. The next morning you'll find a dry prune. That's what's happening to my face.

RAMON: You have a fine face.

LEON: Don't try to flatter me.

RAMON: I mean what I say.

LEON: Then you're a fool. Look at the skin on my forehead. That's where a man's true age shows. In the grain of the skin, right there, where it's tighter over the bones. Between the eyebrows and the hairline. That's where the truth is. I wish I were your age.

RAMON: And I wish I had your mind. I wish I were you.

LEON: I wish I had your skin, and your eyes, and your mouth, and your sex, and your soft hands . . .

RAMON: (*Slightly lifting the razor blade he's holding.*) There's a way.

(FRIDA *suddenly enters.* RAMON *lowers the razor blade.* LEON *has not noticed his movement.*)

FRIDA: Leon, was that you shouting?

RAMON: No one was shouting.

FRIDA: Are you all right, Leon? It was a horrible sound, like a pig being slaughtered.

LEON: Perhaps that's what it was. I'll go see.

RAMON: I'll go with you.

(*They both exit towards the garden.* FRIDA *goes to the window and watches them.*)

FRIDA: Leon! Where are you going? What are you doing? Come back. Don't leave the garden. Don't jump that fence. The road is dark. Anyone could hide behind the bushes and kill you.

I once found a dead dog in that road. It had been shot in the head twice. Its brains were spilled on the pavement. Its eye sockets were swarming with ants. It stank. I poured gasoline over it and burned it. My body smelled of charred dog meat and gasoline for days. It wouldn't go away.

When the tramway crashed, turning me in seconds from girl to monster, from monster to woman . . . that's the smell. What will happen if the flames spread from my legs to my thighs to my belly, which is full of lemonade? It's hot and I drank three glasses of lemonade before taking the tramway. What kind of noise will lemonade and fire make? What smell? What kind of pain?

My father is angry. He smashes the glass of lemonade against the floor. I don't care. It's his glass, not mine, and I already drank all the lemonade. "You can't go to town by yourself! You're not taking the tramway!" I disobey him. But I don't get what I deserve. I don't deserve to grow up so quickly, with so much pain.

It was not my fault. I was almost a child. I didn't know what I was doing. He knew. He should have put me on a leash and tied me to the kitchen door; he should have beaten me up and sent me to bed, hungry. He should have strangled me rather than let me take the tramway. But he didn't. He was weak. It was all his fault. It's his fault that I'm always hungry and thirsty now like that dog dying in an empty road, and nothing, no one can relieve me for more than five minutes. It's all his fault. He was a weak father. And I'm weak with you, Leon. Like him, I'm letting you have a simple pleasure that could cost you your life. I wish one day something would come along and cure me of this need.

Scene 6

(RAMON *is sitting in bed, playing his mandolin.* FRIDA *enters.*)

FRIDA: I didn't know you could play music. Is that a balalaika?
RAMON: This is a mandolin.
FRIDA: It looks like a balalaika.
RAMON: It's a mandolin. I don't even know what a balalaika is.
FRIDA: Something that Russians play.
RAMON: I never heard of that.
FRIDA: There are so many things you haven't heard of.
RAMON: What about you? Have you ever seen a mandolin before?
FRIDA: I have seen pictures in the dictionary.
RAMON: But you never heard the sound.
FRIDA: No.
RAMON: It's a very Spanish sound. Can you hear it? (*He plays a few chords.*)
FRIDA: (*Closes her eyes.*) Yes.
RAMON: Can you hear it?
FRIDA: Yes.
RAMON: Can you see it?
FRIDA: Yes.
RAMON: Can you see the flatlands, dry as a bone, the dust, the wind sweeping the dust on your face? Nothing grows in this soil.
FRIDA: Is that why you left?
RAMON: I wish you didn't ask so many questions and I wish you didn't come here so often.
FRIDA: This is my house and I do as I please.
RAMON: Not with me.
FRIDA: Even with you.
RAMON: If you don't leave this room now, I'll walk out that door and you'll never see me again.

FRIDA: What are you afraid of? We're not even lovers.

RAMON: People don't know that.

FRIDA: What people?

RAMON: Leon, my sister . . .

FRIDA: Everybody knows that I don't like you.

RAMON: You never told me.

FRIDA: Now you know.

RAMON: Why did you come into my room?

FRIDA: I don't know. I heard the music from the hallway. I wanted to see how it came out of your fingers. You have strange fingers—the fingers of a woman, only more brutal. I was curious. Last night I dreamt that you had stuck your fingers into my throat, and made me gag.

RAMON: (*Putting his hands around her throat.*) I wouldn't do that to you.

FRIDA: I find you repulsive.

RAMON: But you came into *my room* . . .

FRIDA: Yes.

RAMON: Why?

FRIDA: I don't know.

(*He lets go of her throat and lies back on his pillow, arms and legs open and relaxed.*)

RAMON: Come here.

Scene 7

FRIDA: (*Voice in the darkness.*) I love this silence. It makes me want to whisper. When I was four years old, I whispered for a whole week instead of talking. I whispered words that came to my mind when I closed my eyes: mamá, México, *amor, crueldad, hambre, crimen; crimen, hambre, crueldad, amor*, México, mamá. My mother asked me what was I doing. "I'm whispering like the volcano," I said. "The volcano doesn't whisper; it hisses," she said. I love this silence.

(*Lights up.* FRIDA *is in her studio painting* RHONDA's *portrait.* RHONDA *is posing.*)

FRIDA: I never cried when I was a baby: I listened. I learned to listen before I learned to talk. My mother thought that I was mute. But I just didn't want to talk. What about you?

(RHONDA *does not answer.*)

You must have looked funny when you were born.

RHONDA: I weighed seven pounds, but most of them were my head. I had such a big head, that my mother thought that I was hydrocephalic. She asked the doctor if he could drill a hole in my skull and drain some of the water out. He laughed at her.

FRIDA: Can that be done? Drain water from a baby's brain?

RHONDA: Perhaps today they can do it. The Russians or the Americans. But not at that time. The only anesthetic we had was chloroform, which kills babies.

FRIDA: But you weren't hydrocephalic after all.

RHONDA: Just a little.

FRIDA: Not even a little. You wouldn't be here with me if you were. You would be dead, drowned in your own water.

RHONDA: To this day, I'm afraid of water.

FRIDA: Move your head a little bit to the right.

(RHONDA *moves her head towards* FRIDA.)

RHONDA: Like this?

FRIDA: Yes. Don't move. You have a small head. Let me see your hands now, on your lap, let me see your fingers.

(FRIDA *paints for a second. Lights down to black*).

Scene 8

(AURORA *is in* FRIDA's *studio cleaning the wheelchair.* FRIDA *enters.*)

FRIDA: What are you cleaning that for? I feel fine.

AURORA: I know. I do this once a month.

FRIDA: I never saw you doing that before.

AURORA: I've always done it once a month.

FRIDA: You make me nervous.

AURORA: Why?

FRIDA: You remind me of a nurse, the last time that I was at the hospital. She'd clean the wheelchair every morning with a wet rag, like you.

AURORA: This isn't wet; it's dry.

FRIDA: That nurse never said good morning to me. All she did was clean the wheelchair. She thought I'd be stuck in it the rest of my life.

AURORA: I'm not like her. I say good morning, good afternoon and good evening. And I smile and I even sing when I clean. Besides, I don't think that you'll sit here the rest of your life.

FRIDA: But you think that I'll need it soon.

AURORA: Well . . .

FRIDA: Well . . . what?

AURORA: I'm finished.

Scene 9

(AURORA *is in* RAMON's *room, touching his bed. He enters and surprises her.*)

RAMON: What are you doing in my room?

AURORA: I'm making your bed.

RAMON: At this hour of the night?

AURORA: I like to start my day early. Like you. (*Pause.*) You look tired.

RAMON: I couldn't sleep.

AURORA: You must have something on your conscience.

RAMON: My conscience is pink, like a baby's.

AURORA: How come you never laugh when you tell a joke?

RAMON: Really? I hadn't noticed that.

AURORA: You didn't laugh right now.

RAMON: That wasn't a joke. It's true I have a clean conscience.

AURORA: It might be clean, but it's not pink. Consciences are white or black. Mostly they're black, because evil is what goes most to the conscience. Goodness sometimes also goes, but that only happens to the saints, not to real people like you and me. When you kill the woman you love, that goes to your conscience forever, like a drop of black ink.

RAMON: Well, I haven't killed any woman I've loved. That's not why I couldn't sleep.

AURORA: What was it, then?

RAMON: You're too curious. That's not good.

AURORA: I like to watch people.

RAMON: What else have you found out about me?

AURORA: All your socks have holes—I mended them. You write letters with blue ink. Everything in your room smells of tobacco—the bed sheets, the curtains, your underwear . . .

RAMON: Where I came from, you would have your tongue pulled out for less than that.

AURORA: That's not the way we do things here.

RAMON: From now on, keep out of my room. Do you understand?

AURORA: I haven't done anything wrong. I go into everyone's room. Even into your sister's room: she doesn't mind.

RAMON: What do you want? (*Pause.*) What do you want?

AURORA: Please, dance with me.

RAMON: Get out of my room.

AURORA: Wait. Please. I promise I won't look in your drawers if you don't want me to. I won't touch anything. I'll just sit here and smell that nice smell of tobacco. That's why I come to your room—I like the way it smells. Please dance with me.

(*She takes his hand. Music starts. They dance. She speaks over the background music.*)

That song was written for me. I remember the night and the man very well. I was 20 and my hair was down to my waist. I smelled like a flower. Young flesh smells like flowers, unless it's sweaty—then it smells like horses. Old flesh doesn't smell. Old flesh has no taste. That night I was a flower. When I opened the door of the bar, the dancing stopped and 50 pairs of eyes stared at me. The older girls were jealous because I had something they had lost forever: I was 20 and I was a virgin. That night, a man who was dying of lung cancer sat at the piano, a cigarette in his mouth, and sang my song for the first time. I paid him with what I had: my body. I never saw him again, but at least he left me a song. The others left me nothing. Each took something from me. The first thing that I lost was my smell. I scrubbed myself every morning, after they had left, to get rid of their smell, that sour smell men have when they get together with women. I scrubbed myself so much that my skin started smelling of soap. Then my hair got bad and I had to cut it. My breasts sagged, the left one more than the right. I became a woman. Too many men, too much booze, too many bad nights. But I'm glad that I still have all my teeth. I may not be 20 anymore, but I know a trick or two. I know life. The rich fuck the poor. The poor fuck the poorer. Me? I just watch and wait.

(*Lights to black.*)

Scene 10

(LEON's *studio. Morning.* FRIDA *tries to pry open* LEON's *desk drawer with a pair of scissors. Then she realizes that* AURORA *is watching her.*)

FRIDA: I know what you're thinking. You're very clever.

AURORA: I didn't know you could read minds.

FRIDA: I don't need to. It's written all over your face. I can read your face like an open book.

AURORA: What does my face say?

FRIDA: "Thief! Thief!" That's what it says. You think I'm trying to steal something from Leon's desk.

AURORA: You are stealing something.

FRIDA: What could it be? Money? He has no money. Letters? He reads them all to me. Papers? He leaves his papers lying on his desk all the time. You don't need to break open a drawer to find them.

AURORA: But perhaps there are some papers that he doesn't leave on his desk, some that he doesn't read to you, some that he hides and not even you have seen.

FRIDA: You're clever.

AURORA: So clever that I'm cleaning your floors.

FRIDA: You don't have to do it if you don't want to.

AURORA: I don't want charity from you.

FRIDA: Is that why you spy on me?

AURORA: What do you mean?

FRIDA: You know what I mean. Is he paying you to spy on us?

AURORA: "He?" Who is "he"?

FRIDA: You know who I'm talking about.

AURORA: No, I don't know.

FRIDA: I saw you dancing with him.

AURORA: I haven't done anything wrong.

FRIDA: You like him. You like him more than I thought.

AURORA: He just reminds me of someone I used to know.

FRIDA: Come back to Earth. Stop rolling your eyes up to Heaven.

AURORA: Can't I have a fantasy? Does it bother you so much?

FRIDA We're not 18 anymore, you and I. No woman over 18 should allow herself to roll her eyes up like a slaughtered cow when the name of a man is mentioned, particularly if the man is a stranger and much younger than her. You want him for yourself.

AURORA: You want him for yourself.

FRIDA: I'm just trying to protect you.

AURORA: From what?

FRIDA: From what happens to women who daydream too much, see too much, talk too much.

AURORA: Are you threatening me?

FRIDA: Yes, I am threatening you. For your own good. Keep out of this.

(FRIDA *exits.* AURORA *goes to the desk and tries to open the drawer with the scissors.*

Lights off.)

Scene 11

(FRIDA *is in bed, moaning in pain.* AURORA *and* RHONDA *stand by the bed, preparing the orthopedic corset.*)

RHONDA: Is she going to die?

AURORA: Don't worry. This happens often. She's used to the pain. (*They start to put the orthopedic corset on* FRIDA.)

FRIDA: Pain doesn't mean anything anymore. That's why I can't stand it. My mother thought each moment of pain was a step on the ladder to Heaven, or at least Purgatory. Pain made her happy. She would dance with pain. To me, pain is useless.

RHONDA: How can you say that? What about your painting?

(*They finish putting the orthopedic corset on* FRIDA *and they help her sit in bed.* RHONDA *sits next to her.* AURORA *sits on a chair and starts sewing.*)

FRIDA: Fuck painting! I'd paint something else—landscape, workers on strike, you. I'd paint you healthy and I'd paint you sick. You could also have an accident one of these days, lose a leg, a finger, and I'd feel it and paint it as if it were my loss. It doesn't have to happen to me. Why me?

RHONDA: Perhaps there is a reason.

FRIDA: I don't believe in God.

RHONDA: I do. Do you see the volcano? Only God knows when it is going to erupt, and who will die. Perhaps I will die and you will be saved. There's a plan and it's fair. I'm healthy but I don't paint; I am not important. No one will remember me after I die.

FRIDA: You shouldn't talk like that.

RHONDA: It's a fact: I am no one.

FRIDA: There's no such a thing as "no one." Besides, if it bothers you so much, you can still do something about it. You're young . . .

RHONDA: No. I like it this way.

FRIDA: No, you don't. Does your brother know how you feel?

RHONDA: He knows everything about me, and I know everything about him.

FRIDA: And what does he think?

RHONDA: You can ask him yourself.

FRIDA: Rhonda! What is the matter?

RHONDA: I'm sorry. It's very hot in here. I suddenly remembered those people in Pompeii who were surprised in the bathtub. (*She laughs.*)

FRIDA: Were they naked?

RHONDA: Yes, naked, with their pricks stuck in the lava . . .

FRIDA: That's very cruel. I always thought you were so happy.

RHONDA: But I am happy, I am very happy.

Scene 12

(FRIDA's *bedroom, weeks later.* FRIDA *is sitting in the wheelchair.* RHONDA *and* AURORA *play cards.*)

AURORA: (*Shuffling the cards.*) This time, Rhonda, I'm going to show you . . .

FRIDA: Help me out of here! Please.

AURORA: Cut. Deal.

FRIDA: Please, help me out of here!

AURORA: Hit me!

FRIDA: Please!

AURORA: I'm out.

FRIDA: Help me, please.

AURORA: Don't listen to her. (*To* FRIDA.) The doctor told you to stay in that wheelchair for a month, at least.

FRIDA: Get me out of here!

RHONDA: I'll help you.

AURORA: (*To* FRIDA.) All right, do it. You want to be an invalid for the rest of your life? Do it. It's fine with me.

(RHONDA *tries to lift* FRIDA *from the wheelchair by the armpits.*)

FRIDA: (*To* RHONDA.) No, not like that. Just hold the chair.

(RHONDA *holds the back of the chair.* FRIDA *lifts herself up to a standing position, stays there for a second, and then crashes forward on the floor*).

AURORA: I told you, *Dios mío, Virgen Santísima*, I told you!

FRIDA: Fucking God, fucking whore Virgin Mary, fucking saints, fucking Christ in the cross, fuck you.

AURORA: I told you.

(FRIDA *and* AURORA *look at each other and laugh.*)

Scene 13

(*Lights go up on the empty garden as the beginning of* Der Rosenkavalier *is heard.* RHONDA *enters the garden, running. She looks with horror at two cows fighting in the distance.* FRIDA *walks in.*)

FRIDA: I like to see the cows fighting. They fight when their milk goes sour. They go crazy. They scratch the dust and moan. The bulls run away in fear. When a cow catches up with one of them, she tears him apart with her nails.

(*Lights dim to black.*)

Scene 14

(RHONDA *has fallen asleep with her clothes on and a book in her hand.* FRIDA *kneels beside her and touches her as she speaks.* LEON *is in the background.*)

LEON: She's not much younger than you.
FRIDA: It's not a question of age. I was never young: I was born old. Look at her face, Leon, isn't she beautiful? Look how empty her face is, a face with no lines, pure as the inside of an apple. Look at her mouth—her lips are so soft and open you can see her teeth. She has no sense of death.
LEON: You're going to wake her up.
FRIDA: She won't wake up. Look at her hands, the skin is so transparent that I can count the veins.
LEON: She's not as beautiful as you.
FRIDA: There's no comparison. I'm an animal, like her brother. I could break her neck with two fingers if I wanted to.
LEON: She may be stronger than you think. (*He takes the book from* RHONDA'*s hand.*) And she's not stupid.
FRIDA: I don't care about that.
LEON: Perhaps you're right when you say that you're an animal.

(*Reading from the page* RHONDA *had marked in the book.*)

"Lay your sleeping head, my love,
Human on my faithless arm;
Time and fevers burn away
Individual beauty from
Thoughtful children and the grave

Proves the child ephemeral:
But in my arms till break of day
Let the living creature lie,
Mortal, guilty, but to me
The entirely beautiful."[1]

(*Lights dim to black.*)

Scene 15

(*A tango is heard.* FRIDA *and* RHONDA *are having dinner, in slow motion.* FRIDA *looks at* RHONDA. RHONDA *averts her eyes. Lights are very dim. The image evokes a faded grey turn of the century postcard. Lights dim to black.*)

Scene 16

(*Late morning, cool and sunny.* AURORA *is making tortillas in the kitchen.* FRIDA *enters.*)

FRIDA: Where's everybody?

AURORA: They all went up there, to take pictures. The girl was wearing your riding boots, and the old man was wearing dark glasses. I didn't see the brother.

FRIDA: No one told me anything.

AURORA: Perhaps they wanted to be among themselves, so they could talk in their own language. What language do they talk in when they're alone? I've heard them. They understand each other very well. They don't need us, except for the feeding. For that, yes.

FRIDA: I really don't mind not going. It's chilly out there.

AURORA: And it's warm and quiet in here, isn't it? I'm making tortillas for you and me. I'm glad they're gone. I hope they stay out the whole day. There are too many people in this house and they all smell different. There's too much confusion.

FRIDA: What are you talking about? We've always had lots of people in this house.

AURORA: Yes, but not like them. They have no home to go back to. When you have a home, you don't bring your worries with you. A real guest has a thin soul; he doesn't occupy much space; you're only aware of him when he eats. These people are not real guests. They're leeches, flies, mosquitoes; sometimes the house is so thick with them that I can't breathe.

---

1. Auden, W. H. "Lullaby." *Another Time.* Random House, 1940.

FRIDA: You're right. The house is very quiet now.

(*They both listen to the silence for a moment.*)

AURORA: *¿Quieres una tequilita?*
FRIDA: No.
AURORA: No?
FRIDA: *Sí.*

(AURORA *pours the tequila for both. They toast and drink.*)

AURORA: *¡Salud!*
FRIDA: *¡Salud!*
AURORA: *¡Qué silencio tan grande! Casi se puede oir el volcán. ¿Tu lo oyes?*
FRIDA: *Sí.*
AURORA: *Suena como agua hirviendo.*
FRIDA: *¿Quieres bailar?*
AURORA: *Vamos.*

(*They hum a Mexican song and dance to it, wildly.* RAMON *appears suddenly on the threshold and scares them. They all freeze.*)

(*Blackout.*)

Scene 17

(*In the garden,* RAMON *is making a hole in the ground with a pickaxe. He's sweating. His shirt is soiled. He wipes his hands and brow with a filthy handkerchief. There's an animal, almost brutal quality about him.*)

FRIDA: What are you doing?
RAMON: I'm going to plant a chestnut tree here, so you remember me when I'm gone—you and everyone else. Two hundred years from now, the tree is still going to be here.
FRIDA: Two hundred years from now, no one will know it was you who planted it.
RAMON: I thought of that. I'll carve my name on the trunk and the date. I can also carve your name, if you want.
FRIDA: No, thanks. I don't want to be remembered like that.
RAMON: A tree lasts longer than a painting.

FRIDA: It's not the tree, it's you. I don't want my name close to yours.

RAMON: Why do you hate me so much?

FRIDA: I don't really hate you.

RAMON: You said you did.

FRIDA: Not now. I don't feel anything now.

RAMON: You're lying. You do feel something.

FRIDA: Nothing. Nothing. You're a very ordinary man. But you stick to my mind like mud sticks to a stone. I can't get rid of you. That's why I sometimes hate you and other times, like now, I get so tired when I see you.

RAMON: I don't want to hurt you.

FRIDA: Then go away.

RAMON: I cannot do that.

FRIDA: Why not?

RAMON: Because I love you.

FRIDA: If you love me, do as I say. Go away.

RAMON: If I go away my sister would leave with me. She won't stay here without me.

FRIDA: Are you trying to blackmail me? You and your sister are not Siamese twins. I'll talk to her.

(*She starts to exit.*)

RAMON: Frida, wait, Frida! Would you love me if it weren't for my sister?

(*Lights to black.*)

Scene 18

(LEON *is cleaning his gun by the window.*)

LEON: Every morning, my grandmother would ask me to braid her hair. She'd sit by the window and look out at the snow. She was always looking out the window, afraid that the village people would come and burn the house down and scalp her. I thought that these people were Indians and that we were pioneers in the Wild West. Our house was a covered wagon. The piano was my black pony. The steppe was the Utah prairie. And the fat Russian dogs were coyotes waiting for the full moon.

(*Lights to black.*)

Scene 19

(RHONDA *is sitting in* RAMON's *bed, in the same way as he was sitting in scene 6.* FRIDA *enters.*)

FRIDA: Where's Ramon?
RHONDA: I don't know. I thought he was with you.
FRIDA: He was. But then he heard some shots in the garden and he ran to see where they were coming from.
RHONDA: Shots?
FRIDA: That's what he said. But I didn't hear anything. I think it was an excuse to run away from me.
RHONDA: Why would he run away from you? He loves you.
FRIDA: I asked him to leave.
RHONDA: Leave? But he loves you. What have we done?
FRIDA: I want you to stay.
RHONDA: I can't stay if he goes.
FRIDA: Why not?
RHONDA: I just can't. Please, let him stay. I'll talk to him. I'll ask him to keep away from you.
FRIDA: That's not going to solve the problem.
RHONDA: What is the problem, then? Tell me.
FRIDA: The problem is that I want you. But I cannot get him out of my mind.
RHONDA: Is that all?
FRIDA: Are you laughing at me?
RHONDA: No, I'm laughing at him running away from you in the garden.

(*Lights dim to black.*)

Scene 19A

(LEON's *studio at night. The room is dark and the only source of light is moonlight coming through the window.* LEON *is by the window, pointing his gun out in the direction of a scratching sound that is coming again from the garden. He crawls under the window, to go from one side of it to the other, as if avoiding gunfire from the outside. The image evokes those in a western.*)

Scene 20

(LEON *throws books at* RAMON. *With each word,* LEON *throws a book.*)

LEON: Utopia.

Savage.

Utopia.

Savage.

Utopia.

Savage.

Innocence.

Melancholia.

Crocodile tears.

A beast, ready to kill and die for . . . for . . .

RAMON: A dream come true. A perfect place to live. Heaven on Earth.

LEON: That's right. A perfect place to live like . . . like . . .

RAMON: Palm Beach, Atlantis, the City of . . .

LEON: No, a real place. Chicago!

RAMON: Chicago is a cruel and filthy place. You get all these shit and piss newspapers flapping on your face. The sidewalks are sticky with chewing gum. Chicago is no Utopia.

LEON: A republic of gangsters.

RAMON: There's blood spattered on every downtown wall. The ice crust over Lake . . . Erie has turned into a blood crust.

LEON: Blood doesn't count.

RAMON: I hate blood and violence.

LEON: So do I. Unless it's absolutely necessary, in which case I enjoy it.

Scene 21

(LEON *has fallen asleep on top of his desk in the fetal position.* RAMON *wields the pickaxe while talking to him.*)

RAMON: Old man, as long as you live I will be in limbo, waiting to put on your shoes. You're so tiny. I can't even fit into your clothes. There's no hope for me. I wish I could stretch you like a rubber doll to fit my frame. I wish I could wear you like a coat. We would be one, then, and nothing would stop us. Too bad that you have bones. You should have been made of rubber or plastic or paper.

Welcome aboard to the ship of fools, too tight to float by itself, everyone lying about his past. Enough; I'll swim to Mexico even if a shark rips off my left leg, the longest of the two. I'll grow it all over again. Sweeten your words, old man, and you may still catch me. I have a weakness for flattery and old age. But I hate beards. What an ugly skin the old shark has. He stinks. He wants a bite of my foot, that same foot that's going to kick him in the head one day.

Patience. You'll soon have your chance to sleep in warm water. Guts will not be spilled; just brains, his and mine. The ladies will stay out of it, lost in their bodies.

The volcano will not explode.

First there is the hair, then the scalp, then the skull, then the brain, then, we'll see. The hand of the surgeon will get to the root of things.

LEON: Were you singing a song?

RAMON: No. I wasn't singing. I am going to kill you.

LEON: I know.

RAMON: I am glad that you know. I am going to kill you because you're wrong and you're dangerous. You make people want everything at once while they can only have a little at a time. You promise miracles but all you give them is words. I am sorry for you because you're old and you really believe your own stories. I am really sorry. But I have to do it. I will always be remembered as the man who killed you.

LEON: Shut up. If you're going to do it, do it quickly.

(RAMON *swings back the pickaxe, then lets it fall over* LEON's *head.*)

Scene 22

(FRIDA's *bedroom, immediately after the murder.* FRIDA *is in bed. She wakes up.* RAMON *enters. He's covered with blood, holding the pickaxe.*)

FRIDA: You killed him.

RAMON: He wanted to die.

FRIDA: You're a liar. He wanted to live. He wanted to see me grow old, he wanted to see me have a child.

RAMON: You can't have children.

FRIDA: Liar! Animal! Why did you kill him?

RAMON: He asked me to kill him.

FRIDA: You're lying. I know he wanted to live. He was harmless. He was so tender with me . . . No one has ever been so tender with me as he was. I loved him. Why did you kill him?

RAMON: I killed him because he made me suffer. Every time I saw him, I suffered. I crushed his head.

FRIDA: Poor baby! I let him kill you. I knew what he was going to do and I let him kill you.

RAMON: I killed him on my own, without you. He's mine.

FRIDA: Where's Rhonda?

RAMON: I sent her away.

FRIDA: What have you done to her?

RAMON: I sent her away.

FRIDA: Rhonda! Rhonda! Rhonda! You killed her, too.

RAMON: I said I sent her away. Are you deaf?

FRIDA: Where is she? Tell me. You have to tell me. Where is she?

RAMON: I can't tell you.

FRIDA: Tell me, please.

RAMON: She doesn't want me to tell you.

Scene 23

(FRIDA *and* AURORA *are cleaning the blood from the floor of* LEON's *studio the morning after the murder. It's 6:00 a.m., just before the sun comes up. Each has a bloodstained rag in her hand. They rinse the rags in a bucket full of bloody water.* FRIDA *is barefooted and in her underdress.* AURORA *is also barefooted. The air in the room is stale.*)

FRIDA: It's cold in here.

(*There is a silence.* AURORA *continues cleaning and does not answer.*)

AURORA: I didn't know that his blood was so bright. I thought it was darker.

FRIDA: Do you remember when I lost the first one? (*She looks at her blood-stained rag.*)

AURORA: The first what?

FRIDA: Baby. (*There is another silence.* FRIDA *cries*). When he came into my room, his eyes were bloodshot. I thought he would kill me.

AURORA: But he didn't. He loved you.

FRIDA: He had small hands for a man. Like Leon. Mine are too big. (*She touches her body in a violent way as she says this*).

AURORA: Don't hurt yourself.

FRIDA: If I had this baby, she might grow up to be a killer.

AURORA: But you can't have any.

FRIDA: Yes, I can. I feel her. She'll have my hands. I'll call her Rhonda.

AURORA: Rhonda is not dead.

FRIDA: How would you know?

AURORA: I know.

FRIDA: How are you and I going to die, Aurora?

AURORA: I'll die of old age. And you'll die of your disease.

FRIDA: Leon wasn't that old. Was he wrong? Did he die for nothing? He wasn't in his right mind.

AURORA: What do I know? What difference does it make? He's dead.

(FRIDA *touches her body.* AURORA *finishes cleaning and puts away the rags and the bucket. She opens the window, letting in the early morning breeze and sunshine.*)

FRIDA: I'm hungry.

AURORA: What would you like?

FRIDA: The air feels good.

AURORA: It comes from the mountain.

FRIDA: Let's go to the volcano.

AURORA: It's dangerous.

FRIDA: I want to go.

AURORA: Let's eat first.

(*They both freeze by the window. Lights dim slowly inside the room, while the landscape and the volcano become more luminous. A Yiddish nursery song, the kind* LEON's *grandmother would have sung, is heard. Lights go to black.*)

Moe Angelos and Dominique Dibbell

O Darn! The World Is Not a Safe Place for Little Buttercups (1991)

Maureen Angelos, a.k.a. Moe, signed up for WOW before there was a space called WOW. As a young New York University theatre student, she attended the second WOW Festival. Dominique Dibbell, a.k.a. Dom, arrived later, after the move to the E. 4th Street space, but her acting skills made her a much-sought-after performer. She was a fixture at variety shows as her character Nancy Bin, a veteran of the women's music festival circuit, who strummed a few songs punctuated by tales from cultural feminism—the essentialist version of the politic, which venerated women's power and biological difference from men—an ethos out of sync with WOW's irreverent, anarchic vibe. Moe and Dom eventually became two of the Five Lesbian Brothers, but they continued to collaborate on their own shows, including *I Wish I Had a Real Gun* and others.

O Darn! The World Is Not a Safe Place for Little Buttercups feels like a postmodern, queer, feminist *Inferno*. The title jabs at the cultural feminist obsession with "safe space," providing a dark but comic reminder that the only way through is through. In the play, en route to the theatre, Manhola falls through an open manhole. Her seven circles of hell include a duel fought between Walt Whitman and a headless General Sherman; a fight between a lesbian couple set in a cultural feminist theatre space; the abstract space of scholarly literary criticism, which offers misery instead of agency; and an encounter with an overgrown child, Buttercup, who seems so stunted by unspecified abuse that she is stuck in a perpetual childishness, vacillating between manipulation and helplessness.

Moe describes the play as fiction, but adds, "Trauma begets revisitation of past trauma or, as Shakespeare more eloquently calls them, 'old woes new.'

In *O Darn!*, Dom and I went down the rabbit hole of trauma to visit our old woes again. We tried to be brave about it, holding each other's hands, not wanting to go, hating it, but going anyway. I think we could only have done this work at WOW. And it sure was fun to play General Sherman and Walt Whitman."

She recalls the process of creating the piece.

O Darn! was created in the context of our own late-20's/early-30's and the fervent, youthful churn of theatre in New York City. As angry young feminists, we really tried to let our psyches run rampant in the process of making *O Darn!* We gently encouraged each other to a place of safety in our rehearsals, which occurred in the typical variety of loaner spaces: some in our tiny apartments, some at WOW, some at a "retreat" we took for a weekend in the country to the upstate shack of our benefactors, Peggy and Lois, and some at the TriBeCa studio of a famous painter for whom my girlfriend-at-the-time worked. At WOW . . . we found a place to be artists, the kind who had day or night jobs but made enough to not have to work two jobs to survive, thereby leaving time in off-hours to make performance not suitable for a commercial context. I recall being tired but driven, as one can only be in the crusade years of life. We had Something to Say.

—*Holly Hughes*

O DARN! THE WORLD IS NOT A SAFE PLACE FOR LITTLE BUTTERCUPS

(*NOTE: This play is written to be performed by two women, playing numerous roles. It should be evident how the roles are divided. MANHOLA falls down the manhole. Psychedelic sequence begins. Black light comes on. Two female performers dance about in a trippy style to Hendrix's "Foxy Lady," animating fluorescent painted cut-outs of oversized eyeballs, rats, alligators, flowers, and a BEAVER. The performers place cut-outs around stage. The two performers, both playing MANHOLA, are identically dressed in manhole hats, shorts and fanny packs. Lost and terrified, they sing.*)

Didn't know where I was going
when I fell down the hole
Hope my underwear wasn't showing
when I was upside down

Don't know if I'll ever see you now
I don't care since I fell down that hole
Don't care if my cats die
since I fell down the hole
Let 'em take care of themselves for awhile
there's plenty of dry food in the bowl
Don't have to see my ex-girlfriend
that's a big relief
I can relax since I fell down the hole

(*One performer exits.*)

Don't start feeling sorry for me
I like it down here
It's warm and it's dark
and I don't feel no fear
The gravity's stronger
it's pulling me near
Mother Earth, she wants me in her hole.

(*Second performer, now dressed as a naked* WALT WHITMAN *with wild beard and flopping genitalia, enters.*)

I think I see Walt Whitman
I thought he was dead
I must be tripping
or maybe I just hit my head
I can't feel my body
but that's nothing new
I am the same since I fell down the hole.

(WALT, *crouched on a rock, is composing a poem for his boyfriend.*)

WALT: . . . His strapping manhood I did ride all through the willowy night . . .
No, no, that's not right. Let's see . . . tenderly the young blacksmith, with
calloused hands, worked my tool—no. When first your column I did pon-
der, with gaze transfixed upon its engorged grandeur—no, no, no. Um . . .
throbbing, veiny, noble! Yes, noble grandeur!
MANHOLA: Excuse me, Mr. Whitman, can you tell me where the ladder is?
WALT: Hello, strapping lad!

MANHOLA: Well, I'm not a boy actually, I'm a lesbian.

WALT: Oh, my mistake.

MANHOLA: Happens all the time. Can you tell me where I am? I'm a little pressed for time. I'm late for the theater.

WALT: Oh, you must mean those feminists!

MANHOLA: I guess so. I mean some of them are feminists . . .

WALT: Oh, here's what you do—you go down the way until you see a big green neon sign that says DO NOT ENTER. You go right in and walk past Beaverkill Pond, taking care not to step on the beaver lodge. You walk for five miles divided by five and there you are. Do you have provisions?

MANHOLA: (*Checking contents of fanny pack.*) All I have left is my energy vitamin pack from the Korean market on Second Avenue. I had a thing of Naya water but I musta dropped it.

WALT: Hmm. I'd better give you something for your journey. (*Hands her Whitman Sampler.*) Here. They're homemade.

MANHOLA: Um. Thanks. I'm trying to stay off sugar, but thanks anyway. See you.

(MANHOLA *exits.*)

WALT: Ungrateful lesbian. Now let's see, where was I? "I hope you have plenty of blankets to keep you warm and that they are feeding you well. Did you get the fruitcake I sent last month? I have enclosed a poem I just wrote for you. I hope you like it. Everything here is fine. I am awaiting your safe return. Please don't get your balls shot off, for as you know, this is my favorite part of you. Love and kisses, Walt." I hope he likes this poem.

(*Courtesy of Walt Whitman's* Leaves of Grass:)

"O tan-faced prairie-boy,
Before you came to camp came many a welcome gift,
Praises and presents came and nourishing food, till at last among the
    recruits,
You came, taciturn, with nothing to give—we but look'd on each other,
When lo! More than all the gifts of the world you gave me—"
The blow job.

(*Enter headless* GENERAL SHERMAN. *He carries his brain in a jar.*)

But who is this gentleman who comes clad in uniform of wars gone by! He strikes a manly figure. Indeed, methinks I knew him once. For once, he had a head with forehead high and noble like the flagpole and eyes terrible and cruel beneath his fire-red hair. But his action is humpy! For this is the soldier brave who cut a burning swath from Atlanta to the sea! Hello General! And how's your mighty sword hanging today?

SHERMAN: What? Oh, hello poet.

WALT: You can call me Uncle Walt, all the soldiers do.

SHERMAN: My men call me Uncle Billy.

WALT: Where are you going Uncle Billy, clad in your fine dress burial uniform?

SHERMAN: Well, I'm on my way to the Museum of Body Parts in Washington, DC, to visit my head. As you can see, I don't have a head. They cut it off, you see. Those damn Army surgeons wanted it for their damn museum. 'Cuz I'm a military genius and they thought if they looked inside my head they'd see how the whole thing operated. Pretty clever, huh? So every year on the anniversary of Bloody Shiloh, six score and nine years hence, me and Grant and Lee and ol' Stonewall meet up there and drink a toast to our heads, have a cigar. The guard knows us. He lets us in when everybody's gone. Long live the Union! Long Live the South! We have a good chuckle. War is hell. But it really wasn't as bad as they say. I miss that war. Sing me a poem about the war, Uncle Walt.

WALT: A-hem.

(*Courtesy of Walt Whitman,* Leaves of Grass:)

"Vigil strange I kept on the field one night;
When you my son and my comrade dropt at my side that day,
One look I but gave which your dear eyes returned with a look I shall
    never forget,
One touch of your hand to mine O boy, reach'd up as you lay on the
    ground,
Then onward I sped in the battle, the even-contested battle,
Till late in the night reliev'd to the place at last again I made my way,
Found you in death so cold dear comrade, found your body son of
    responding kisses (never again on earth responding)
As onward silently stars aloft, eastward new ones upward stole,
Vigil final for you brave boy,
(I could not save you, swift was your death, I faithfully loved you and
    cared for you living, I think we shall surely meet again,)
Vigil for comrade swiftly slain, vigil I never forget, how as day
    brightened,

I rose from the chill ground and folded my soldier well in his blanket,
And buried him where he fell."
Copyright Walt Whitman.
General, though you have no eyeballs, I can tell you are weeping.

SHERMAN: Oh, that poem is so sad! It reminds me of my dearest dead friend, James B. McPherson—a brave soldier he. Shot once through the breast by a Rebel sharpshooter at the fall of Atlanta. O, how I wept when they brought his crimson gurgling body to me on a door abruptly torn from its hinges.

WALT: Let it out Uncle Billy. It's good and manly to cry.

SHERMAN: I had a son once. (*Pulls out tiny coffin.*) Darling Willy. He got sick on the boat and died. The entire thirteenth regiment came out to bury him. I couldn't make the funeral. You're so lucky you get to be a poet. You know I painted once?

WALT: Really?

SHERMAN: In the army after the Seminole wars. But I had to give it up. I had to discipline myself. You know why?

WALT: No.

SHERMAN: Because I started to love it more than war, that's why. And you know what else? No one ever loved me. The one chick I really dug didn't love me. She wouldn't marry me. You know why? I'll tell you why. She said my eyes were cruel. They weren't that bad were they?

WALT: Well . . .

SHERMAN: After that I became a hard man. My life was empty and lonely and then you know what happened? You know what happened? Guess!

WALT: You became a general?

SHERMAN: Yes! I became a general and I started killing people and burning things up. And then my life started to have some meaning.

WALT: You miss your friend, huh?

SHERMAN: McPherson? Best damn man in God's creation.

WALT: So, um, you guys were pretty close, huh?

SHERMAN: Yeah, I guess so.

WALT: Did you ever bunk together?

SHERMAN: Once in a while we bivouacked!

WALT: So was he tall?

SHERMAN: As a Florida pine!

WALT: Big hands?

SHERMAN: Big! Big and manly!

WALT: Did he wear jockeys or boxers?

SHERMAN: Ol' Jimmy, God bless 'im, he never did wear underwear.

WALT: Mmm. Now I'm getting the picture. So did you have sex with this guy or what?

SHERMAN: No!

WALT: Well, do you wish you did? Are you going to try to tell me you didn't think about it once?

SHERMAN: Well, there was that one time at West Point when we were both really drunk and we started wrestling and—hey! Wait a minute! I'm no homo! You're the homo! You're the one who got a boner just talking about it!

WALT: Just because I espouse a philosophy of manly adhesion is no reason to call me a homo!

SHERMAN: Oh yeah? What were you in the war? A nurse! A nurse! A nurse! A nurse!

WALT: Oh, and you're such a big man! Burns a swath from Atlanta to the sea but too chicken to suck your best friend's dick!

SHERMAN: Fairy!

WALT: Closet case!

SHERMAN: Fudge packer!

WALT: Manic depressive!

SHERMAN: You shut up about that!

WALT: Make me!

(*They fight. It is an uneven match, as* SHERMAN *has no eyes.* WALT *becomes bored and exits.* SHERMAN *bumbles around looking for his brain.*)

[. . .]

(*At the cultural feminist theatre.* DIERDRE *goes back up the ladder, starts hanging lights.* ROBERTA *holds it for her. Helps her, hands her tools. They are sweet and flirtatious with each other.* ROBERTA *snakes extension cord up through hole in the knee of* DIERDRE's *jeans.* DIERDRE *comes halfway down ladder. They kiss and make out on the ladder. Voiceover of a "happening" text begins. It is spoken in the manner of a strident feminist.* DIERDRE *and* RO-BERTA *exit halfway through the recitation.*)

VOICE-OVER: The play is happening. Now you are watching the play. Have you ever seen two women kissing? How does it make you feel? Are you aroused? Are you nervous? Do you feel ashamed? Do you wonder what they are going to do next? Do you wonder what they do in bed? Do you know what they do in bed? Is this your best fantasy or your worst fear? This play is asking you questions. This play asks you to look at your oppression as a woman. This play asks you to examine your own feelings of homosexuality. This play asks you to stand up and shout when you are angry. This play asks, Why are you resistant to these ideas? This play asks, Are you ashamed of your body? This play asks, Do you say no to yourself more than five times a day? This play asks, Are you turned on? This play asks you to empower yourself by going home and masturbating. This play asks you to make your boyfriend or husband fuck you the way you want to be fucked. This play asks, Why do you always make the eggs in the morning? This play asks, Why are you always naked on the cover of *The Drama Review*? This play asks you to kiss your best girlfriend on the mouth. Of course, this play asks you to take off all your clothes. This play asks you to quit your job. This play asks you to stop wearing pantyhose. This play asks you to look at your own oppression. This play asks you to look at how you oppress others. This play asks you to look at war. This play asks you to see it, hate it, stop it. This play asks you to jump the turnstile. This play asks you to wear the hairstyle. This play asks you, Where is all the good theater? This play asks you to make your own play if you don't like this one. This play asks you if you are a right-on woman.

[. . .]

(MANHOLA *has collapsed in tears on the floor.* BEAVER, *wearing overalls and nail apron and pushing a broom, enters.*)

MANHOLA: Hi.
BEAVER: (*Glances up at her briefly.*) Hello. (*Returns to work.*)
MANHOLA: Are you a beaver?
BEAVER: Yeah.
MANHOLA: Oh, I was wondering if you could help me get this manhole off my head. It really hurts.
BEAVER: Of course I can. You sure asked the right species. I can do just about anything. We beavers are very handy. Kind of like you lesbians.

(BEAVER *helps her take off manhole.*)

MANHOLA: Thank you, Beaver. Do you know what time it is?
BEAVER: I guess it's like around eight or something.
MANHOLA: Maybe I can still make the show.
BEAVER: Can I help you make the show? Is it made of wood?

MANHOLA: No, I mean, I have to get to the theater to see a show.

BEAVER: Where?

MANHOLA: Oh, back over there . . . somewhere. I'm not sure which way it is now. Gee, I'm sort of disoriented.

BEAVER: Well, the moss grows on the north side of the trees. Does that help?

MANHOLA: Yeah, okay. North. But where's a tree?

BEAVER: The table is made of a tree. Let's look at it. There's some moss back here. This is north.

MANHOLA: Well, I uh . . . uh . . .

BEAVER: There is south. And their cousins East and West.

MANHOLA: Thank you, wise Beaver. But the problem is I'm not quite sure where we are so it's hard to tell where anything else is even with directions.

BEAVER: What is it with you people? You always want to know where you are. You are here, my dear. Isn't that good enough for you?

MANHOLA: Beaver, I'm feeling pretty weird. Do you think you can tell me something about the beavers and their simple way of life?

BEAVER: Sure, sad lady. I'll sing you a little song. Here, I made this guitar today. I chewed it out of a tree. Can you play guitar? (*Hands her guitar.*)

MANHOLA: No. I'm not very musical.

BEAVER: Hmm. (*Throws magic leaves on her.*)

MANHOLA: Wow!

BEAVER: OK, it's in the tune of P minor.

O we're big fat beavers

O our life's not meager

Plenty of wood all around

And our lodge is warm and sound

O we're not the beavers

that you thought we were

We're really the manifestation of the goddess

embodied in fur!

A European trapper my grandma spied

He said, Beaver, I'll tan your hide

Nothing was the same from that day

Now we work at night to stay out of their way

MANHOLA: Let me sing one!

In Montana we built a dam

Longer than any built by man

They blew it up with dynamite

We built it back overnight!

BEAVER:
We work all autumn to get it done
When winter rolls around we have some fun
Come over to the lodge, it's warm and dry
We'll serve you up a slice of our willow pie!
MANHOLA:
In days gone by our cousins did
Mostly disappear from the trapper's bid
But now we do live a happy life
Cause we've got karma on our side!
TOGETHER:
O we're big fat beavers
O our life's not meager
Plenty of wood all around
And our lodge is warm and sound
O we're not the beavers
that you thought we were
We're really the manifestation of the goddess
embodied in fur!
MANHOLA: If only I was a beaver everything would be ok. But I'm not.
BEAVER: Every girl has a beaver inside.
MANHOLA: I can't find mine.
BEAVER: You can't be somebody until you find your beaver chakra.
MANHOLA: Your beaver chakra! Which one is that?
BEAVER: That's your ninth chakra.
MANHOLA: I thought there were only seven.
BEAVER: No. They left the other two off because they were too powerful and the men became scared of them.
MANHOLA: I'm too tired to find my beaver chakra. I just wanna lie down. This whole thing has been too much for me. I just want to sleep forever and wake up when it's all over.

END OF EXCERPT

Susan Young

WOW Women in Their Own Words

WOW gave me a sense of home and security when I first moved to New York. It became a base for my aspirations. I never saw myself becoming a theatre person or being an actor, but I have creative aspirations. I'm a very project-oriented person, and I'm always in a creative mode. WOW gave me a great release for that. It also became a social home. It connected me with people with whom I was meant to have lifelong relationships.

WOW made me more comfortable being who I am. I felt the freedom to express my selves in lots of different media. I met Amy Meadow, with whom I've had an almost twenty-year relationship. I met Peggy and Lois. I haven't been actively involved with WOW for almost ten years or more, but Peggy and Lois call me, and we still collaborate on the visuals of their shows.

Holly and I collaborated on a lot in the beginning on stage props and visuals. She and I would go out on the streets of New York and pick up junk and make props out of it. This was super low budget and spontaneous, but that was the foundation of a production value to me. That still stays with me, and I run a two-million-dollar feminist-type business now—for women—which operates from many of the same production values.

Alice Forrester and I had a great collaboration for a period of time. We just threw around ideas and made props. They were kind of Brechtian. Something had to be able to change onstage; it had to be able to become something else. A person could become a chair or a lamppost. It was a very expressionist time. It didn't have to be realistic at all. This was a very high period of creativity for me. We spent virtually no money at all. Everything was handcrafted; we would never go to a store and rent a costume. I'm an expert patternmaker, an expert dressmaker. Everything fit really beautifully. I always wanted the women to look just terrific.

I wanted to have fun with the girls; I wanted to be part of the lesbian crowd. But at the same time, I wanted to make theater history. That was a private goal, but I feel like we did that. I wanted to do it in a very big, exquisite way that gained a lot of recognition, not because it's calling out for it but because it's so exquisite it can't help but bring attention to itself.

I came to WOW with very high organizational skills and professional skills, but experimentation always had to be a part of the process. You had to take it all in. You had to commit to the process. I hope that if there was nothing else I contributed to the aesthetic there, the women onstage always looked incredible and sexy. I always felt disappointed if the curtain opened and the audience didn't gasp. The idea is to move people in a visual way.

How to Write Autobiography with Someone's Hand over Your Mouth

I remember when Diana fell down the elevator shaft and we were
standing outside while the paramedics used the Jaws of Life to
get her out of the bottom. I was wondering if the city would close
WOW down. I went to the pay phone at LaMama and called Paula
Ettelbrick, who was the staff attorney at Lambda Legal Defense at
the time, to get her advice. Of course, the most important concern was Diana, but I remember also thinking, what will we do if
WOW has to close? I felt like it was my home. I couldn't imagine
life without it. We used to joke about how we'd get old together
and be a bunch of eighty-year-old dykes and still be doing these
goofy shows together.

—Lisa Kron

Every American-raised queer person is a solo performance artist. We are all
versed, knowingly or not, in the many genres and subgenres of live actions
associated with this bratty don't-call-me-a-field field. I don't think I know
of any L or G or B or certainly T person, and certainly no one in this book,
who hasn't had the experience of seeing a meal with one's family of origin
turn into a futurist salon, with every word leaving your mouth a provoca-
tion, an upending of social niceties, sometimes by intention, sometimes not.
Marinetti urged his outraged audiences to "throw an idea, not a potato," but
queers get both. Ideas get thrown at you—ideas about what it means to be
female, to be a member of this family, this community, this planet. The pro-
verbial book gets thrown at you, the book of religion, of the medical and
legal establishments.

And we are expert at body art and durational performances. Our bodies are canvases. We take risks with them in bed and on the street. We find
that chopping off your hair is as upsetting as cutting yourself in front of a

group of art connoisseurs. We undergo and endure conditions as rigorous as walking the Great Wall of China from one end to the next because we are propelled to do so by unruly desires, by something within us that refuses to shut up. Our lives are—as I say in my performance *Dog and Pony Show: Bring Your Own Pony*—compositions only in a John Cage sense of the word. By rejecting the heterosexual marriage plot, we find ourselves living by luck and happenstance.

But if we are skilled in all these types of performance, we excel at the autobiographical storytelling solo work that began to emerge in the late '80s. Every one of us carries around enough personal stories to fill up at least one *Moth Radio Hour* boxed set. In part it's our heritage as Americans; we're born into a culture that values stories told in the first person. We're born into a history told often as a series of individual triumphs. This embrace of individualism clearly has pitfalls. But the personal narrative has played a leading role in social justice movements, from slave narratives to the consciousness-raising groups in second-wave feminism, where women got to the political by first mapping the personal.

But autobiographical storytelling is also specifically queer. The coming-out story is the lingua franca of American queer experience. The first time we step into a gay space—whether an actual space, like a community center or a bar, or a virtual space online—we offer up these stories as the price of admission. We narrate how we came to understand ourselves as different, as refuseniks to the standard narratives of gender and sexuality. Those stories can carry us, at least for a moment or two, across the fault lines of other charged identities, like race or ability or age.

Whatever separates us, we all have this in common: our first stories start at the same place. We woke up one day with the knowledge that we were different, that we were wrong. This is the first of many comings out. That moment when we realize we are different, even if we can pass for a regular pink-wearing girl, we know we are not what we are supposed to be. We don't have to go to a special workshop in Bushwick or Silver Lake to be schooled in conflict or stakes. From Day One, we're spies, we're outlaws, and the first story we tell is to ourselves. That story is designed to keep us safe, but the first story we tell is a lie. Even when we move into the truth, we remember how to lie. Lies are a useful part of the truth. Later we'll come out again and again and again. We have different stories for different occasions, told in different registers, from the rant to the poetic. Even in a moment when the public mood in America seems to be shifting toward tolerance and even the embrace of LGBT people, the simple act of coming out can be costly. We can still lose our jobs, our families, or our lives.

The autobiographical stories in this section are often inventive, following Tim Miller's admonition, "Everything I'm about to tell you tonight is true, and some of it really happened." We've had to invent ourselves, so we've sometimes created fictional selves that feel closer to the truth than what might turn up in a police report. Take the case of Carmelita Tropicana, who found she could perform herself when she crafted an alter ego of refashioned, formerly toxic images of *latinidad*. We've mastered many forms of delivery. We are able to say Kaddish with our mouths shut. In these scripts, we tell the truth with an awareness of the risk in such an act, and with the knowledge that truth is something we are continually inventing.

—*Holly Hughes*

Carmelita Tropicana and Uzi Parnes

Memories of the Revolution/
Memorias de la Revolucíon (1987)

There were many firsts with *Memories of the Revolution/Memorias de la Revolucíon*. It was my first play and it was cowritten with Uzi Parnes. It was the first time Carmelita Tropicana, the alter ego I created at WOW, appeared along with Pingalito Betancourt, my other male drag persona. *Memorias* premiered at WOW and then went on to PS122, and it marked the first of many Tropicana/Parnes collaborations.

As a collaborator, Uzi brought a comic flair, knowledge of musicals, and a visual eye that were very fitting for *Memorias*, a multimedia play. Since *Memorias,* he has continued to build a solid career as a filmmaker, director, and actor. His film and video works have been presented at the Museum of Modern Art, the Anthology Film Archives, and the Berlin International Film Festival. He's also a photographer of downtown performance legends, including Jack Smith. And he's been an actor who has appeared in the theatre work of Ethyl Eichelberger, Jack Smith, and Kestutis Nakas.

With *Memorias,* as with other collaborations, we took on multiple jobs. Uzi wrote, directed, and designed, and I wrote, acted, and produced. In addition to *Memorias*, we presented *A Clamcracker Suite* and a workshop of *Candela*, plays that added Ela Troyano to the mix as a collaborator. All these plays were an anomaly for WOW since Uzi was allowed to be involved in a way that no male had before or since. He was regarded as my family, since he was living with Ela, my sister, and ran Club Chandalier with her, where the WOW girls performed regularly. Uzi had also acted in Holly's show at WOW, was writing about the influence of Split Britches in his doctoral dissertation on pop performance, and appeared as Lois Weaver's lover in Sheila McLaughlin's film *She Must Be Seeing Things*.

We both felt lucky to have a pool of talented actors to choose from at WOW and found that an effective shortcut was to write parts expressly for them. At WOW auditions were unthinkable, but the talent was plentiful. It was great to have WOW girls—none of whom were Latinas (a word that came into the lexicon in the '80s)—perform Cuban characters. They all brought inimitable accents—some a bit more Polish than Spanish—to their roles. Uzi was thrilled to have an all-female cast playing both female and male drag.

Memorias is a comic satire. The title nods to Thomas Gutierrez Alea's influential film *Memories of Underdevelopment*. The play is a mix of Carmelita's memories as she reenacts her history and my own exilic memories and those of my relatives, especially my father, who was a *comandante* in Castro's revolution. His revolutionary stories, his defection, and his escape by boat fed the play. The song and dance numbers "Yes, We Have No Bananas," "Siboney," and "Besame Mucho" are fun, but they also aim to critique Cuba's colonial, ethnic, and gender politics. —*Carmelita Tropicana*

MEMORIES OF THE REVOLUTION/
MEMORIAS DE LA REVOLUCÍON
Written by Carmelita Tropicana and Uzi Parnes
Directed by Uzi Parnes
Set design by Uzi Parnes
Lighting design by Joni Wong
Staged-managed by Mary Patierno
Projections by Ela Troyano
Costumes by House of Chandalier and Quinn
Memorias de la Revolucíon was first presented as a work-in-progress at WOW in 1986. In 1987 it was presented at PS122 with only one cast change: Annie Iobst replaced Holly Hughes in the roles of Brendah and Tropicanette.

CAST
Carmelita Tropicana/Pingalito Betancourt: Herself
Brendah/Tropicanette: Annie Iobst
Brendaa/Tropicanette: Alison Rooney
Machito/Tropicanette: Maureen Angelos
Capitán Maldito/Tropicanette: Kate Stafford
Marimacha/Tropicanette: Peg Healey
Juanita/EI Tuerto/Go-Go Dancer: Quinn
Rosita Charo Rosita Charo/Tropicanette: Lisa Kron

Lota Hari/Nota: Diane Jeep Ries
The Virgin on Film: Uzi Parnes
Act I: Havana, 1955
Act II: Lost at Sea in a Rowboat, 1955
Act III: New York City, 1967

(*The action takes place in the middle of the ocean in a rowboat.* CARMELITA *has escaped with* LOTA *and* MARIMACHA. *It is nighttime.*)

CARMELITA: How long have we been here, Marimacha?

MARIMACHA: Let's see. Night . . . mmm. I will say about 20 hours.

CARMELITA: We should see Key West already. We should go right, not left. Why did we listen to the German?

LOTA: I heard that. It's because Germans make the best precision instruments in the world. My instrument in the tropics is not so precise.

CARMELITA: Great, Lota.

LOTA: I'm trying to find our course due north by northwest. It takes a little time. It takes something you hot-tempered Latins don't know—how to be—quiet.

MARIMACHA: Well, when you find it, please let us know. I'm tired of rowing.

CARMELITA: I'm hungry.

MARIMACHA: I'm starving. (MARIMACHA *remembers she has a candy bar she is hiding from them and sneakily takes a bite.*)

LOTA: I also.

CARMELITA: (*Seeing* MARIMACHA *chewing.*) Marimacha, what you got?

MARIMACHA: Nothing.

CARMELITA: Milky Way. Give me some.

(*They fight over the candy bar.*)

MARIMACHA: I was about to offer you some.

(*A ship's horn is heard.*)

MARIMACHA: Carmelita, look, the Love Boat.

LOTA: *Das Liebe Boat.* The Love Boat.

CARMELITA AND MARIMACHA: (*Getting up and yelling.*) We're here! Save us! *Estamos aquí!*

LOTA: Sit down, both of you. They can't see us.

CARMELITA: Lota, get up and scream. Maybe they hear us.

LOTA: They can't hear us. Stop rocking the boat. We will capsize.

CARMELITA: *No tienes sangre en las venas. Tienes hielo, hielo, hielo.*

MARIMACHA: You are frozen, frozen, frozen.

LOTA: I heard you the first time. Sit.

CARMELITA: You don't order us no more. You hear? Enough. We row for 20 hours and for what? Nothing. Look at my hands. I'll never get to play the castanets anymore.

MARIMACHA: I didn't know you played the castanets.

CARMELITA: (*Punches* MARIMACHA.) Why don't you do something good—like fish. You told me you were a fisher of women. Prove it. Catch us fish with your precision instrument.

LOTA: Very well. I will teach you both how it is done. First the hose. (*She removes her stocking.*) I need something to attract the fish. Earrings.

CARMELITA: No, it's the only pair I take out of Cuba. I can't.

MARIMACHA: We are starving and you're thinking of jewelry. Look over there. (*She grabs the earring out of* CARMELITA's *ear.*)

CARMELITA: (*Smacking her.*) Marimacha, how can you? You know who you talk to? Look at me. You have become an animal.

MARIMACHA: (*Crying.*) I'm sorry Carmelita. I don't know what comes over me.

CARMELITA: (*Comforting her.*) What happen, baby?

MARIMACHA: Remember the Maine. I lost my mother, my father, my two older brothers in a boat at sea. Ever since then I have such memories. I can't go to the beach. If I see suntan lotion, I start to shake.

CARMELITA: Come over here, Marimacha. It's okay. You are fine, Marimacha. Let it all out.

MARIMACHA: Thank you, Carmelita. I needed that.

CARMELITA: (*Giving her the earring.*) Here, Lota, do what you have to do.

LOTA: (*Attaching earring to hose.*) Here, Marimacha. Like this. I am sorry, Carmelita, I call you hot-tempered Latin.

CARMELITA: It's okay, Lota. You teach us how to fish. We survive. You are masterful with the hose.

LOTA: I learned to fish in the Black Sea. Black—your eyes are black. *Schon.*

CARMELITA: *Schon?*

LOTA: Beautiful. Your hair is *schon.* Your mouth is *schon.*

CARMELITA: Your nose is *schon.*

(*They are in an embrace about to kiss when* MARIMACHA *interrupts.*)

MARIMACHA: Help, hey, you guys. The fish. The fish. I lost the fish.

CARMELITA: I lost my earring.

LOTA: I lost my head.

(*The sound of a storm is heard. The waves start to get rougher.*)

LOTA: Sit down. We will capsize.

MARIMACHA: I see a storm ahead.

CARMELITA: Lota, where are we?

LOTA: *Mein Gott in himmel.* I think we are approaching the Bermuda Triangle.

MARIMACHA: The Bermuda Triangle?

LOTA: Bad currents. The most powerful ships like the Love Boat have been swallowed.

(*Storm sounds are heard: thunder, waves crashing.*)

CARMELITA: Marimacha, give me your oar.

MARIMACHA: I'm gonna die like my brother, my mother, my father. I wanted to die in the revolution. Not here. (*She cries.*)

LOTA: Marimacha, hold on two more minutes and it will be over. Hold onto the side of the boat.

(*Finally the storm subsides, and both* LOTA *and* MARIMACHA *fall asleep. Two angels appear and open doors to a backdrop triptych with painted cherubs on either side. In the middle panel is a screen for a film projection of an apparition of the* VIRGIN *Mary on 16mm film.*)

VIRGIN: Carmelita, Carmelita.

CARMELITA: What is this? Am I hearing things? Marimacha, Lota, wake up.

VIRGIN: *Shalom alechem vee geyste?* I'm Mary, the Virgin. You have been chosen by the Goddess herself to be the next hottest Latin superstar, but you gotta wait a little.

CARMELITA: I always knew my destiny.

VIRGIN: But listen, there's a little problem. There is a difficult road ahead. Cuba will no longer be your home. Her revolution will not be your revolution. Yours will be an international cultural revolution.

CARMELITA: But what about my brother, Machito?

VIRGIN: Hold your oars. Fate will have you meet your nemesis, Maldito, and when you do, you'll know what to do. As for that *geshtunke* brother of yours, you, too, will be reunited. Where was I? Oh, the revolution. Let it be your art. Your art is your weapon. To give dignity to Latin and Third World women: this is your struggle. If you accept, you will be gifted with eternal youth. You will always be as you are today, twenty-one.

CARMELITA: Nineteen, please.

VIRGIN: Okay, but you will suffer much. Spend years penniless and unknown until 1967.

CARMELITA: That is a lot of years, but for nineteen is okay. I accept.

VIRGIN: But listen, Carmelita, there is more. You must never, ever, ever . . .

CARMELITA: What? You are killing me.

VIRGIN: Or all the years will return, like to that nasty Dorian Gray.

CARMELITA: Never do what?

VIRGIN: Never let a man touch you. You must remain pure, like me.

CARMELITA: Never let a man touch me. Believe me, to Carmelita Tropicana Guzmán Jiménez Marquesa de Aguas Claras, that is never to be a problem. (*She winks.*)

(*The film of the* VIRGIN *ends as lights change and* CARMELITA *sees land.*)

CARMELITA: Marimacha, Lota, wake up. (*They wake up.* CARMELITA *is ecstatic.*) Look! It's Miami Beach!

(*Blackout.*)

END OF EXCERPT

Claire Moed

How to Say Kaddish with Your Mouth Shut (1988)

Claire Moed was a constant presence at WOW during its first ten years. She dolled up as Marilyn Monroe, and she appeared at variety shows as our in-house Joan Rivers to offer off-color, feminist commentary on the looks we'd cobbled together. She performed in numerous productions and finally, at a WOW retreat, when a canceled show presented a challenge, Moed heard herself volunteering to write and produce a new play in a few months' time.

How to Say Kaddish with Your Mouth Shut is a reworking of Moed's own upbringing as a kind of lesbian *Waiting for Godot*. Grace is a stand-in for the author, who announces at the top of the show, "Before we begin this evening I would really sincerely, and whole heartedly like to stress that this is a work of fiction and any resemblance to any living or dead relatives who happen to be here tonight is purely coincidental."

Moed leaves interpretation of the title open. Kaddish is the Jewish prayer for the dead. Are the characters dead, the waiting room situated in the afterlife? Or is their dynamic paralyzed, as if in rigor mortis? Or is the under-the-breath Kaddish a way to summon death, perhaps metaphorical or psychological, death as a kind of deliverance from a situation that seems deadly and inexorable? —*Holly Hughes*

HOW TO SAY KADDISH WITH YOUR MOUTH SHUT
Directed by Kate Stafford
Sets and Costumes Designed by Susan Young
Lighting Design by Joni Wong
Lights Operated by Joni Wong and Babs Davy
Sound Design by Vincent Girot

Sound Operated by Peg Healey
Stage-Managed by Elizabeth Edman
Assistant-Stage-Managed by Peg Healey
Assistant Director, Lisa Kron
Set Assistant, Amy Meadow
Production Assistant, Nancy Swartz
Script Editor, Deb Margolin
Script Consultation, Joni Wong and Lisa Kron
Photos by Eva Weiss
Publicity by Mary Ward
Postcard/Program Design by Morgan Gwenwald
House Managers, Nancy Swartz, Maz Troppe, and Lisa Kotin
Maintenance Manager, Babs Davy

*This play is dedicated to my late cousin, Martha Wyatt,
who was the first woman judge in her county.*

CAST
Grace Goddess: Imogen Pipp
Patrice Goddess: Lisa Kron
Mother Goddess: Claire Moed

Characters in order of appearance
GRACE GODDESS, a young woman who attempts to dress in "downtown"
    fashion but ever so slightly misses the mark. Her purse is oversize and
    overfilled with every possible feminine necessity.
PATRICE GODDESS, her older sister, who attempts to dress in more
    business-like clothes but ever so slightly misses the mark. She carries a
    portable office and school in several politically correct tote bags.
MOTHER GODDESS, their mother, a pianist, who no longer wears skirts
    or dresses but doesn't miss a thing. She carries with her more bags than
    is humanly necessary.

Scene One

*(The entire play takes place in a hospital room, preferably a waiting room.
There should be a couch and several chairs downstage. Some of the stage de-
scriptions and instructions included with this script are those used during the
WOW Café production in January 1988.)*

(*Lights come up while a cheerful Beethoven etude plays.* GRACE *enters from stage right.*)

GRACE: Welcome. And thank you for coming. Before we begin this evening I would really sincerely, and whole heartedly like to stress that this is a work of fiction and any resemblance to any living or dead relatives who happen to be here tonight is purely coincidental.

(PATRICE *enters from stage left.*)

PATRICE: Freud says there is no such thing as a coincidence. What are you doing, Grace? Are you talking to yourself in the mirror again?
GRACE: Whatever you do, don't stand up in the middle and shout that's not the way it happened.

(MOTHER GODDESS *enters from upstage center.*)

MOTHER GODDESS: I'm going to laugh the whole night through. Grace, what are you doing? Are you talking to yourself in the mirror again?
PATRICE: She said some parts aren't funny.
MOTHER GODDESS: I'm going to laugh especially hard through those parts.
GRACE: For those of you who don't know what Kaddish means, it's the prayer for the dead. I've said it several times. It's been said for me several times. Only problem is . . . at the time we were still alive . . . Get it? You're only supposed to say it when someone is dead. How many *goyim* are out there anyway?
MOTHER: Grace! Who taught you to speak like that? I certainly didn't. *Gentiles*, damn it, gentiles. Are you sure you're my children?
PATRICE: You've said *goyim*. I, of course, only say *schikza*.
MOTHER: Patrice! Where did you learn that kind of language? In my day we'd say she comes from a certain milieu.
PATRICE: In your day, you said *goyim* and *shikza*.
MOTHER: I never said that. Ever. Or pregnant. I never said pregnant. Except when it was with thought.
MOTHER, PATRICE, GRACE: I AM PREGNANT WITH THOUGHT.
MOTHER: Or bra. One should always say brassiere.
PATRICE: Whether you wear one or not?
MOTHER: I gave them up when I gave up my ex-husband.
GRACE: Why do I always get the feeling I am listening to Mother Goddess's version of Funk and Wagnall?

PATRICE: I remember looking up the words *fuck* and *clitoris* in Funk and Wagnall. In sixth grade. But for years I mispronounced them because I never heard anyone say them.

GRACE: What? You said *fooock*? I'm going to *fooock* you?

PATRICE: No, Grace. Clitoris. I thought the emphasis was on the *toris*. As in cli-TOR-is. Do-You-Mind?

GRACE: No-I-Don't-Mind.

PATRICE: Thank you.

GRACE: You're Welcome.

MOTHER: Well, I don't know what to say.

GRACE: Prayer is like a shotgun. Don't ever pray for anyone you truly love. Don't. And if we got too guilt-ridden for our unspoken massacre we'd stab ourselves a few times for good measure, you know, to even things out. Drinking, smoking, playing piano, clipping coupons.

PATRICE: I resent the implication that being money-conscious is a destructive habit, whereas drinking, smoking and playing the piano are. And the incident of which you speak concerning the seventeen cent coupon with no expiration date for a twelve ounce box of Product 19, clearly indicated that I had justified reasons for pressing a suit against false advertising as the owner of the Gristedes had a poster clearly stating that the item was on sale and in the store and I had walked from 103rd street to 77th to redeem it. And it was Sam's favorite cereal!

MOTHER: You walked from 103rd to 77th for a man?

PATRICE: My Husband.

MOTHER: A Ma . . . You Married A Man!?

GRACE: And we were dying.

PATRICE: Yes, a Man. Some people in this world do that, you know.

GRACE: Dying of each other. Vampires sucking the last bit of sanity from one another . . .

MOTHER: I don't know what is worse, the man part or the marriage part . . .

GRACE: . . . Years and years of silent battering, moistening our lips shut and drawing our eyes back like a cannon about to shoot, and mouthing into our brains, "*Yisgadal v'ysikadash sh'me rabboh . . .*"

MOTHER: Grace! Where did you learn *those* words? Perchance this man plays an instrument?

PATRICE: Folk guitar.

MOTHER: AAAHHHHH!

GRACE: . . . *beolmo,d'hoo ossid leis-chadto . . .*

PATRICE: Grace! Cut the dramatics! Mother, I told you last week I married a—

GRACE: . . . All I can say is how fitting it's at Beth Israel Emergency that we are awaiting the results of our work of years, gasping for air we're waiting, waiting, waiting for one of us to finally drop, waiting, waiting, waiting . . . (*Addressing the audience.*) There was this summer. The first summer. I didn't speak to anyone for months. I probably did, but I don't remember. I just remember walking up Broadway, the old Broadway of sleaze and slime. I was carrying this bag of donuts because that's all I knew to buy to feed myself. And this guy goes, "HEY FAT GIRL." I remember that. I was staying at Patrice's violin teacher's house. He needed a plant-waterer house-sitter, I needed a home. I talked to myself to the television. I ate all his carob ice cream. I kept replacing it so he wouldn't know I ate it. And I kept eating it some more. I must've replaced it four or five times. Hamburgers. I made myself loads and loads of hamburgers. Then I'd go stare in his full-length mirror, naked, and look at my body and see a stranger. I had no idea I had breasts. They were there in the mirror but not on my body. I remember this one night this kid being beaten up by this cop by this movie theatre. Everyone stared. It was summer. It was hot. I was the fat girl.

MOTHER: (*Addresses audience.*) I used to say that my children believed in the women's liberation movement. They want their mother *and* their father to wait on them. I tell you, it is very painful being a parent, especially if you don't remember becoming one. I mean, one day I was practicing Beethoven's Sonata No. 26 in E flat. The next day I was pregnant. With thought. I tell you if I don't breathe for 20 minutes in the morning the whole day is wasted. Who wants to remember a mistake that lasted 37 years. Well . . . I had no preparation for having children. None. Absolutely none. Oh, I have been asleep. But I will tell you this. I never spoke down to them. I would ask, "Do you have to make a bowel movement?" None of this gobbly-gook. On one of their first birthdays, Patrice, no maybe it was Grace, in any event, on one of their birthdays they received a birthday card from Jean Van Hieny, or was it Dana, and I, I handed it to one of them, and I said, "This is Yours. Your Personal Mail." I wanted them to know from the very beginning That I Respected Their Privacy. Why, I used to walk down the hallway very loudly so they'd know I was coming and not think I was spying on them. Well, I do have a personal relationship with my students . . . (*Puts headphones back on.*)

PATRICE: Oh, yeah? I was very happy with my schedule today. I had four appointments with potential violin teachers and one judge. I lead a very, very busy life. I left you all behind when I left you all behind. I don't consider my new life to have any connection to you or our "relationship." Just because you're family doesn't mean you have to like each other. Family is just incidental biology. I have Sam. I don't really need any of you. Sam and I have a very close and loving relationship together. He is so sweet and vulnerable. If I wanted to, he'd even give me tap dancing lessons, if I wanted to. He's my family. We have a very lovely home together. It was very hard to leave you behind when I left you behind. I had to leave. I had to leave. I had to leave. I felt bad for years, leaving you like that. I had to leave. I just couldn't protect you from her or the other or the music or . . . I had to get out to save my life. I am sorry, I couldn't save yours, also. I tried. Every time I passed the old neighborhood I would throw out an imaginary life raft and try to pull you a little further to safety. You had to stay. You were littler. I felt so responsible, leaving you like that. Especially when you started disappearing into your face, I felt so responsible.

END OF EXCERPT

Sharon Jane Smith

Threads from the Tailor's Grand Daughters (1989)

No one called her simply "Sharon Jane"; her name was preceded by the modifier "the lovely." She was and is lovely physically, tall, with long, softly wavy auburn hair and a smile on a face that recalls the beauty of the upper Midwest. She is also blessed with a lovely temperament. She radiates generosity, optimism, and a can-do spirit. Her presence alone could defuse tension as the band of misfits did battle in our noncooperative cooperative. Arriving early in the Café's stint on E. 11th Street, accompanied by her then partner Becky High, Sharon Jane remained at WOW after many of the founders left, assuming leadership responsibilities and shepherding the organization through several transitions: from a leaderless group of renters to an incorporated not-for-profit that owned its own space, and from a mostly white herd of biological women to a more diverse flock with women of color and trans folk in positions of power.

Sharon Jane grew up in a large, Catholic, blue-collar family in Winona, Minnesota. Most summers she would return to live on the Mississippi in a houseboat called the *Peach Palace,* returning with stories and songs about popping barrels under the *Palace* to keep it afloat. Her connection to the place and her family baffled me. Most of my friends who migrated to New York from other places dreaded going back and wanted desperately to establish themselves as New Yorkers. In my mostly middle-class white circles, it was assumed you loved your parents but you didn't like them. Sharon Jane was fluent in two places, maintaining a low-rent, bohemian, bicoastal existence, an eccentric wherever she landed.

In *Threads from the Tailor's Grand Daughters,* Sharon Jane's desire to make her own path shines, illuminated by her loyalty to place, to class, to a stubbornly nonmaterialistic vision of art making. She was the valedictorian of her high school class and recalled being offered a full scholarship.

> The University of Minnesota was recruiting students so I was invited. It was a mathematical thing. . . . Grade points. They didn't really want me, S.J. The reason I knew was because they showed U of M football movies. . . . I remember thinking it was a strange idea to show football films to recruit us. We were all girls, except Lowell Polachek. He was the tall, skinny mathematics genius. . . . There I was in the Holiday Inn with my parents having ham and scalloped potatoes and a Jell-O salad listening to the advantages of a college education at the University of Minnesota. I was dressed up. There was no way I was gonna go to college at the University of Minnesota. . . . It was a good school but I was anxious to meet the real world. I was glad for my mom that she didn't have to cook supper that night. She didn't get to eat out much.
>
> Whatever I was wearing, I didn't feel comfortable. . . . I didn't know these other girls. They were from the public high school. They all seemed blond and pretty. I felt more like Lowell looked; gangly. I may have gotten my period during the dinner and worried that it showed. . . . I just wanted to go home, to my room. . . . I was gonna get a job instead, at a resort up North. Then I was going to travel. First I was going to go to my room.

Smith uses the motif of weaving—of threads in the most literal way—to recall spending time in her grandfather's tailor shop, playing with spools of thread as quietly as possible, finding connections between stories of life on the Mississippi, imaginary encounters with admired eccentrics (mostly of earlier generations, including Josephine Baker, Liberace, Greta Garbo, and Elvis), framing her mandolin playing as a feminist act of class loyalty, and celebrating what others might bemoan: the need to juggle day jobs full of physical labor with making music. Her queerness is always present. It's part of what marks her as different wherever she goes, but it's one of the many threads she works into the fabric. —*Holly Hughes*

THREADS FROM THE TAILOR'S GRAND DAUGHTERS
(*Music, film, and stories*)
Written by Sharon Jane Smith
Directed by Heidi Griffiths
Lighting by Claudia Giordano
With Terry Dame, Gail Freund, Beverly Bronson, Mary Patierno, Lise
   Tribble, Imogen Pipp, Heidi Schwartz, and Barky Barkyville

For Christopher Whorton

I tried to say goodbye to the boy down the street. He played the mandolin too. He moved to New York when he came of age, just like me. We were both "different." I knew it when I met him at the ice-skating rink when I was in seventh grade. He talked differently than most boys. He caught hell for it. We acted in plays together in high school. I was sure he would be famous for his acting, someday. I competed with him for that place in the sun, theoretical as it was. I was afraid there wouldn't be room for both of us. I was also afraid that I might be just like him; a faggot. A girl faggot of course. We were both "different," that's for sure. I gave him hell for it, in my competitive way. We both got our mandolins stolen in the city that never sleeps. I accumulated spare mandolins and insurance policies. He never bought a new one. He became a chef instead and lived dangerously close to Hell's Kitchen. He brought the virus to our hometown to die. I vacationed there, never knowing. I was sure he would be famous for his acting someday.

A New Game Called "Tell Me Everything"

Tell me everything. Tell me anything. Tell me your story. Give me your spiritual thread in one minute, please. Tell me where you were going in that car, who was driving, what you wore. Any of the boring details. I want it all. How fast can you tell me a story you don't know but surfaces when I demand it? Tell me everything. You can tell me anything. How do you win the game? By telling a story you didn't know you knew.

These Hands

These hands are dangerous, you warn me. Specifically the fingers; even more specifically, the fingernails. You are not the only one to mention the way they feel, across your back. They can be very convincing. You may be convinced you want something you do not need. Pleasure. Yes, I am the lucky one. Blessed with these hands that give pleasure I thought we all had. 'Til my mom showed me an old photograph of her father, with his family. I saw bits of my own family in their faces and with horror realized my great-grandfather had no fingers in the photograph. There was something very hard in his face.

"How did he lose his fingers, Mom?"

"He froze them, out driving the buggy caught in a blizzard. There was no doctor near the farm in North Dakota," she added. His wife had to cut them off for him. I imagined the kitchen table.

You are a tougher great-grandmother than I will ever be. I haven't even met a winter that cold yet. Now, I treasure every fingertip I touch, every cold shoulder I scratch.

EZ Method Music #4 (Killing Time and Keeping Time)
(SJ distributes mandolins to cast.)

It started out as a way to kill time. I didn't learn the correct posture for playing the mandolin 'til it was too late. I had already slouched into my own style. I was seventeen; what did I know about music? I thought a mandolin was meant to be cradled, hunched over. When I took it into the music store to have a bridge put on it and to string it up, the clerk told me, quite matter-of-factly, "Nobody plays these anymore." The "folk renaissance" had not reached my part of America yet. I knew I'd been born in the wrong century. I stuck with it anyway. (I don't care how it's tuned, just play the damned thing.) It gave me immense joy to discover the first song I stumbled onto. Perhaps it can be played again, but never with the same hypnotic power. All of my adolescent sex drive found its way to my fingertips. Strung up, in these strings. To listen is the only way to learn music. To listen while one's fingers run, instantly pulling passion as if it were play. Remember the passion you put into your playing? No one paid you to be creative. You just did it. You weren't a fool, you were a child. You've lost that playfulness now. Some one has convinced you there are rules. Not to the music, to the business. That is what sometimes pinches your fingers. My mom suggested I wear a glove on my hand to protect my fingertips from those biting strings. I was proud of my flat fingertips. It meant I was serious. Mom was ahead of her time. Gloves are very fashionable in music nowadays. What did I know? I was just bent over a belly-shaped box, as women have for ages. The woman and the mandolin; a painting done at least seven times by seven great painters in their days. One sold for $2 million at Sotheby's in 1984 and I learned my lesson. The money's in painting. It's a visual age. A lady who had an identical act in this day and age would have a very hard time gigging.

The Day I Won Lotto

I may not have told you about the day I won the Lotto. $12 million, yeah. I never knew how to bring it up. Actually, it was just a close call, but it changed the way I view the game. I had four of the numbers right and the other two were reversed versions of the correct numbers. But with my semidyslexic brain I looked at the numbers on my card, then at the numbers posted, back at my card . . . again at the numbers posted, and for a few moments I knew what it felt like to be terribly rich. It was terrible, for me, Sharon Jane Smith. There was something I learned, terribly quick, that I must share with you. I felt a burst of energy shoot from my brain, still trying to sort out the real numbers from the dyslexic numbers and then the energy drained to my feet. Somehow, my heart was dragged with it and in a flash I saw all of my life become insignificant to the fact that I had won a large sum of money. It was not a good feeling. It was that sinking feeling. It felt more like the hand of doom than a lucky day and I immediately planned how I could keep this a secret so it wouldn't ruin my life. I didn't want to be remembered as the lady who won $12 million. It wasn't enough. I was even sorry I would have to carry this secret with me but I'd be damned if I was gonna let a lump of cash get in the way of my life. There are worse dark secrets, I consoled myself, trying to rise to the occasion. I was suddenly aware of what I could not be, as a millionaire. A folk musician as a millionaire? I would just be another mandolin-playing millionaire. My life's work would be ridiculous. No one believes the wealthy have feelings. How many rich blues singers are there? "Sharon Jane and the Idle Rich"? Great name for a band, but . . . this can't be my life. Sure enough, I was right. I'm *not* the type to win $12 million. Before I had time to say out loud, "There must be some mistake . . . ," I realized it had only been a close call. I laughed at myself. I laughed at my fears. I was relieved to win $20 for the four correct numbers. Later, I wondered if there was someone out there who had felt the same way about sudden wealth and had never turned in their winning ticket because they didn't want to change their life. Cashophobia? Is that what this is? Fear of money? No it's fear of being mistaken for a pile of money. I couldn't afford it.

I felt immense relief when I realized I hadn't won. Like waking from a nightmare in which I am doomed to fill out tax forms. When I regained my composure, I laughed at what my face must have looked like. I don't play the Lotto much anymore. I got too close for comfort. I wouldn't wish that feeling of losing control over one's destiny on anyone. With the wealth goes responsibility, to, to . . . one's accountant.

Untitled

When I was very young I walked off of a sandbar, into the river, over my head. My eyes were wide open and the water looked brown. My nose hurt, I couldn't breathe. As I sunk the light got dimmer and the more I struggled to regain my footing the more I lost control. Suddenly, I was being swallowed by the river. I panicked. I couldn't fight the power of the water and gave in to the river, for a moment. It was a brief moment of peacefulness and I sensed I was going somewhere else when I was jerked by the arm from the water. My older sister was rescuing me. As my face came out of the water, I was crying and spitting water. My sister was laughing, probably at how spooked I looked. It was my first experience with fear of drowning. The smell and the taste of the light above the water becoming more faint, as I sank, remains vivid. A year later I met a little boy who never returned from that underside of the river. We had the same birthday, me and Jesse. He was two, when he dropped to the bottom of that water. The "terrible twos," yes. Ran off the porch of a boathouse and wasn't found 'til a week later; after the boathouse had been burned in revenge. His renegade uncles blamed the owner of the house. Torched it late at night, no one home. I guess the custody battle would finally end. Little Jesse's body was found under the charred remains of a boathouse. The drowned rise, but not from the dead. They rise from the river, just to remind us how easily we slip in.

EZ Music Lesson #1043 (Musical Snobbery)

You don't like "folk music." Honey you don't like folks. Let's be serious for a moment. What is the opposite of folk music? Machined music. Music made by something other than people. Non-folk music. For you who don't identify with the past, the vacuum sound. Star Wars sounds. Well I'm gonna invent synthesized folk music, sweet synthesized soul, I know you're out there. Singing in a black hole, to the universal disc jockey.

I'd Clean Up

I've had a history of cleaning. When I got out of high school, I took a job as a maid at a resort in northern Minnesota. First exposure to lesbians. Then I had a job cleaning classrooms and offices at the College of St. Teresa. I grew up across the street from it.

Mapping the halls of higher education I'd say. I also found myself cleaning on a steamboat, in churches, museums, restaurants, and, of course, a glass factory. At a certain point I embraced this fact and not much later I found myself in New York. I was walking on E. 12th Street in my new neighborhood. I met up with a street man and his shopping cart of miscellaneous wares for sale. All around him were piles of books, shoes, mirrors, a parachute, quite a selection, actually. He laughed and spoke rather eloquently, in a way. He immediately responded to my vibe. He knew a real impulse shopper. I bought the parachute, some books, and the whole box of mirror stock, various sizes. He was delighted at my rampant consumerism but more impressed that I understood his rambling talk. He was a street prophet of sorts, wanting to give me as much information as he could in what he and I knew would be a short meeting. As I attempted to carry my load of goods away he smiled and said, "Honey, if I had a face like yours I'd clean up."

I have been following his advice ever since.

Untitled

In the fall and the spring, approximately 10,000 Whistler Swans pass through the Mississippi River Valley. They sound like a crowd at a football game—or maybe I associate the two sounds. Anyway, they only come to one spot: Weaver, Minnesota. That's where they want to stop and that is it. Nowhere else will do.

> I met a woman who tricked me,
> taught me my
> own song
> back again.
> More than echoing.
> Low and behold
> she was a weaver.

Never Gamble, Ladies

I know only one card trick. Watch as this completely innocent deck of cards eats this dollar bill. See, it ate it.

Never gamble, ladies. It doesn't become you. It makes you appear foolish. Couldn't have that. It makes you appear mannish.

But if you must gamble, never gamble more than you can afford to lose. It doesn't become you. It makes you appear mannish and rebellious. If you appear this way, you're likely to be mistaken for a rebellious man. No one can afford that. Even successful British rock stars admit that owning up to one's rebellious nature can be "the biggest mistake of your career." You can move quickly from commercial product to commercial leper with just one or two words. I figure, start out as a commercial leper and work your way up. Maybe no one will notice, after awhile. Maybe they'll forget it mattered. Maybe they'll forget . . . I forgot what I was saying.

Can I deal you in?

Threads from the Tailor's Grand Daughters

I'm gonna find the right wardrobe if it kills me. The suit that makes me stand up straight. Show off my shoulders. No slouching baby. No slouching toward anywhere but deep, deep down. If the clothes make the man, what are we made of?

These Clothes Between Us

Don't let these clothes get between us. | Nobody knows these threads that lead us | one to each other, | over again | nobody knows these threads that lead us. | Don't tell me it breaks | and don't tell me when. | The mending is only as strong as the thread. | Let me now rest in the granddaughter's dreams. | Let me now dream in the granddaughter's bed.

Liberace's Boat

I dreamt I was on Liberace's boat, cruising the Mississippi. The boat was huge and looked like the ones the Czar and his wife vacationed on, in the early 1900s. The wood was a rich brown with beautiful brass fittings and railings. It was crowded with Liberace's friends, partying on every deck. Lee was dead. I knew that even in my dream state. My brother and his family were the only people I knew on the boat. My brother piloted the boat for a while. The men on deck talked of Lee and his music. They argued over who would get his music, now that he was dead. They didn't mean the sheet music or the videotaped performances, or even the copyrights. They meant the music that floated in the air and disappeared. But I loved the ride. I felt Liberace was there, watching from above, smiling of course. The party was great until one man threatened to throw another overboard, behind his back. It was still that fight over the music. Who will get the music? It was an ugly fight and I awoke missing Lee, and his antique boat. I could feel another war starting over "Who will own the sound?"

Threads from the Tailor's Grand Daughters

You may recognize the thread of a story.

You mean the threat of a story.

I mean the story, for God's sake.

The story was the same. The daughter was different. She had a different way of dressing.

END OF EXCERPT

An Interview with Sharon Jane Smith
by Carmelita Tropicana (December 2001)

WOW Women in Their Own Words

CARMELITA TROPICANA: What attracted you to WOW at the beginning?

SHARON JANE SMITH: Well, it was the women . . . The social aspect of these women gathered together who wanted to do theater, who wanted to do art . . . it wasn't clearly defined, it could stretch anywhere between theater, performance, music, what have you . . .

CT: Had you written and performed elsewhere before you came to WOW?

SJS: Yeah, I was a folk singer. I actually had written what I called "low key musicals," which used my songs, which were not Broadway-style song-and-dance. I had written them into two-character plays, where basically two women met and conversed in different situations and then traded songs with each other. But I had never staged any of them. I wrote them but I never produced them.

CT: Do you think there was a WOW aesthetic when it began?

SJS: I think that it was an aesthetic of breaking all rules, of not worrying about it, a just do it kind of approach that I liked. And it was anti-elitist in terms of art.

CT: What do you mean?

SJS: Well, you know how art can get so hoity-toity or so academic and so up-tight about what it is, and that sort of cripples you, because you don't want to take that risk. Whereas this was a small enough venue, and a supportive enough group that had a sense of humor about mistakes. That's one of my favorite parts of theater, really, is what happens accidentally. It's very real.

CT: You share that in common with Jack Smith, who was always saying that it's really exciting when things happened on stage where you have to watch the actor think.

SJS: When they're thinking on their feet, that's true. Time stops because they have to be real, they have to be in the moment; they can't be 10-pages ahead of it. And speaking of Jack Smith, that was one of my favorite moments at WOW, when Jack spent five hours in the dressing room getting ready and meanwhile, outside that dressing room, we were discussing whether we should really have a man performing. It was a very heated discussion. Some people felt very passionately that a man should not perform. I thought, Jack Smith broke all the rules as a performer and I was honored that he was there. Quite honestly, I didn't care whether he was a man or not. But I guess that's when you realize if you're a true separatist or not.

CT: To Jack, everything was art; he lived in art time. So he went to WOW and he was just standing in a corner with a lamp-shade on his head, while people were discussing whether a man should perform there. He was unplugged. We were so upset. My sister [Ela], yelled, "Do you know who this man is or his queer work?"

SJS: That was one of my favorite moments at WOW. He was so focused getting ready for what he was going to do. There was something about those quiet moments in the dressing rooms; those were often the beautiful times at WOW for me—watching a performer get ready.

CT: What have been some of the other most difficult moments at WOW?

SJS: The most difficult moments are those moments when you see the personalities clash because someone is not getting recognized or respected. You know who gets in trouble are those extremely aggressive women, who come in and they want to get their show and they're going to figure out a way of breaking the rules to get it and they're going to get other people to help them. In the normal sphere of theater, that probably works fine, that super-aggressive thing. But this group of women wanted to be equal and have the same rules.

CT: At WOW, there never were any written rules.

SJS: Well, now we have a stage/house manager manual. Lynn Hayes helped put together the first house manager manual, and the producer's manual, so there are certain rules. But still, there are people who are able to break or stretch the rules. There's no enforcer, there's no one who enforces those rules. That's the anarchistic aspect of it.

CT: Do you think that WOW is anarchistic?

SJS: It fluctuates, depending on who's involved. But yeah, there's an aspect of it that is anarchistic.

CT: Do you think that WOW had leaders at the beginning?

SJS: In the beginning, certainly yes: Peggy, and Lois, and Holly, and Susan Young. It fluctuated depending on projects and the producers. When Susan was living in the space, she had a leadership role. But in general, I would say it was a bunch of misfits who gathered together. Lesbians are suspect of leaders. They want to be more egalitarian than that. Or else they're loners—they work best alone.

CT: You worked at WOW at the beginning and you still work at the Café now. Tell me about what you see as improvements.

SJS: There's a whole new generation who has come to WOW because of the information that has been transmitted through books and magazine articles about WOW, or performers talking about WOW. So when they come, there's a history they've already heard about. Maybe they have dreams attached to that; usually the dream is about doing their own thing. They take risks that I would never have dreamed of taking when I was a teenager. It's safe because it's a different town and they're not going to run into people they know, necessarily. It's a haven and they look forward to that.

CT: Are they gay and lesbian?

SJS: Some are, some are not, but they understand the history of WOW. They know that it was started by lesbians and they are very respectful of that. WOW has become more racially diverse in the last five or ten years, through individuals who have connected to others and made others feel welcome there.

CT: You mean before we didn't connect?

SJS: Before—we were trying.

CT: You said your function at WOW was "bringing levity"—

SJS: Bringing levity to solve crises, though I'm not always that successful. The problems that come up between personalities are universal. It's just that we haven't had a group of women gathered together like this often. Our society pits us against each other. I value whatever information I have, and I share information I have with people. I'm not threatening because I'm not trying to take anything away from them.

CT: Why do you still hang out at WOW?

SJS: I must need a group of women that I can connect to. Because I don't go to church anymore and I think I probably want to connect to other people who want to do art. Because it's already set up, it makes it easy for me and I'm always curious what people want to present on stage. No matter whether I like it or not, I'm curious what they envision on stage.

CT: But why not a different group? There are other groups.

SJS: There are?

CT: Well, you can form a group or you can do theater someplace else.

SJS: Theater somewhere else, I don't think it offers the same kind of . . . I used to work at PS122. People there come in, they do their show, they're in a panic, and they leave. I don't see it as connecting to people, when you're not doing a show, and you're thinking about things or reacting to other things that other people have done. WOW is already set up. I think of it like a home. It has that safety too, where I can experiment and feel safe, and it's no big deal if I fail.

CT: Do you think that WOW works very much on a friendship/communal level?

SJS: Yeah, at its best, that's what it does. It allows the women a space to present their work and they can become friends in the process. They can meet other people that they wouldn't necessarily meet. Where would I have met you if I hadn't met you at WOW?

CT: In the first 10 years, it was easy because we were all in the same neighborhood. Now, people are coming from many of the other boroughs to get to the meetings.

SJS: I come to WOW because it gives me a group of women I can bounce ideas off of, and because there's a camaraderie. We all need theater, whether we're going to be stockbrokers or teachers or bankers or mailmen. We need theater.

Eileen Myles

Feeling Blue (1988)

Eileen Myles was a frequent WOW audience member. By the late '80s, she had become the poet laureate of bohemian lesbian nation, able to channel the rhythms of Beat poetry through the prism of queer feminist experience. Certainly, there was no shortage of excellent lesbian poets, but Myles's gritty bravado, her quirky humor, and her focus on the urban over the pastoral aligned her with WOW's sensibilities.

Feeling Blue was Myles's first foray into performance, her first "play," as she disarmingly confesses early in part 1. This confession is not an apology; it's a gesture that speaks at once of vulnerability but also of boldness. It's almost as if she were saying, "Hey, watch me, no hands!" Like many WOW members, Myles placed her bets on her desire to be heard and her belief that her sense of urgency would more than compensate for any lack of familiarity with dramaturgical conventions.

Part 1 is a monologue drawn from Myles's experience. Part of the narrative follows a now familiar trajectory of coming-out tales: the early signs that she was not like other little girls, flashes of forbidden desire, an urge to jump boys and threaten them with a beating until they "gave." She dazzles with her ability to distill beauty from the daily. But Myles effortlessly leaps from the facts to the fantastic. She's always inserting her experience into the frames of pop culture, much as gay photographer Deborah Bright collaged herself into iconic movie stills, interrupting the assumption of heterosexuality with her visibly queer body.

Myles imagines conversations with Madonna. She recasts her romance as a western that unfolds on the Lower East Side and in Paris. She insists on being as sexual as a character from a Tom of Finland drawing, "a small man with a big dick." It is a dangerous world; her girlfriend, the Cowbunny, keeps a gun under her bed with her sex toys. But danger is not to be avoided; she asks us if we know how sexy it is to be kissed by a beautiful woman with a gun.

Part 2 is an escalating confrontation between a mother and a daughter. Both feel betrayed and judged by the other. In part 3, three characters with shifting gender presentations—Taffy, Lady, and Sparkle—hold forth on their competing cosmologies, while a television, called the "Teevee" in the script, interrupts with Jenny Holzeresque aphorisms and a sign flashes "The Door to the Moon."

Feeling Blue, parts 1, 2, 3, was presented at WOW in June 1988 as a staged reading with Myles, Peg Healey, Karen Crumley, and Danine Ricereto performing. Part 1 was performed as a solo piece at PS122 in the fall of 1988, with a full production following in the spring of 1989. In the latest production, the performers were Eileen Myles, Rebecca Moore, Richard Boes, and Will Scheffer. —*Holly Hughes*

FEELING BLUE
The Characters
SHE, a woman in jeans, jean jacket, cowboy boots.
MOTHER, a woman dressed in baseball cap, striped tee-shirt, Converse high-tops.
DAUGHTER, a woman dressed in baseball cap, striped tee-shirt, Converse high-tops. Could be played by the same actor as "SHE."
TAFFY, a woman dressed in battered tuxedo. Could be played by "SHE" and "DAUGHTER" actor.
SPARKLE, a woman or man in hat and tuxedo with shorts. Mute throughout.
LADY, a tall woman in a black dress. Could be played by "MOTHER" actor.

Feeling Blue, Part One

(*The stage is set to resemble a TV talk show. Three yellow chairs at left center face the audience. Behind the chairs is a screen upon which images are shot throughout. Just upstage of center sits a stool with a candle on it. After a few moments, a woman walks out from stage left. She wears cowboy boots, jeans and a jean jacket. She carries a rope. She stops at center stage and begins hesitantly.*)

SHE: Welcome to "Feeling Blue, Part One." (*Gestures towards the empty chairs.*) Some of my guests this evening are My Angel in Paris—otherwise known as "The Cowbunny"—The Virgin Strip, a combination of Madonna and that statue outside of my window; Joan of Arc (*kneels, then gets up*), the female individual as she stands, a monument to her, her total . . . feeling. It's a figure—I mean, the one that dances, that prays, that goes to war, um, the one that gets left alone . . . like this. Let me be honest with you. This is my first play. Yes. It is. Originally, it was called *One, Two, Three* and I don't know where *Feeling Blue* came from. I guess I just was, you know. And I wanted to move out into something that had more room. (*Gestures around into the spaciousness of the stage, kind of seeing it for the first time.*) Nice, huh? I don't really know much about conversation, interaction. So I thought I would start out with me. I would start with something I know— me. And I would do that for a while and then move on to something different. Two people talking . . . That'll be Part Two. Then Three. It's amazing, though. I am one person standing here, but I am filled with dreams. I am not just one person. I am every other "one person" in my culture. (*A picture of Madonna flashes on the screen.*) I like Madonna, I really do. She has a ton of nerve. I wish she was my girlfriend. I would say to her, "I think it is a riot what you do." I don't understand the impulse from the gut. But that doesn't matter. She's who she is, I'm who I am. We like each other. You know, you really don't have to understand other people. You can just look at them and feel for a moment all their brain cells churning and the blood pumping through their veins, and realize they have come from a whole different configuration of family, were born at a different point in time, even just a few years, it makes a big difference, had different sexual experiences . . . you know, you look at them and in one stunning moment you realize, she is someone else—she is not me! (*Pause. starts playing with the rope.*) My girlfriend is a cowboy and she moved to Paris. I call her the Cowbunny. She is in a rodeo and she wears a white hat and a white cowgirl outfit and has the prettiest cowboy boots you ever saw in your life. She has a gun. (*Points at audience.*) You know how exciting it is to be with someone, particularly a woman, who has a gun. She sort of kept me in line with that gun. Even as she was kissing me I would think a beautiful girl with a gun is kissing me. It was so exciting. She had one of those beds with drawers and she kept it right there, just like you might keep your sweaters or your sex toys. She had a gun. She used to work on a ranch on Second Avenue. I'd ride by on my horse and there'd she be with the dogies. She'd come home real late after a hard day at the ranch and she'd smell like horse, and sweat, and dogie. And she'd break into that old song:

No time to understand them just ride 'em, rope 'em, brand 'em . . . And we'd laugh and she'd begin to take her clothes off.

(*Instrumental intro to Madonna's "Material Girl" begins to play. Blackout. Music fades. Lights go back up.* SHE *stands center stage.*)

I live in this little studio on 3rd Street between First and Second Avenue. Funny place for a cowboy to live. And I face that cemetery between 2nd and 3rd Streets. (*Turns and addresses someone backstage left.*) Hey, let's have a map. (*Beautiful, blonde, '50s-style woman rolls out a map.*) Here we go. I move in here in 1977. Don't even know who I am. Only know I'm sad. There's all these trees outside my window. That's something. Okay, that's May. Summer passes, Labor Day, everything—(*waves hands frantically*) just like . . . traffic, you know, time, cars . . . then, one morning . . . I wake up in October, my whole orientation has changed—my heart is broken . . . over a woman! And I look out the window, the leaves have fallen, because it is *fall*, and there she is, Mary, Christ's mother standing there, looking up at me. This is a vision. A vision in stone, but a vision just the same. I think, Oh my God, I have either done something very right or very wrong. *God's mother is looking in my window.* Thank you! That's all I could think to say. I guess she's The Virgin Strip. (*Beautiful woman brings out a slip of paper.* SHE *reads it. Looks up.*) Thank you. Thank you. Thanks a lot. Yes, it's this incredible forgiving quality of life, or Nature, that I would like to celebrate tonight. Every year, the Virgin undresses outside my window, she sheds her leaves and she looks up at me and I have to explain my year to her, what I'm doing with my life. She's like "Okay, I stand naked—now what about you?" I think of Marilyn calendars. I admire the dignity some women have in their faces as they lie there, naked, curled up on silk in front of the eyes of the world. If I could have that much dignity, openness. (*Pause.*)

I would take it to war. What do you think of fighters? I used to like to fight. I used to hang out by the little path that opened up into the ballpark, and I'd say, "I can take you!" I'd say that to every boy who passed by. We'd wind up rolling in the dirt, getting burrs all over our socks, and sometimes I'd make the boys cry. I didn't hit them in the face, I never wanted to hurt them and I frightened myself when I made them cry. I only wanted to dominate them. I wanted to sit on their stomachs and pin their arms back and say, Okay, do you give? And unless they said yes they could not get up. Those were my rules. And I was pretty much dressed like this. Around that same time I was given the Classic Comics version of Joan of Arc. She was great. She had her hair cut like I did and she rode a horse. She left her family and she didn't have to get another one like most girls. She got an army. Naturally, she was faulted for things that generals don't usually get faulted for—like the way she dressed, and her manners and her general lack of . . . *savoir faire*. Though she did speak French. Joan of Arc was a French cowboy. All through grade school I worshipped her. When it came time to be confirmed—this happens to Catholics in around seventh grade; it's how they try and distract us from puberty—we'd all get to pick new names and these are the names we use in the imaginary army. We are soldiers of Christ. I don't know what this army ever does though I suspect when the Chinese Communists come to stick chopsticks in our ears and try and make us deny Christ—that's when the giant glowing army rises up in our chests and we get to yell, "Kill me, stick those chopsticks in my ears because I am not Me today, I am Joan!" (*Pause.*)

I took Joan for my confirmation name. All the other girls took "Brigitte" amidst much giggling. What is this, why does everyone want to be "Brigitte" this year? Because we all want to be French sluts, that's why. The Cowbunny, "My Angel in Paris," told me that all high school girls are little sluts, or want to be. Untrue. I did not want to be a slut. I inadvertently got on the boy-boat, not the girl-boat. I wanted to be Bobby Vee and get all my girlfriends pregnant.

You know, I don't remember anyone being very interested in what kind of names boys took for confirmation. They seemed to have names enough. It was the girls who were looking for their real names. The Brigittes and Joans. (*Pause.*)

Puberty was like a Hall of Mirrors. I dutifully had crushes on the boys my girlfriends wanted to make out with. Through these crushes, I would become them. I could picture it. I would roll on beds with my girlfriends in my mind.

Last Halloween just for fun I dressed up like a man. Kind of a little faggot with a big dick. I looked like one of those Tom of Finland guys. I wore a little Greek cap, and black stretch pants and Li'l Abner boots and a sailor shirt and I had a rose on my forearm and one on my chest and I even had a small tuft of curly black hair on my chest. I had a moustache and sideburns and a little curl up here. (*Puts her hand through her hair.*) I was cute in a certain way. I went to a party downtown and I noticed gay men liked me a lot, so did straight women, and gay women were divided. Some thought it was a riot, even really liked it, I thought. Others couldn't handle it. Leonard (*slide of Leonard flashes*), who helped me get dressed, sent a photo of me as a man to the Cowbunny. She didn't like it a bit. (*Pulls letter out of her pocket.*)

I just got a letter. Now's as good a time as any. (*To the wings.*) Could we have a little music? (*Country western strings play. Like Skeeter Davis.* SHE *reads.*)

I don't know what I'm doing here.
Paris is like an ashtray.
It's like spending your whole day on the platform at Union Square. My
    horses can't get enough to eat.
That snow stopped
our show for two
weeks. And then
the Metro broke.
The dollar is plummeting.
I wish that we could
drive to Texas and
eat some Bar-B-Q
Je t'embrace
Cowbunny

(*Music fades.*)

Why did the Cowbunny want to go to Paris? (*Pause. Moment of befuddlement. Throws down letter.*) Because she's not Me! How does she do it? Do you know what I mean? When I read about someone I admire or even am fascinated by I think, How did Hitler do it? How did he do it? I zip to the end of the book to see when they "kicked the frame," as the Buddhists put it. I mean *died.* 'Cause I want to know . . . maybe I'm them. Could their soul have slipped into mine? Sounds kind of dirty doesn't it? Someplace in the year 2008 Joan Baez gets reborn. She's been dyin' for it. She's got some songs and she's looking for a life-style in the most literal of ways. Here she comes again.

(*Slide flashes of Moonbeam McSwine.*)

She's Moonbeam McSwine. It's a kind of Russ Meyers's reality after the Apocalypse and this whole planet looks like Dogpatch. Big women rule—picture it! Even now I think the whole '80s strategy of glorifying big, sexy women is sort of an homage, a farewell to sexual stratification. (*Pause.*)
    I picture myself an eleven-year-old tomboy walking up to Moonbeam McSwine—"Hey, do you want to hang out with me?" (*Shrugs.*) Al Capp

did not resemble Li'1 Abner. By now, sexual stratification does not exist. Arnold Schwarzenegger does not marry Moonbeam McSwine. He marries a Kennedy. Most of the men who look like Abner are gay. The Abners get the Abner and the Moonbeams get small men with power. I think the day of the medium-sized androgynous person is upon us. (*Pause. Lifts a boot up on a stool. Pulls a handkerchief out of her pocket and shines the boot.*)

The atmosphere is totally sexual, isn't it? I don't get to be this woman every year. I think I mentioned that I went to Catholic schools. I like to move through a variety of uniforms. If I think of Brigitte Bardot in a Catholic school uniform I just die. I never thought of "sexy" as a possibility for myself. There were girls I remembered being good at math and now here they were breaking all the rules with make-up and earrings and intensely rolled up skirts and they had breasts and really big beautiful legs and what confused me is their boyfriends were short and fully employed as oil burner repairmen. They had big greasy hair and cars and cigarettes and these guys would wait outside for Doris and Debbie and Donna, and the guy would put a hand on the girl's shoulder and they would move real slow down Medford Street to his car. I could never see falling for one stage of my development over another. Caught. If you had a boyfriend like that, then you would be pregnant and married real soon. I mean these girls weren't exactly going off with Roger Vadim. In junior high, I used to like to talk dirty to these girls. It was the best I could do as far as bonding with them. (*Pause.*)

It wasn't even like the sexy girls who liked garage mechanics were necessarily dumb. Doris wasn't. Just really impatient. Had to get in that car. There it goes. Now she's just a dot. A writer I really admire describes a woman sitting there as a fountain. Her existence as a fountain. He's right. It's hard to imagine "being" as just being still. He was being a man observing a woman he loved. Her existence is a fountain. Her light is wrinkling there right in front of you. (*Pause.*) I think of pulling identities out of myself like scarves. Imagine pulling colorful scarves one by one out of the top of your head. (*Flash Brigitte Bardot.*) I started studying Brigitte to see what all the hoopla was about. She's perfect. That's what it was. *And God Created Woman*— what a great title. Did you hear the story recently about Prince trying to woo her? Sending her truckload after truckload of roses. Don't you get it, he screamed. I'm Prince. I think he wanted to make a movie with her. She wouldn't even return the call. Who is this Prince, she asked. Talk about an Angel in Paris. (*Pause.*) But *And God Created Woman* is it. Roger Vadim put Brigitte in a little French town and every man in town was vying for her. Let her ride a bicycle, let her skirt blow mostly open while she walks down the street. She gets a little drunk. Everyone freely calls her a tramp because she's really too beautiful for life. It disturbs them. That's why she's in the movies. Her absolutely perfect youth has become a myth.

(*Neil Sedaka's "Breaking Up Is Hard to Do" plays. Fades.*)

    The color of puberty is lavender. In 1963 it was. My next door neighbor looks like Annette Funicello and everything she owned was orchid. That color. It was like blood slowly coming to the surface of the skin. It was like swooning.

(*Blackout. Lights up.* SHE'*s holding a card.*)

I send a postcard to Paris. It reads:

December
The black branches
rattling against
a lavish purple
sky. My hope
is that I
will see
you again.

   END OF EXCERPT

WOW Women in Their Own Words

The first WOW festival in 1980 seemed like the coolest lesbian bar I had ever seen. Everyone was droll and far-out and stylish and druggy. It was really electric and alluring. Then there was the skinny WOW on E. 11th Street. That's where I first saw Holly's *The Well of Horniness*. It seemed like such a huge play for such a small place. The occasion of her play gave me hope because the play was campy and ironic and cheesy and over the top and mostly just smart and funny. It established a feeling for how lesbian culture could be. I was a little nervous about this wonderful, temporary lesbian festival being planted in this skinny little theater place. But once I saw *The Well of Horniness*, I realized that the size of the space was not the point at all. What was important was how unlike any other space it was and how much you felt like you were seeing and hearing something new—from dykes.

By the time WOW was on E. 4th Street, I was really impressed: their own theater. Because I was and am a poet, I never thought of it as "my" space. But these were the theater people who were "like" me. I saw Diane Torr's first drag pieces at WOW (and took part and was naked in front of an audience for the first time and then slipped on a big dick) and saw the Five Lesbian Brothers, which on first viewing struck me as genius as, say, Nirvana or Jefferson Airplane. A group had slipped into something bigger than its parts; a genius called the Five Lesbian Brothers had "occurred."

I've always been enraged by how much WOW *isn't* New York, in a way. I've seen so many "firsts" there, so many stunning nights of theater and total avant-gardism and kitsch and darkness, and yet the work at WOW is never regularly reported in the *Times* or the *Voice*. Nonetheless, WOW strikes me as the preeminent theater space of its time. Café Cino, in the '50s or '60s, was punier and only so historic because men did their early work there. If we can survive lesbian theater being lesbian and treated as such then we will probably have surmounted the greatest obstacle ever thrown in the path of a human being.

To be a female human talking about loving (or hating, but mainly obsessing on) other female humans is to ultimately derail the greater purpose of the birth process which is to create men. WOW is an abysmal failure on an historic scale in that it has ultimately produced decades of dangerous and vital women. (August 23, 2000)

Women and Children First: Outstanding Perk or Tool of Oppression? (1992)

Barbara Davy (Babs) is one of the founding members of the Five Lesbian Brothers, the acclaimed company of writers and performers formed at WOW. Babs is also the author of three solo shows and has appeared in Maria Maggenti's films *The Incredible True Adventure of Two Girls in Love* and *Puccini for Beginners.*

Babs is the only Brother who did not have a theatre background. By day she worked as a Whitney Museum registrar. By night she accompanied her sister, Kate Davy (an academic who went on to write *Lady Dicks and Lesbian Brothers: Staging the Unimaginable at the WOW Café Theatre*), to shows at WOW. In 1984 Kate was covering the burgeoning East Village performance art scene for *TDR: The Drama Review*, in an issue that featured all the productions happening on the same night (November 30). Kate's evening included two stops: WOW and Club Chandalier, spaces that shared many of the same performers. Babs found both the performances and the women in the shows compelling. Soon after, she went to WOW and joined.

At WOW women quickly recognized her acting talent, and she was cast in numerous shows: *Paradykes Alley, Paradykes Lost, Rabbit Plantation, A Clamcracker Suite, Into Temptation, Of Men and Steamboat Men,* and *Guitar Boy.* As a member of the Brothers, she began to write plays that were presented at WOW: *Voyage to Lesbos* and *Brave Smiles: Another Lesbian Tragedy.*

Bab's first solo show at WOW was *Women and Children First: Outstanding Perk or Tool of Oppression?* Deb Margolin directed her debut, which was followed by *How I Drank My Way through Heterosexuality*, which was presented at a Dance Theatre Workshop Festival. Her last solo show, *Blest Like*

Me: Psychopharmacology and Salvation, was presented at WOW's 30th Anniversary Festival in 2010.

In *Women and Children First,* she explores her '60s suburban childhood of love, loss, and open-heart surgery amid her family's alcoholism. She includes stories of her experiences as a museum registrar and guides us through the process of organizing and coding works of art. The excerpt included here is the story of her surgery, told from the perspective of a child who is on an emotional roller coaster. She is trying to grasp the immensity of a life-and-death issue and is shocked to find out that, while others knew about her heart condition, she'd been kept in the dark her whole life.

The play's language is simple; the comedy shirks sentimentality. Babs tells the story as if she's in a show-and-tell in front of her grammar school class, holding the get-well cards her classmates had sent. She confesses that she always wanted to tell the story of her open-heart surgery and asked her teacher, who thought it would be inappropriate because the story might scare her classmates. At WOW she finally gets to tell her tale.

Babs confesses that her secret childhood fantasy was to be one of the June Taylor Dancers and to act in a sitcom. Her show-biz dream was realized, if a bit modified, by acting at WOW and in Maggenti's films, writing her solos, and becoming one of the talented Five Lesbian Brothers.

—*Carmelita Tropicana*

WOMEN AND CHILDREN FIRST: OUTSTANDING PERK OR TOOL OF OPPRESSION?

When I was nine years old, I had open heart surgery to correct a congenital defect. And everything came out okay; the trouble came when I tried to re-enter my life just three weeks later. Because after open heart surgery, third grade, the Brownies and Confirmation (becoming a soldier of Christ) just seemed unimportant somehow. And nothing my teacher Mrs. Burvenich could tell me was as interesting as the experience I had just been through. My friends, Laura Mallany, Roxanne Checka, and Greg Magrime, all signed the autograph bear given to me by my favorite nurse at the hospital, Nurse Barb (*shows autograph bear*), and would gather 'round as I told stories of my trip there, and they were very receptive, which was good because telling these stories was the only thing I found meaningful in those days. Greg especially enjoyed these sessions. Greg was the kind of kid who once had a jar in his desk with a couple of fleshy orbs floating in some liquid (*produces jar with skinned plums floating in water*) and a story about the virility of the family dog, the constant crying at the door to get out, the frequency of canine pregnancy in the neighborhood and his father's uncontrollable rage the evening before in connection with all of that. Greg needless to say found my real life stories from post-op irresistible. But soon I realized I needed to reach a larger audience and I thought that story hour at school would be a good forum. My story had a broad base of appeal and story hour was well-attended, a perfect match! So I approached Mrs. Burvenich with my idea and I thought that she would be impressed with my willingness to be so candid about such a personal ordeal and that she would recognize what a unique educational opportunity this would be for everyone. Instead, she was non-committal and said something about "we'll see" and when story hour came and went without a nod in my direction I knew she thought I was showing off. This was Catholic school and that sort of behavior fell into the "Cardinal sin" category I think. I now know it was more the "true story" nature of my grisly tale that put her off. And that she would not look forward to moderating the Q&A that would follow such a story hour or the many calls from irate parents to her home that evening. And so I remained frustrated . . . until tonight. I have recently observed the 27th anniversary of the "story hour that never was"; Mrs. Burvenich has, I'm sure, long since left this world for the next, there isn't an eight- or nine-year-old in the house and so I have determined that now, finally, It Can Be Told!

The focus of my remarks tonight will be a little different than they would have been all those years ago for James Fizenberger, Christine Trutwin, Mara Keen, Patti Bortoulousse, and all the gang at Assumption School. No, tonight I'll be talking less about how they made the incision starting from here (*indicates chest area*) and went around my side (*indicates line going around side to the back and up towards neck*) to my back and then up five or six inches. And how they put my little arm in a sling and cranked it up enough to get their big surgeon hands inside my little nine-year-old chest. And, "Oh, still not quite enough room, let's get the saw out and remove a couple of those ribs. There, now we can see what we're doing." No, I'll be talking less about that and more about the fact that they called the procedure "smile" surgery because of the shape of the incision. (*Smiles.*)

I was diagnosed four years before the actual surgery but I wasn't told until three days before I was admitted into the hospital. And, I found out later, *everyone* knew but me! All the kids on the block knew and never let it slip. My best friend, Diane Pafiolis, who always got to be married to Paul McCartney when we played Wives of the Beatles, and who forced me to play doctor on the threat that she wouldn't be my friend anymore and then left me on her porch face down with Crayolas in my butt for her mother to find me prone, obediently waiting for the doctor to return, Diane never breathed a word about "smile surgery"! I can directly trace the foundation of my adult paranoia to this point in my life, a point when everyone was walking around thinking I was a goner and no one was telling me. And I have proof! I have family movie footage of me, suitcase in one hand, Raggedy Ann in the other (*picks up suitcase and Raggedy Ann*), walking out the front door of the house and down the sidewalk toward the camera until my little face filled the frame—repeatedly! My dad wanted to get several takes because he wasn't sure it was going to be a round-trip to the hospital. The thing that was most upsetting to me was that I felt fine.

Doctor Ray Anderson followed me in "clinic" for the years between my "diagnosis" and "cure."

Yes, they gave me a number and tracked me not unlike the noble wildebeest you have oft seen on *Wild Kingdom*. My body was observed, measured, weighed, poked and listened to ad nauseam and for what, I ask you? My file is full of letters like these. (*Reads first of two letters.*) "June 1, 1962, A.U.H. 987360" (*looks at audience*). That would be me. "I examined this five-year-old girl on May 29, 1962. Barbara was first noted to have a heart murmur about two or three weeks ago when examined on a routine visit. She has never had any definite cardiac symptoms, and her general health has always been good. Examination showed a very well-appearing girl weighing 43 pounds and measuring 44 inches in height." Etc. . . . "In the meantime, I think the girl can be treated as a normal youngster, being allowed full activities."

(*Reads second letter.*) "The findings two years ago indicated a coarctation of the aorta. The girl has done very well in the intervening time, with no cardiac symptoms. Her general appearance was very good on this visit." Etc. . . . "I expect she will get along very well in the meantime and need not be restricted in her activities in any way. Thank you very much for the opportunity of seeing this very pleasant little girl again." (*She feigns modesty.*) You have to agree there doesn't seem to be any hard evidence that there was a problem. It wasn't like they could take an x-ray and say, "Ah, there it is, let's go after it!" I felt fine, and based on these letters, I would like to know what the matter was? I was asymptomatic and under no restricted activities. Sure I turned blue in the Richfield pool during swimming lessons, it was seven a.m. and the water was 50 degrees! Everyone had a hard time catching their breath. No I think these guys got ahold of a shiny new heart lung machine and they wanted to try it out! My folks didn't even have to pay for the operation! Now that is suspicious!

A couple of days before surgery, Mom and Dad gave me the bad news. It was a Sunday morning.

I had just loaded up on ham and eggs, I was feeling pretty good and Mom and Dad started acting weird. Mom said she had a surprise for me. I remember them using the term "surgery," but I didn't know what it meant. And they were both so busy "downplaying" the whole thing that I decided I was merely going back for more tests, and that the only difference was that this time I would be staying over night at the hospital. In fact missing school was sounding pretty good to me, especially when mom told me, "You know you don't have to go into the hospital until Wednesday but if you want to you can stay home Monday and Tuesday" (I guess they thought I should be able to spend my last days anyway I wanted to). They gave me a new lavender comb and brush set and a new pair of pajamas and the trip was really shaping up.

Then Mom brought out the World Book. (*Shows* World Book.) This was my sister Kate's idea.

My mom and dad were so freaked out about the whole thing that I think they were planning to just pull up in front of the hospital and drop me off. My sister said, "No I think you better tell her a little something about it." (*Shows fabulous* World Book *color transparency overlays of the human body.*) You can see here that the skeletal system overlays onto the muscles, and here we have the organs, and every one of them is numbered and very clear. And here is number 37, the aorta, and Mom said, "They are either going to put something in or take something out or sew something up, they aren't sure what, but they're going to make it better." Things were coming together for me now. I was beginning to understand that the word surgery meant operation.

This then would explain their agitated behavior and over-animated expressions, and then Dad chimed in about how they called it "smile" surgery, and, why, and the whole picture snapped into focus. Adrenaline cruised through my system screaming *fight or flight! Fight or flight!* To which I responded, Fight who? Fly where? I bravely held my ground and decided to call a few friends to tell them my big news and diffuse some of the panic, only to be told that they already knew.

On the appointed day, Mom and Dad admitted me into the hospital. The night before surgery a minister made a visit to my room. I should have told him that I was Catholic and given him the boot. I should definitely have told him that I was in the middle of an enema. Instead, I listened politely to this very pleasant and smiling man who seemed harmless until he wanted to know about my nail-biting habit. I sat on my bed pan shocked.

This was not the sort of comfort I had in mind. I really didn't need to be reminded of my human frailty the night before major surgery. I think some encouraging words about my strength and resilience would have been in order. He wanted to know if my mother had ever tried nail polish to help me stop. I wanted to know where he learned his bedside manner and what kind of church lets a guy like this loose in a Children's Heart Hospital? And anyway did he really believe that fingers chewed enough to be noticed from a distance of 50 feet would respond to Revlon? I told him nothing so far seemed to work (because in fact my mother had tried nail polish). I should have told him to go fuck himself, that if he didn't mind I needed some time alone, that I had a little nail biting to catch up on before going under the knife.

Around midnight, a guy dressed like a gangster came into my room. He had a big storm coat on and a fedora that cast a shadow over his face. He introduced himself as Aldo Castanada, my surgeon. I thought, Impressive, a gangster and a cutter. He asked me to explain what was going to happen the following day and was impressed with my understanding of the procedure. I'd been coached with the fucking *World Book*! It was all very reassuring except that I couldn't help thinking he should be home getting some sleep instead of prowling around the hospital in the wee hours of the morning before our big day.

Later that night, I was carried on a gurney to a room where I was left alone with a man who banked towels around my arm and emptied a hypodermic full of something into it. Then, when my arm was numb he picked up a scalpel. He never spoke but this is how he sounded (*makes grunting noises*). We were never introduced. After that I only ate what they put into my arm.

I have some get well cards that I saved. And I know that the senders all meant well but each one seemed to upset or piss me off in some way. Because open-heart surgery makes you cranky. I had a hard time catching my breath because of the rib thing and everything. I was too weak to make a fist. Nurse Barb and I had a date every night to walk the halls because I was favoring the incision at about a 45 degree angle. (*Demonstrates bending completely sideways.*) My brother told me years later while we were decorating the Christmas tree that he took one look at me and my 107 stitches right after surgery and thought to himself, "She was a good sister while she lasted." So that's the state of affairs when these get well cards start rolling in.

END OF EXCERPT

WOW Women in Their Own Words
As the World Turns: Twenty Years Later (2004)

SUSAN YOUNG: WOW's legacy was some of the great feminist theater of the '80s: Peggy and Lois, Carmelita, Deb Margolin, and The Five Lesbian Brothers, and all the work that Holly has done ... it all evolved out of that very raw, raw sense of theater and that need to project those images.

CARMELITA TROPICANA: There was nothing out there for us. There was just nothing. We made outsider art.

SY: But we made the mainstream pay attention to us, finally, because there was inherent talent and skill. The more traditional society came to us. But think of what a great community it was in those years.

LOIS WEAVER: It was so un-self-conscious. We weren't making art. We were just making theater 'cause we had to. We really had an enormous freedom because we didn't care. We really didn't care. And we'd try anything.

PEGGY SHAW: When Holly did the BOW WOW, which was Boys of WOW and Women of WOW, the Boys of WOW would all be recorded in all the books. The women of WOW weren't. That's how history wrote itself, isn't it? That's why this book has to get written! At the same time, Lois and I ventured out into the more heterosexual performance world. We performed as James Dean and Katherine Hepburn. And we really stood out. People were, like, astounded. We stood out because we had rehearsed. You guys were describing how we just had half of an idea and we'd get up and do stuff, but we also had an incredibly professional aesthetic. If people were going to come in here and see us, then we were going to work hard and we were going to give something. What we all shared was our work ethic, which was very strong, very different. Every one of us had a different one. But to this day, when I walk into a theater that's well-known or come across a group that's well-known, I think, "My god, we had much stronger professionalism."

[. . .]

PS: There are still the same issues now at WOW. The subjects don't go away. Life is not something you solve and then you go to the next life. The same problems exist now at WOW . . . Men in the space. How much input do men have? And who's supposed to be running it? Why weren't you there? Why didn't you do this? You can't have a show, you weren't here enough.

LW: How are we going to have grants without an official, hierarchical structure? Can we raise money without that? If we have that, how does it look? What does it look like?

[. . .]

CT: One of our problems at WOW had always been people of color. How do we get people of color? So, we tried different things. We would try having a festival to bring people in. But again, WOW's this place that, you know, if you get in there, you have to do it. You have to involve yourself in it.

PS: Then we gave—I mean this is the classic—and we gave Sunday nights to the East Coast Asian Lesbians. Because we have this space and the original people who had the space had to continually open it up to other people. It's like being in someone else's home. How do you do that? Without feeling like a colonialist?

CT: You have to really want to do it. When I started out, I sort of split myself. I was doing stuff at WOW with all the WOW women. But I did *Memories of the Revolution* with Uzi Parnes and with all of the WOW women. They all had different fake Latino accents. Some had Polish accents, some had German accents—that's Latino. Then I had INTAR [*INTAR was and remains one of the most important Spanish-speaking theatres in the country.*], where the name "Latino" started coming up and we were finding our roots. I was split between the lesbian and the Latino. A lot of times, at INTAR, they were giving me money to develop a show, and I would bring the WOW people in. It was like trying to mesh your worlds, which sometimes was very difficult to do. I was exotic—I'll take that. 'Cause you can take something that starts as a negative, perhaps make it a positive. I know I could play my cards right, in the space. Because I was a woman of color. You know I could play the race card and no one would say . . . as much.

I came to WOW and then I met Ana Maria Simo, who started Medusa's Revenge, the Lesbian Avengers, and Dyke TV. And where did I meet this Cuban-American? With you guys. I hadn't met her before—and we lived two blocks apart. WOW tried to address race. Maybe it wasn't successful in some ways. But it wasn't for not trying.

LW: I'm glad you brought up Medusa's Revenge, which was the first—as far as I know—the first lesbian theater in New York. It started in 1977, on Bleecker Street. Magaly Abalau and Ana Simo started it. They produced lesbian theater, lesbian performance, and cabaret; they had parties. They were really a precursor to WOW. It was a different kind of space, a different aesthetic and structure, but they were really there. When we started the first WOW festival, because they had lost their space, they gave us their lighting equipment. Some of the equipment we still have at WOW came from them.

PS: I went to their space once and did a performance about a water bug from my apartment. It was an awesome basement place. It was another endless investment of time, 'cause you didn't just walk in there and do a gig and get paid and leave. You had to invest yourself in the space. And Magaly and Ana had a different aesthetic than me and Lois had. But they are the ones who said to us, "In order for love to grow, you have to have a space."

[...]

PS: WOW became a teaching organization. Sometimes I regret that we all didn't become a big theater company, which was the original idea. The beauty of not doing that is that we were all able to blossom in our own directions. But as every year passed, more and more women came in. It was tedious to teach them, or to say to them, "You can't do that." People would come in and say, "I want to get a grant," and we'd all roll our eyes and say, "A grant will be the end of us." We had to soften our edges and we had to be teachers.

LW: I think that conflict between order and chaos is what you're talking about. We really celebrated the chaos because it allowed us all to be different. At the same time we all craved a certain kind of order. Maintaining chaos in an orderly fashion was one of the challenges that we all worked with. And, like you said, wouldn't it have been great if we could have all become a company. At the same time, that would have completely choked the individual, chaotic nature of the way that we created. We were always slightly struggling against those two realities. That's one of the things that I'm really proud of: that constant desire to balance the order and the chaos is still there.

My own personal challenge is that Peggy and I came to WOW with certain seniority because we had started it. I came to it with a certain leadership experience. It was hard to balance that personal skill, and my desire to see the organization run smoothly, with the desire to keep it a collaborative collective. I wanted to have my input acknowledged without threatening the collectivity. In retrospect, sometimes I wish I could have been able to just acknowledge what I contributed and, at the same time, not have been overbearing.

CT: We're all friends so we all know conflict is good. Women at that time were not supposed to be leaders. Because we couldn't say we were leaders, WOW's a collective. That's true. But certain operational things happen even within a collective. Some people lead more and others follow more. But being women, and being feminists, you couldn't be a leader. So we had this *huge* fight, that was really one of the most painful big meetings at WOW, because who was the leadership? Lois was a leader; Peggy was a leader, but she wasn't called that. Peggy was responsible for getting us the space on E. 4th Street. There were things that you guys were very knowledgeable about.

Then there were fights that have nothing to do with what the fight is about. Peggy and I fought about wood. Wood was the big thing.

LW: Well, some people can move wood and some can't.

CT: It wasn't about the wood. It was about leadership, about acknowledging responsibility. So, who carries wood is one thing, and who does the books is another, and you don't want to call yourself a leader, but what are you putting into WOW? It was very tricky. Other people emerged, too, who had put a lot of stuff into the space. It was one of the very painful but very good moments at WOW when we had to realize that a lot of the feminist way of behaving was perhaps not the best because it was—

PS: It was silencing.

CT: It was like, "You know who we are, but we can't really be that."

PS: I think it was also a class thing. I always took the abrupt, confrontational . . . I didn't hold myself back. Eventually, I had to get a chiropractor and blood pressure pills and wrote a show, because everyone was saying, "Shut up Peggy, you sound just like my father." I eventually made a show called *You're Just Like My Father*, because I cause arguments all the time because I'm so stupid and opinionated and I'm an asshole and I say everything on my mind. A lot of women coming into WOW were not prepared to engage that kind of aggressive behavior. I was very aggressive. Ellen Bialo taught me to sit back in my chair, but I can't sit at WOW meetings like that; I was going to have a heart attack. I cause disruption, I'm abrupt and make people fight me. A lot of my role was that, that kind of abrupt behavior, or aggressive behavior, or opinionated things that made other people have to stand up to me.

But conflicts are important. They taught us all a little bit more about how to deal with things that happen in life, and how to deal with challenging people. We all had to deal with different types of personalities all the time. When someone creates conflict, the way you react to it is often as much a learning thing as it is when something positive is put out.

LW: Conflicts also highlighted the sense of the "non-organizational organization." There was no organization that someone could come to and say, "I don't want to work with this person because I feel physically threatened," for example. There was no structure for dealing with that, so it would get dealt with in the way that everything got dealt with: some of us took it on board. I would say, for example, "If this person doesn't feel quite safe in the space, we have to figure out how to deal with this." These conflicts brought up representation, censorship, and structure. They forced us to talk about order, chaos, communication, group dynamics, and power.

CT: As always at WOW, something would happen at the meeting and then there would be the other back-story. It becomes like the game, Telephone. WOW functioned as a family, too. If the family took in people who have a relationship, and they're fighting, are we supposed to step in and be the judges of that relationship? We're all being very positive about the space but you don't want to just present the rosy picture. Great things happened, but there were also things that could have broken us.

LW: The conflicts we had about power do touch on the limitations of some feminist organizations. Had we been able to acknowledge certain kinds of power and act on that, we wouldn't have been as vulnerable to attacks over power when they happened.

CT: WOW is a girl's club. When I had a fire, I called you [Lois] and you set up a whole system of helping me. So it really does work as a community.

PS: It's about community theater. But another conflict that caused a lot of women to leave WOW was about men. When WOW started, it was about inclusiveness. But there were women who had to work with men all day and they wanted WOW to be separatist and not even have men allowed in the door—almost like the Michigan Women's Music Festival. The women at Michigan want ten days when they do not have to deal with one man. And that's kind of like what it was with some of the WOW women. We didn't know how to deal with it. And then they left.

LW: It wasn't even a political principle. It was about, this is a girls' club and no men allowed. No boys allowed.

PS: But we never dealt with that, as a group. We didn't have a mechanism to deal with it.

LW: It was never about "no men" in any capacity. It's always been about degree, that the women maintain some degree of control and ownership.

[. . .]

PS: WOW was a place, a building, a structure in which people could form work that was viewed by other people. The satisfaction to me was finding a space that we could afford, the second WOW. I worked all my neighborhood contacts. It took me almost a year to get that space. Every day, I went to Cooper Square and made sure that we were going to get it. It took a year out of my life. That is very satisfying to me, to create something that is going to continue.

Lois and I took a year off to enhance our reputations and to call back all the academics who had been calling us, who we were ignoring. We decided to take a year off so that we would be written about, so that people wouldn't have to just do it again and get lost again. The satisfaction is having a place where anybody could come in if they had the stamina.

But I also feel a responsibility to teach. I got my aesthetic from Hot Peaches; they got it from the Angels of Light and the Coquettes, from California. They passed it on to me and I felt like I needed to pass it on to someone else, so that anybody could get up and tell their story.

[...]

LW: WOW replaced a lot of things for me. Like church.

PS: Yes, definitely.

LW: It replaced church, 'cause church was the place where you could perform and you could do interpersonal stuff and you could be a leader. And you thought about things and you had socials. So it replaced church for me. And it definitely replaced family. It functioned like that for a long time. I don't think it functions that way anymore, but somehow, the connection still exists, even though it's not the tight nucleus that it once was. That was real important for me. It still is very important to me, that I've had that in my history.

[...]

LW: I have two kinds of favorite moments. One set is the things that raised questions for me. And the other is the butch/femme nights, which we did in 1983, when people were just beginning to reclaim butch/femme. We did the butch night, and it was such a celebration, then we did the femme night and it was such a struggle.

CT: Such a loser of a night.

LW: It was such a loser night and it was so hard and we all *knew* why it was hard, but we couldn't *say* why it was hard. We just couldn't . . . we couldn't swagger, in a femme way. That raised such huge questions for me that I think I'm still trying to answer, about how butches could display and femmes had such a hard time displaying in that context. That was massive for me.

The things that I love the most are all of those things that were born out of necessity, in quick moments, when people grabbed their most creative selves together and made something big happen.

PS: I just want to tell one story about necessity, when we were having fun performing Holly's show, *The Lady Dick*. One of my characters was Mickey Paramus. The show started with me killing eight women with my song. We put outlines around their bodies around the floor. Then Mickey was sitting at a bar and every night Holly, who's not a trained actor, bless her soul, would kick open the door at WOW, come in, and *grab* me, physically, really painfully, and do "Lethal Weapon," which is one of the best-written monologues of all time. Absolutely the most beautiful monologue, however, I could not hear one word, because she *mauled* me every night. And every night, she'd spit in my face.

CT: She was lethal.

PS: It was scary for me. Every night after the show, I'd say, "Holly, you can't do that, I am not the real person. I'm Peggy standing there. You cannot hurt me physically. You can't jump on me and spit in my face." She wouldn't stop. 'Cause she didn't know how to stop.

CT: She couldn't. She didn't know.

PS: So one night she came out, and I couldn't—my body physically wouldn't—so when she kicked open the door, which made everyone scream, I mean everyone jumped, my body went into this physical like—So she came at me, and I went, "Somebody call 911, this woman is not in the show! She's not in the show!" And I went out into the audience. Well, Kate Davy [*Kate Davy is a feminist academic who wrote about* The Lady Dick *and was in the audience that night.*] wrote four pages about breaking down the [fourth] wall. When the academics started writing about us, we realized that our aesthetic was a moment and it was challenging everything.

[. . .]

PS: I did the Buddhist exercise of making a space every day, of going there every morning and washing the floor. I loved washing the floor. Those are some of my favorite moments: having a key to a space. I open the door—no one was in there, right? And I could go there any time of day. I could wash the floor and nobody was in there. I could put on music, right? This was our space. It was an incredible feeling. It was like owning something that was lesbian. It was a brand new feeling. I got that. I still have that feeling. I still crave it, sometimes. I don't have a key to WOW now.

CT: I don't either.

LW: I don't either.

PS: I still sometimes crave going in there at night and putting on music and just . . .

LW: Washing the floor.

PS: Washing the floor.

CT: Or painting the space.

PS: Or painting the space.

CT: A different color.

LW: Or cleaning the dressing room.

PS: Cleaning the dressing room. Or Susan sneaking in there and bringing all the curtains home and ironing them and bringing them back and hanging them correctly. Or whatever you do when you're private and alone. Having a space to make work is an awesome thing. (May 1, 2004)

Contributors

Moe Angelos has been one of the Five Lesbian Brothers, who have received a Bessie, an Obie, and other dustable honors, since 1988. She has collaborated with the Obie award–winning Builders Association as a performer and writer since the last century and has appeared in several Builders' productions in several countries on several continents. She has been involved with the WOW Café since 1981 and has appeared in the work of many Off-Off-Broadway luminaries, including Carmelita Tropicana, Anne Bogart, Susan Young, Holly Hughes, Lois Weaver, Kate Stafford, Brooke O'Harra, Half Straddle, and the Ridiculous Theatrical Company, to name a few. Moe works in United Scenic Artists 829, assisting with Hollywood magic when she is not treading the boards. To hear more of what she has to say about show business, visit http://madehereproject.org/ and browse the artists.

Babs Davy is a founding member of the Five Lesbian Brothers, whose plays have been published by Samuel French. Also in print are *Five Lesbian Brothers (Four Plays)* and *The Five Lesbian Brothers' Guide to Life*. Babs has authored three solo performances: *Women and Children First: Outstanding Perk or Tool of Oppression?*; *How I Drank My Way through Heterosexuality*, the story of a teenage "closet case" living in a single-parent household dominated by happy hour; and *Blest Like Me: Psycho Pharmacology and Salvation*, a recovering Catholic's triumph over mental illness via the "good news" of group therapy and a pile of sacramental psychopharmaceuticals. Babs can be seen as "Accounts Payable" in a feature film co-written and directed by Madeleine Olnek, *The Foxy Merkins,* which premiered in Los Angeles at the Sundance Institute's Next Weekend Film Festival in 2013 and was an official selection of the 2014 Sundance Film Festival NEXT category. She also appeared in two Maria Maggenti films, as the "Waitress" in *The Incredibly True Adventure of Two Girls In Love* (1995) and the "Softball Dyke" in *Puccini for Beginners* (2006), which debuted at the Sundance Film Festival and was nominated for a Grand Jury Prize.

Dominique Dibbell is a cofounder of the Five Lesbian Brothers and a writer and performer. She was awarded an Obie for her performance in the Builders Association's *Jet Lag*. *Lady*, a film she made a long time ago with Ira Sachs, continues to be pondered by queer studies majors. Her writing has been published in the *Los Angeles Times Magazine*, *The New F**k You*, and a handful of other places. She lives in Los Angeles with her wife and son.

Jill Dolan began her career as a feminist lesbian theatre and performance critic by attending performances at WOW in the early 1980s. She's indebted to all the women collected in these pages (and many others) for years of laughter and inspiration. Among other books and essays, Dolan is the author of *The Feminist Spectator as Critic* (1991/2012); *Utopia in Performance: Finding Hope at the Theatre* (2005); *Theatre and Sexuality* (2010); and *The Feminist Spectator in Action: Feminist Criticism for the Stage and Screen* (2013), all of which include discussions of work by performers who began at WOW. Dolan writes the George Jean Nathan Award-winning blog, *The Feminist Spectator* (http://feministspectator.princeton.edu) and edited Peggy Shaw's Lambda Award–winning play collection *A Menopausal Gentleman* for the University of Michigan Press (2011). Dolan is the Dean of the College at Princeton University, where she teaches on the faculty of the English Department, the Program in Theatre, and the Program in Gender and Sexuality Studies.

Alice Forrester began her work at WOW as a stage manager for the second WOW Festival and spent the next ten years with the women of WOW, serving brie and Rolling Rock at its 330 E. 11th Street location, touring with Split Britches, set designing, directing with Heidi Griffiths, playing with Lynn Hayes and Debra Miller, and, in retrospect, preparing for her second career as a drama therapist. Now Alice is the executive director of Clifford Beers Clinic, serving families living with traumatic stress and trauma, paying for her PhD, and living in New Haven, Connecticut, with her wonderful partner, Pam Linder, and three wonderful kids, Elisabeth, Daniel, and Camille. Her life experiences at WOW inform every aspect of her current daily life:

believing that anything and everything is possible . . . and, as Peggy Shaw is known to say, that "the only way home is through the show."

Lynn Hayes's WOW life began as a food advisor to the original 11th St. WOW Café, meeting with Holly Hughes and suggesting toaster oven menu choices. She became a WOW girlfriend, lead actress in *Snow Queen,* and Kiki of all trades. Lynn, with Alice Forrester, Debra Miller, and other WOW gals transformed the old Coney Island doll factory on East 4th St. to the new WOW Café by installing the wooden floor and building the dressing room tables with lumber "donated" from her "real job." Encouraged to write a play, Heidi Griffiths advised, "write about what you like," and *Guitar Boy* was born. *Starstruck, Playground, Drag Night at the White House, A Strong New Chord, Somewhere Along the Way,* and the song, "It's Hard to be a Dyke in NYC" soon followed. Owner of Country Girl Productions, Lynn attributes her self-confidence and success to the amazing, free-spirited, courageous women of the original WOW.

Peg Healey, WOW girl and founding member of the Five Lesbian Brothers, relocated to California, where she has written on and off for film and television. She currently lives in the Antelope Valley where she breeds and raises race-bred quarter horses with her wife, Toni Perkins, at their Rollfaster Quarter Horse Ranch.

Holly Hughes is a writer and performer. She is the author of *Clit Notes: A Sapphic Sampler* and coeditor of other collections, including the Lambda award–winning *O Solo Homo: The New Queer Performance,* with David Román, and *Animal Acts: Performing Species Today,* with Una Chaudhuri. Her work has been presented internationally to a range of responses. On the one hand, she has received funding from the National Endowment for the Arts and Creative Capital's MAP Fund and been awarded two *Village Voice* Obies and a 2010 Guggenheim Fellowship. On the other hand, she was notoriously defunded by the NEA and denounced as a child pornographer in the US Congress. So she has some nice certificates and a pile of hate mail, much of it with return addresses. She is now a professor at the University of Michigan, where she directs the Bachelor of Fine Arts in Interarts Performance program.

Lisa Kron is a writer and performer whose work has been widely produced in New York, regionally, and internationally. She wrote the book and lyrics for the musical adaptation of Alison Bechdel's graphic novel *Fun Home*, with music by composer Jeanine Tesori, which was nominated for the Pulitzer Prize and won five 2015 Tony Awards including Best Book, Best Score, and Best Musical. Lisa's other plays include *Well, 2.5 Minute Ride* (Obie Award), and *The Ver**zon Play*. Honors include a Guggenheim fellowship, the Doris Duke Performing Artists Award, the Cal Arts/Alpert Award, and the 2014 Lortel Award for Outstanding Featured Actress. Lisa is a proud founding member of the Five Lesbian Brothers and she considers her years at WOW the foundation upon which all her subsequent work has been built.

Deb Margolin is a playwright, performance artist, actor, and founding member of the Split Britches Theater Company. She is the author of nine full-length solo performance pieces and the recipient of a 1999–2000 Obie award for Sustained Excellence of Performance. Deb was awarded the 2005 Richard H. Brodhead Prize for teaching excellence at Yale University and the 2005 Kesselring Playwriting Prize for her play *Three Seconds in the Key*. Caryl Churchill's play *Seven Jewish Children* inspired Deb's piece *Seven Palestinian Children*, which was written to continue the dialogue investigating the Israeli/Gaza conflict and has been presented internationally alongside Churchill's work. Her play *Imagining Madoff* premiered at Stageworks Hudson in the summer of 2010 and opened the 2011–12 theater season at Theater J in Washington, DC. Her most recent solo work, entitled *GOOD MORNING ANITA HILL ITS GINNI THOMAS I JUST WANTED TO REACH ACROSS THE AIRWAVES AND THE YEARS AND ASK YOU TO CONSIDER SOMETHING I WOULD LOVE YOU TO CONSIDER AN APOLOGY SOMETIME AND SOME FULL EXPLANATION OF WHY YOU DID WHAT YOU DID WITH MY HUSBAND SO GIVE IT SOME THOUGHT AND CERTAINLY PRAY ABOUT THIS AND COME TO UNDERSTAND WHY YOU DID WHAT YOU DID OKAY HAVE A GOOD DAY*, explores the 1993 Clarence Thomas/Anita Hill hearings. Deb received the 2008 Helen Merrill Distinguished Playwright award. She teaches in Yale University's undergraduate Theater Studies Program. Deb's two newest multicharacter plays are *TURQUOISE*, which ran in workshop at Dixon Place in NYC, and *What Difference Does It Make?*, which premiered in August 2015 in New Orleans, directed by Deb's son Bennett Kirschner. Her newest solo play, *8 STOPS*, was commissioned by the Kimmel Center in Philadelphia, presented there, and then produced by All For One at the Cherry Lane Theater in April of 2015.

Debra Miller's involvement with WOW began at the first WOW Festival as a dance company manager and sound engineer for the main festival theater. As a collective member, she was active in running the space and, to the chagrin of many, acting. Her other credits include the Santa Cruz Bozo Collective, *Patience and Sarah, Largely NY–Bill Irwin* (Kennedy Center/St. James Theater), and work in San Francisco nightclubs, as well as film forays (*Lez B Friends: A Biker Bitch Hate Story, Gigi Goes to a Book Club,* and assorted cameos). Debra's writing includes theatre and film reviews, erotic short stories, and two unproduced short screenplays. She has worked professionally in the film industry and as a programmer for OUTFEST, the Ann Arbor Film Festival, and the American Film Institute Film Festival. Her first homo-humor how-to e-book, *Assisted Loving: How I Stopped My Homo-Centric Life to Take Care of My Elderly Father,* is available on Amazon.

Claire Olivia (C.O.) Moed grew up on New York City's Lower East Side when it was still a tough neighborhood. A WOWette from the early days of 11th Street, her plays delved into relationships desperate to thrive and her fashion shows revealed the little known historical fact that all fabulous styles came from Lesbian revolution. An Elizabeth George Grant for Fiction recipient and a Rockefeller Media Arts nominee, her short stories, flash nonfiction and dramatic works have been published in several anthologies and literary reviews. She chronicles the heart and soul of a disappearing family and a city in the throes of extinction and evolution on IT WAS HER NEW YORK (myprivateconey.blogspot.com). The rest of the time she writes, shoots, works a day job, and lives with her partner, fellow writer Ted Krever and two cats in New York City.

Eileen Myles has published more than twenty collections of poetry, fiction, nonfiction, plays, and libretti including *I Must Be Living Twice/new & selected poems* (2015), *Inferno (a poet's novel), The Importance of Being Iceland, Not Me,* and *Chelsea Girls,* reissued this year. With Liz Kotz, she edited *The New Fuck You/adventures in lesbian reading.* Her plays and solo performances include *Joan of Arc/a spiritual entertainment, Patriarchy, a play, Feeling Blue Parts 1, 2 & 3, Leaving New York , Modern Art,* and *Our Sor Juana Ines de la Cruz,* which she wrote for Alina Troyano, all produced at WOW and PS122. She's received a Shelley Prize, a Warhol/Creative Capital grant, a Guggenheim fellowship, and a grant from the Foundation for Contemporary Art. She is a Professor Emeritus of Writing at UC San Diego. She lives in New York.

Madeleine Olnek has written and directed over twenty plays—all comedies—presented in downtown New York City venues, frequently to sold-out crowds. She often collaborates with Deb Margolin and actors Dennis Davis, Susan Ziegler, Cynthia Kaplan, Lisa Haas, Jackie Monahan, Alex

Karpovsky, Rae C. Wright, Sally Sockwell, Kevin Seal, and members of the Five Lesbian Brothers. Other frequent collaborators include filmmaking partner/producer Laura Terruso, choreographer Stormy Brandenberger, and costume designer Linda Gui. Madeleine has made several movies (including a film version of *Codependent Lesbian Space Alien Seeks Same,* available at www.codependentlesbianspacealienseekssame.com), which were official selections of the Sundance Film Festival. She received a master of fine arts in creative writing from Brown University on full scholarship and an MFA in film from Columbia University, where she received the William Goldman Screenwriting Fellowship, as well as the Adrienne Shelley Prize for Best Female Director. Her latest feature, *The Foxy Merkins*, premiered in 2013 at Sundance's first festival in Los Angeles.

Uzi Parnes is a New York-based filmmaker, photographer, curator, and actor. Presentations of his work have been shown internationally, most recently in a career survey at The Arsenal Institute for Film and Video Art (Berlin, 2012). His dissertation, *Pop Performance: Four Seminal Influences,* was published in 1988 and has become an influential reference for scholarship around Jack Smith's work. Parnes was founder and co-director with Ela Troyano of the legendary 1980's performance club "Chandalier."

Diane Jeep Ries has a long history of creating art, performance, beauty, and spiritual development. A veteran drag king since the 1970s, an original member of the WOW Café, and hairstylist for many WOW productions, Jeep is also a published writer, director, and seasoned producer. Now an ordained interfaith minister, Reverend Ries is the founder and pastor of the God Garage (www.godgarage.net) for those whose spirituality is outside the box and not from a big-box store. She also maintains a private spiritual counseling practice. Her performance expertise informs all her life-cycle ceremonies and service sermons. She has spoken at the Unitarian Universalist Congregation of the Palisades, the Southampton New Thought Spiritual Center, and the International Day of Peace at the United Nations' Tillman Chapel. Jeep believes she is called to bring love, laughter, understanding, acceptance, communication, dignity, and authenticity to those in need.

Alison Rooney spent the 1980s performing solo theater pieces at all the downtown haunts, from on top of the bar at 8BC to Franklin Furnace. She hammed it up in many a WOW extravaganza and then some. Her play *Rabbit Plantation*, first produced at WOW, went on to win Australia's Playworks competition and was performed at the Belvoir Street Theatre in Sydney.

(Much) more recently, her play *Eddies* was a Lark Theater Playwrights Competition finalist. She currently lives in the Hudson Valley, where she is an arts journalist for local online and print media and a member of World's End Theater, where she recently directed a staged reading of Charles Ludlam's *Medea,* in much the same spirit as *Waaay Beyond the Valley of the Dolls,* though not on a stage strewn with pills, Hostess snowball wrappers, and empty bottles, alas.

Peggy Shaw is a performer, writer, producer, and teacher of writing and performance. She cofounded Split Britches and the WOW Café in New York City. She is a veteran of Hot Peaches and Spiderwoman Theater and has collaborated as a writer and performer with Lois Weaver and Split Britches since 1980. Her more recent Split Britches collaborations include *Miss America* (2008), *Lost Lounge* (2009), and *Ruff* (2012). She has received three Obie awards, the 1995 Anderson Foundation Stonewall award, and the Foundation for Contemporary Performance Theatre Performer of the Year award. Her book *A Menopausal Gentleman: The Solo Plays of Peggy Shaw,* won the 2012 Lambda Literary award for LBGT Drama. The book, edited by Jill Dolan, includes scripts of her solo performances *You're Just Like My Father, Menopausal Gentleman, To My Chagrin,* and *Must—The Inside Story.* Peggy was the 2011 recipient of the Ethyl Eichelberger award for the creation of *Ruff,* a musical collaboration that explores the experience of having a stroke. She is the 2014 recipient of the Doris Duke Artist Award.

Ana Maria Simo is a New York playwright, essayist, and fiction writer. Born in Cuba, she was educated in France. Her plays include *Without Qualities, The Opium War, Truth, Kuh, Ted and Edna, The Bad Play, Going to New England, Penguins, Alma, What Do You See?, Pickaxe, Dungeon,* and *Exiles.* They have been produced in New York City at PS122, the Bessie Schonberg Theatre, Theater for the New City, INTAR Theatre, the New York Shakespeare Festival's Latino Festival, Duo Theatre, and WOW, and at the Walker Arts Center in Minneapolis. She has also made important contributions as a lesbian activist, cofounding projects such as Medusa's Revenge, the first lesbian theater in New York, in 1976; the direct action group the Lesbian Avengers, in 1992; Dyke TV, a public-access show dedicated to lesbian programming, in 1993; and *The Gully,* an online queer magazine, in 2000. She is currently writing *North,* the second novel in a trilogy.

Sharon Jane Smith is a songwriter, playwright, and storyteller who has worked at the WOW Café since 1982 with artists Holly Hughes, Terry Dame,

Beverly Bronson, Moe Angelos, Heidi Griffiths, Rebecca High, Lois Weaver, Carmelita Tropicana, Peggy Shaw, Lynn Hayes, Babs Davy, Lisa Gluekin, Laura Marie Thompson, and Elize Tribble. Her work has also been performed in New York City at Dixon Place and PS122. Her theatre writing includes *Threads from the Tailor's Grand Daughters, Of Men and Steamboat Men, The West Wasn't Won on Salad, Cabaret de la Gay (in D minor), The Truth about Gypsy Byrne,* and *Crooked Slough Dike Road and Other Stories.* In 1998 she was awarded a New York Foundation for the Arts Fellowship by her peers. Her music is available at A Repeat Performance, the shop she runs with Beverly Bronson in New York City. She is currently writing "Confessions of a Shopkeeper."

Alisa Solomon is a professor at Columbia University's Graduate School of Journalism, where she directs the masters concentration in arts and culture. She is the author of *Re-dressing the Canon: Essays on Theater and Gender* (winner of the George Jean Nathan award for Dramatic Criticism) and *Wonder of Wonders: A Cultural History of "Fiddler on the Roof."*

Split Britches was founded by Peggy Shaw, Lois Weaver, and Deb Margolin in New York City. Since 1981 these artists have performed as a trio, in duets, and in solos, both independently and under the company banner. Projects collaboratively written and performed by Shaw, Weaver, and Margolin include *Split Britches, the True Story; Beauty and the Beast; Upwardly Mobile Home; Little Women, the Tragedy; Anniversary Waltz;* and *Lesbians Who Kill.* Visit their site at www.splitbritches.wordpress.com.

Carmelita Tropicana (Alina Troyano) is a writer, performance artist, and actor born at the WOW Café. She is an Obie recipient whose work includes the plays *Memories of the Revolution; Carnaval* (with Uzi Parnes); *Chicas 2000; Single Wet Female* (with Marga Gomez); the monologues *Milk of Amnesia* and *With What Ass Does the Cockroach Sit?;* the performances *Chicken Sushi* and *Homage to Jack;* and the film *Carmelita Tropicana: Your Kunst Is Your Waffen,* written and directed by Ela Troyano, which won the Teddy award at the Berlin Film Festival and was shown on PBS. Her work has been produced or presented at PS122, INTAR Theatre, Hebbel Am Ufer in Berlin, Centro Andaluz de Arte in Seville, Centre de Cultura Contemporanea in Barcelona, and the Andy Warhol Museum in Pittsburgh. She is currently working with Ela Troyano on *Ursa's Tail, for SB,* a sequel to *Post Plastica,* a play with video and art installations that premiered at El Museo del Barrio in 2012.

Lois Weaver is Professor of Contemporary Performance Practice at Queen Mary University of London and an independent artist and activist. She was cofounder of Spiderwoman Theater and WOW and artistic director of the Gay Sweatshop in London. She has been a writer, director, and performer with Peggy Shaw and Split Britches since 1980. As part of *Staging Human Rights,* Lois taught in women's prisons in Brazil and the United Kingdom and, in 2006, became artistic director for *Performing Rights,* an international festival on the themes of performance and human rights held in London, Vienna, and Glasgow. Her experiments in performance as a means of public engagement (www.publicaddresssystems.org) include the *Long Table,* the *Library of Performing Rights,* the *FeMUSEm,* and her facilitating persona Tammy WhyNot. Lois and Tammy are engaged in an ongoing research project, *What Tammy Needs to Know about Getting Old and Having Sex,* and present their findings in a lecture performance, *What Tammy Found Out.* Lois is a 2014 Guggenheim Fellow.

Susan Young first encountered WOW in the mid-1980s at the Bellevue Hospital performance of *Split Britches.* She so gravitated to its unique feminist intelligence and creativity that she ended up acting in and designing costumes and sets for numerous WOW shows. She also designed for Split Britches on *Upwardly Mobile Home, Belle Reprieve,* and *Dress Suits to Hire.* In 1989 Susan was awarded a *Village Voice* Obie award for sustained excellence in costume design and an American Theater Wing costume design award for *Tale of Two Cities* at the Ridiculous Theatrical Company. In the early 1990s, Susan became a patternmaker in the garment industry. Gradually, over twenty years, she became the manufacturing leader of the large, lovely, global Women's Wear company. She now spends her time traveling the world to develop her products. She agrees with Alice Forrester in saying that "much of my ethics and the sensibility that gets me around the world with good production values come from my experience at WOW."

Further Reading

Carr, C. "No Trace of the Bland: An Interview with Holly Hughes." *Theater* 24, no. 2 (1993): 67–75.

Case, Sue-Ellen. *Feminism and Theatre.* Houndsmills: Macmillan, 1988.

Case, Sue-Ellen. *Feminist and Queer Performance: Critical Strategies.* New York: Palgrave Macmillan, 2009.

Case, Sue-Ellen, ed. *Split Britches: Lesbian Practice/Feminist Performance.* New York: Routledge, 1996.

Davy, Kate. *Lady Dicks and Lesbian Brothers: Staging the Unimaginable at the WOW Café Theatre.* Ann Arbor: University of Michigan Press, 2010.

Davy, Kate. "Outing Whiteness: A Feminist/Lesbian Project." *Theatre Journal* 47, no. 2 (1995): 189–205.

Dolan, Jill. *The Feminist Spectator as Critic.* Ann Arbor: University of Michigan Press, 1989.

Dolan, Jill. *The Feminist Spectator as Critic.* 2nd ed., with a new introduction and bibliography. Ann Arbor: University of Michigan Press, 2012.

Dolan, Jill. *The Feminist Spectator in Action: Feminist Criticism for Stage and Screen.* New York: Palgrave Macmillan, 2013.

Dolan, Jill. *Presence and Desire: Essays on Gender, Sexuality, Performance.* Ann Arbor: University of Michigan Press, 1993.

Dolan, Jill. "Seeing Deb Margolin: Ontological Vandalism and Radical Amazement." *TDR: The Journal of Performance Studies* 52, no. 3 (Fall 2008): 98–117.

Dolan, Jill. *Theatre and Sexuality.* New York: Palgrave Macmillan, 2010.

Dolan, Jill. *Utopia in Performance: Finding Hope at the Theatre.* Ann Arbor: University of Michigan Press, 2005.

Five Lesbian Brothers. *The Five Lesbian Brothers (Four Plays).* New York: Theatre Communications Group, 2000.

Five Lesbian Brothers. *The Five Lesbian Brothers' Guide to Life.* New York: Simon & Schuster, 1999.

Hughes, Holly. *Clit Notes: A Sapphic Sampler.* New York: Grove Press, 1996.

Hughes, Holly. "Faith Not Lost: Holly Hughes Interviews Lois Weaver about Split Britches' *Lost Lounge* (2009)." *Women & Performance: A Journal of Feminist Theory* 22, no. 1 (2012): 135–40.

Hughes, Holly. *The Well of Horniness.* In *Out in Front: Contemporary Gay and Lesbian Plays,* edited by Don Shewey, 221–51. New York: Grove Press, 1988.

Hughes, Holly, and David Román, eds. *O Solo Homo: The New Queer Performance.* New York: Grove Press, 1998.

Kron, Lisa. *In the Wake.* New York: Dramatists Play Service, 2012.

Kron, Lisa. *2.5 Minute Ride and 101 Humiliating Stories.* New York: Theatre Communications Group, 2001.

Kron, Lisa. *Well.* New York: Theatre Communications Group, 2006.

Margolin, Deb. "*Index to Idioms:* A Performance Novel." *TDR: A Journal of Performance Studies* 52, no. 3 (Fall 2008): 160–73.

Margolin, Deb. *Of All the Nerve: Deb Margolin Solo.* Edited and with an introduction by Lynda Hart. New York: Cassell, 1999.

Meyer, Richard. "'Have You Heard the One about the Lesbian Who Goes to the Supreme Court?' Holly Hughes and the Case against Censorship." *Theatre Journal* 52, no. 4 (2000): 543–52.

Muñoz, José Esteban. "Choteo/Camp Style Politics: Carmelita Tropicana's Performance of Self-Enactment." *Women & Performance: A Journal of Feminist Theory* 7–8, nos. 14–15 (1995): 38–51.

Muñoz, José Esteban. *Disidentifications: Queers of Color and the Performance of Politics.* Minneapolis: University of Minnesota Press, 1999.

Shaw, Peggy. *A Menopausal Gentleman: The Solo Performances of Peggy Shaw.* Edited and with an introduction by Jill Dolan. Ann Arbor: University of Michigan Press, 2011.

Solomon, Alisa. *Redressing the Canon: Essays on Theatre and Gender.* New York: Routledge, 1997.

Torr, Diane and Stephen Bottoms. *Sex, Drag, and Male Roles: Investigating Gender as Performance.* Ann Arbor: University of Michigan Press, 2010.

Troyano, Alina, with Ela Troyano and Uzi Parnes. *I, Carmelita Tropicana: Performing between Cultures.* Edited by Chon A. Noriega. Boston: Beacon Press, 2000.

Acknowledgments

This project has been in development for many, many years, and many people have helped immeasurably along the way. We'd like to thank all the WOW women, past, present, and future, for their sustaining vision of a theatre that continues to be unique and vital. Thanks to all the contributors for their work and for the images everyone provided to allow readers to visualize what it meant to inhabit E. 11th Street and E. 4th Street during those ten years.

Thanks, in particular, go to Kate Davy, who worked on her own book in conjunction with ours for many years and provided images and information along the way; to Eric Glover, our editorial assistant at Princeton; to Susanne Shawyer, whose keen editorial eye, copy editing, and suggested revisions brought us much closer to completion; to Katie Welsh, whose precise, careful, and efficient proofreading and ace editorial assistance allowed us to get the book to press; to Sara Warner, whose smart and supportive reader's report for Michigan provided the last set of suggestions we needed to finish; and to our editor at the press, LeAnn Fields, who stuck with this project through the long years of its genesis and execution.

Thanks to Holly's wonderful rotating crew of assistants—Caitlyn Couture, Bryan Heyboer, Amanda Krugliak, Jim Leija, Brian Lobel, and Amadeus Scott—who worked hard on this project over the past twelve years. They transcribed interviews, retyped, scanned, and proofread nearly illegible primary documents. Holly also thanks the Penny W. Stamps School of Art and Design, the Institute for Research on Women and Gender, and the Office of the Vice President for Research at the University of Michigan for generous funding in support of the research for this book.

Thanks to Uzi Parnes and Ela Troyano for their support and for making Club Chandalier a second home for WOW performers.